Alice. Pleasance. Liddell.

THE RED KING'S DREAM

or

Lewis Carroll in Wonderland

CHRIST CHURCH, OXFORD, IN THE 1860s

THE RED KING'S DREAM

DREAM

or Lewis Carroll in Wonderland

Jo Elwyn Jones &
J. Francis Gladstone

JONATHAN CAPE
LONDON

First published in 1995

1 3 5 7 9 10 8 6 4 2

© Jo Elwyn Jones and J. Francis Gladstone 1995

Jo Elwyn Jones and J. Francis Gladstone have asserted their right
under the Copyright, Designs and Patents Act, 1988
to be identified as the authors of this work

First published in the United Kingdom in 1995 by
Jonathan Cape
Random House, 20 Vauxhall Bridge Road, London SW1V 2SA

Random House Australia (Pty) Limited
20 Alfred Street, Milsons Point, Sydney,
New South Wales 2061, Australia

Random House New Zealand Limited
18 Poland Road, Glenfield,
Auckland 10, New Zealand

Random House Africa (Pty) Limited
PO Box 337, Bergvlei, 2012 South Africa

Random House UK Limited Reg. No. 954009

A CIP catalogue record for this book
is available from the British Library

Papers used by Random House UK Limited are natural,
recyclable products made from wood grown in sustainable forests.
The manufacturing processes conform to the environmental
regulations of the country of origin.

ISBN 0-224-04020-0

Printed and bound in Great Britain by
Butler and Tanner Ltd, Frome, Somerset

Contents

LEWIS CARROLL'S OWN ILLUSTRATION
FROM 'ALICE'S ADVENTURES UNDER GROUND'

I began a poem the other day in which I mean to embody something about Alice (if I can at all please myself by any description of her) and which I mean to call 'Life's Pleasance'.

Lewis Carroll, Private Journal,
13th March, 1863

I pray thee oh God, help me to overcome Temptation: . . . help me to remember the coming hour of death – for of myself I am utterly weak and vile and selfish. Lord, I believe that Thou canst do all things. Oh deliver me from the Chains of Sin! . . . Amen! Amen!

Lewis Carroll, Private Journal,
6th March, 1864

Preface

OUR LIFE-LONG interest in the 'Alice stories became a quest when, by chance, we discovered a link between a family forebear, William Ewart Gladstone, and the Reverend Charles Lutwidge Dodgson, a mathematics don at Christ Church College, Oxford, in the years before Gladstone (himself a Christ Church scholar) became Prime Minister. We had long suspected that real Victorians were hidden in the characters Dodgson invented for the two stories for children he published under a pseudonym, Lewis Carroll, in 1865 and 1871. Their full and correct titles are *Alice's Adventures in Wonderland* and *Through the Looking-glass and What Alice Saw There*, and both are illustrated by the political cartoonist for *Punch* magazine, John Tenniel. These were the last drawings Tenniel ever produced for books intended for children. An earlier version of *Wonderland* was eventually published in Carroll's own hand and illustrated by himself. It was called *Alice's Adventures Under Ground*, and it is still available in a facsimile edition.

Why have these books remained so well loved, by adults as well as children, for more than a century? 'Mad as a Hatter' has crept into the language. Tweedledum and Tweedledee have become metaphors for equal and opposite. Or we say, as Alice did, 'curiouser and curiouser'. Their humour is not gentle: the Dormouse is pushed into a teapot, the White Knight falls head first into a ditch and is unable to right himself as his armour-clad legs flail in the air, and the Queen of Hearts' favourite occupation is executing people. In the midst of all this violence

9

the polite and sensible Alice represents a way of coping with a mad, mad world. Could she represent more than this?

We knew that Dodgson, who lived at Christ Church all his adult life, first told the 'Alice' stories to young Alice Liddell, daughter of the Dean of Christ Church, a reformer whom Dodgson did not like. His pen-name, 'Lewis Carroll', came to him one weekend in February 1856 when he was pondering the overlap he felt deeply between dream and reality. Playing the kind of word game he had enjoyed since childhood, he derived 'Carroll' from the Latin for Charles – Carrollus. In a kind of charade, his mother's name 'Lutwidge' became 'Ludovic', 'Louis' and then 'Lewis'. Later in life he confessed to putting himself in the 'Alice' fantasy as the clumsy Dodo. It was the nickname by which he was known to his close friends because of the way his pronounced stutter made him introduce himself as 'Do-Do-Do-Dodgson'.

In that same spring of 1856 he took up photography and soon excelled in portraits of little girls. Less well known are the photographs he took of prominent personalities in adult Victorian society, many of whom were known to Alice Liddell and entertained by her father. Reality became dream, and Dodgson became Carroll.

He began to photograph Alice Liddell when she was four years old. They met frequently, and often went rowing on the river Thames with her sisters and Carroll's friends. Abruptly, when she was eleven, Alice's mother put a stop to Carroll seeing her and burnt his letters to her. Mrs Liddell fancied a royal marriage for Alice and Carroll had no place in the Liddell circle of high society. Besides, Oxford dons were celibate by law until 1871. None the less Carroll nursed a personal as well as a moral and professional grievance against the liberal Liddells, and they were not the only power-brokers at Oxford or at large in Victorian society whose behaviour he despised.

Living as we do in part of Mr Gladstone's country house in North Wales, a short walk from the library where his vast collection of books and Victorian pamphlets are now housed, we had begun there with a startling discovery – a hitherto little known pamphlet by C. L. Dodgson which sets out a mathematical

DREAM AND REALITY IN *JUDY* MAGAZINE — MR GLADSTONE
REFLECTING ON HIS LOSS OF THE OXFORD SEAT

formula for a fairer system of counting the votes in a Parliamentary election. Why had Gladstone kept a paper outlining Carroll's views on proportional representation? It prompted us to look up the record of the 1865 election when Gladstone lost his seat in the House of Commons as Liberal M.P. for the University of Oxford, coming third in the poll against two Tory opponents.

Before eighteen months had passed we had read a great many Victorian lives, letters and collected works and had visited the places where Carroll's strangely occluded life unfolded. We had found the original of Carroll's photograph of the biologist Thomas Henry Huxley, taken at the time of the Oxford debate over Darwin's theory of evolution. Almost certainly Carroll attended the debate, and this connected Huxley and Carroll in a way that had not been done before. The literary critic, William Empson, had suggested in 1935 that the fictional Alice's changes in size were an allusion to Darwin's theory of evolution, and indeed Darwin had been hurt at seeing himself caricatured as a dog. A *Beagle* puppy? The Puppy that charged at the diminished Alice in the wood? If we were not the first to suspect that real Victorians were concealed and subtly lampooned in the 'Alice' stories, no one had revealed the full extent of Carroll's parodies, nor imagined that he had written a *roman a clef* and thrown away the key.

Here was a new slant to Carroll's inventiveness.

Much has been lost in the century since Carroll's death. The most crucial material covering Carroll's contacts between 1858 and 1862 may have been destroyed deliberately. Even that which survives has not all been made available to the public. We examined the handwritten list Carroll made in his diary of the 104 little girls he befriended and photographed (or planned to do so) as he prepared 'Alice' for publication, a list omitted from the published version of his diaries and not mentioned in subsequent books about Carroll. The list appears incongruously opposite the prayers that he thought worth recording. We uncovered a new aspect to his relationship with the celebrated actress, Ellen Terry, and unravelled some of his sly jokes at the expense of the Pre-Raphaelites.

In the end what we found confronting us, as in a mirror, was no less than the secret identities of the Ugly Duchess, the mad Hatter, the White Rabbit, the Cheshire Cat, the Tiger-lily, the Walrus and the Carpenter and many other Carroll characters. Here was persuasive evidence that Carroll concealed what he thought about the moral and intellectual climate of his day in a story told on the river to his favourite child-friend. What interested us most was how he articulated his enigmatic private life in the midst of all the conflicts that were going on around him.

By the end of his life in 1898 close to 180,000 copies of *Wonderland* had been sold and a decade later the number in circulation had risen to about 600,000. *Looking-glass* was equally successful, and both books have been translated into Russian, Japanese, French and a score of other languages. They have also been made into films, ballet, television programmes and theatre productions. The collection of different editions made by Alice Liddell and her son now occupies twelve yards of shelf space at Christ Church. Apart from *The Hunting of the Snark*, little else of Carroll's is read today .

Can all this success for 'Alice' be put down to nothing more than a few childish drolleries, as Carroll tried to pretend? It seems unlikely from a man who loved anagrams and puzzles, who was a code maker and a code breaker.

At the end of the second book, Alice wakes up. She knows she has been dreaming. She knows too that the Red King has been asleep and dreaming within her own dream. So, she wonders, who has really dreamed her adventures? 'You see, Kitty, it must have been either me or the Red King,' she muses. Is Lewis Carroll telling us about the 'looking-glass' aspects of the world he inhabited and that we all experience in one way or another as temporal reality? He constantly played these games of metamorphosis, and if he almost always succeeded in covering his tracks, he did leave clues in the consistent pattern of his logic.

For us, the black-suited clergyman, mathematics tutor at Oxford and brilliant photographer of little girls employed his wild and violent sense of wit to mock the new and diverse ideas of an entire generation, and in so doing created a fantasy masterpiece and took his secret – as he intended – to the grave.

CHAPTER ONE

The Lion and the Unicorn

SOME TIME in the 1850s an Oxford don, the Reverend Charles Dodgson, gained the confidence of a little girl called Alice Liddell who was the daughter of the Dean of his college, Christ Church. At the age of twenty-four, when Alice was four, he began to take photographs. Alice and her brother and sisters were some of his first subjects, encouraged by their parents who were among the first Victorians to see the charms of this new medium of portraiture. After early failures, Dodgson's control of technique improved and outdoor exposures began to produce an image on bright days. Helped by improved chemicals, success became more frequent. Even so, keeping little children still for up to a minute was not easy. And, if they were still, would they be in the right mood? To solve this problem, which was soon to make him a master of child portraiture, Dodgson relied on his gift for story-telling. The stories he invented were about odd creatures, part human, part animal, often grotesque. Some were made of playing cards. The most concentrated of all his models, Alice, became the centre of these narratives. When they were written down, Alice became 'Alice'. So long as the Oxford sky was not dark and dull it was even possible to take pictures of the children on rainy days.

It was raining on that Saturday morning when our search began to take shape. We were at home in North Wales and had planned to spend the day in the mountains of Snowdonia with an American friend, David Walker, a clergyman and administrator in the Episcopal Church in Arizona who was on

sabbatical leave and working at the Library W. E. Gladstone*
had founded in the village. Hoping the rain would stop, David
had said he would first go into Chester, and we agreed to meet
him at the library later in the morning. What we knew about
Lewis Carroll then was little more than we could recite during
the ten minutes' walk to the library.

He was born in 1832 in rural Cheshire. Later his entire family moved to Yorkshire. His father was an erudite, classically-
educated clergyman with a sense of humour, who wrote to his
son Charles on the boy's eighth birthday a letter describing the
Mayor of Leeds on a plate and covered in custard with almonds
stuck into him. This type of humour reminds one of Carroll's
'Alice', but without the jokes on language.

Carroll grew up surrounded by sisters. There were eventually
eleven Dodgson children, of which Carroll was the only boy in
the first five. Carroll's mother, Frances Jane Lutwidge, was her
husband's first cousin. Little is known about her except that she
had a strong sense of duty as a daughter, wife and mother.
Carroll could be cold or kind as the mood took him. With children, and especially little girls, he tended to be kind having an
adult personality that was strange, repressed and shy. He also had
an imagination that ravelled and unravelled yarns of thought
and abstruse puzzles, as did Alice's cat with its ball of wool. He
was not too shy to commission photographs of himself in which
he displayed a deadpan and righteous face.

His mother's early death, at the age of 47, just as he went up
to Oxford as an undergraduate, was devastating. Perhaps he
locked part of her personality in a childish world of his own creation. Only in a child's world, weaving tales and inventing
games, does the adult Carroll cease to be ill at ease.

At the age of fourteen Carroll had been sent to boarding-
school at Rugby which was, if *Tom Brown's Schooldays* is to be
believed, rough for a boy like Carroll with a stutter, plain looks
and a fascination for puzzles. In 1851, a place was found for him
at Christ Church, Oxford, by an old acquaintance of Carroll's

---

* A short biography of each of the Victorians of importance to our argument is
in the Bibliographical Register, pages 277–290.

father, Canon Pusey, a conservative High Churchman of the school who thought the purpose of Oxford University should be the training of clergy and little else. Isolated from the aristocrats at Christ Church, who spent their time hunting, Carroll worked hard and was clever enough to gain First Class Honours in mathematics – the best of his year. He was offered a college position, first working in the library and then teaching mathematics. He embarked on the process of taking Holy Orders (a requirement of all junior Fellows) and was to remain resident in Christ Church until he died.

In 1855, Henry George Liddell was appointed Dean of Christ Church and Head of the College. By that time he had five children, of whom Alice was the fourth. He was a reforming liberal aristocrat, a friend and supporter of Gladstone's. The appointment signalled a turbulent period in the university's history, a time of controversies. That we knew from glancing through *The Annotated Alice* by the American mathematician Martin Gardner. What we did not know was the extent to which Carroll participated in these controversies.

The library we were approaching in the rain was named after the local Welsh patron saint, St Deiniol. It has some bias towards Mr Gladstone's own interest in the classics, church history and his own politically turbulent times. Indeed it originated with the fifty thousand or so books which he had collected and carried in wheelbarrows up Hawarden Hill in what became a pet project of the years after his eightieth birthday.

The building is of red Cheshire sandstone in a late Victorian theological style, with leaded windows and a gothic atmosphere about it. It is necessary to ring a bell and, on admission, walk down a red tiled passageway that leads into the reading-room. The tiles are noticeable because one's heels echo in an otherwise hushed atmosphere of study. David Walker had not returned from Chester, so to pass the time we went into the reading-room, a dark, wooden-vaulted room with books to the ceiling. No one was there apart from a young clergyman in a dog-collar, sitting near the books on doctrine. There was a large book with a picture of the *Mona Lisa* open in front of him. While waiting, we glanced through the catalogue of pamphlets.

In the main subject headings, Church History came next to Denmark, Denmark to Disestablishment (particularly of the Irish Church), then came Doctrine, then Drink (legislation and taxation on alcohol), the Eastern Question and the atrocities in Bulgaria, followed by Education and Ireland. We must also have noticed the heading under Elections at Oxford.

David Walker had still not arrived, so we turned to compilations of *Punch* cartoons of which the Library has a large holding. Among these was a cartoon relating to Mr Gladstone losing the election at Oxford, a serious set-back in his political career, although one from which he recovered.

'Mr Gladstone is the Unicorn,' one of us blurted out.

'No, he's not,' the other said. Husband and wife teams have their advantages and disadvantages. The theological student looked up with an air of contempt. Carroll would probably have done the same when he was supervising noisy undergraduates in the Christ Church library.

One of the few references in *The Annotated Alice* to a real Victorian being hidden by Carroll was in the *Looking-glass* scene where the Lion and the Unicorn fight. Hadn't *The Annotated Alice* said this was to do with Gladstone and Disraeli? There in the card index, next to a Carroll who wrote on seventeenth-century Christian schismatics, were entries under Carroll, L. Among them was Martin Gardner's book. His note said 'it was widely believed that the Lion was Gladstone and the Unicorn his political arch-rival, Benjamin Disraeli'. It was a diffident note which concluded that 'there is no proof of this'. He accepted that, as John Tenniel, the political cartoonist for *Punch* who illustrated the 'Alice' books for Carroll, made many caricatures of the Liberal Gladstone and the Tory Disraeli and sometimes of both of them together in various guises, it was possible that such an identification might be correct.

Why, we wondered, did Carroll use Tenniel? Why did he want a political cartoonist for a children's book? In any case, was Gardner right about the Lion and the Unicorn? Was there not something about the portrait of the Unicorn, in Carroll's words and Tenniel's drawing, that suggested Mr G? In other words, if Mr Gladstone was in the scene, would he more likely be the Unicorn than the Lion?

UNICORN, ALICE, LOOKING–GLASS CAKE
AND LION – by John Tenniel

There were other entries under Dodgson, one a sermon given by Carroll's father at Ripon Cathedral and purchased by Gladstone. There was also a pamphlet, dated 1885, by C. L. Dodgson entitled *The Principles of Parliamentary Representation.* C. L. Dodgson? . . . Charles Lutwidge Dodgson? Surely Carroll was not writing about parliamentary representation?

Outside it had stopped raining. There was dappled sunlight on the lawn and around the old yew trees at the entrance to Hawarden Church where Mr Gladstone worshipped, several times on any Sunday when he was at his country home. A cat crossed the library lawn with a flapping half-alive grey pigeon in its mouth. The pigeon had lost its head but went on flapping.

★

The particular *Looking-glass* scene with the Lion and the Unicorn is a complicated set-piece. The Hatter and the Hare enter as the White King's Anglo-Saxon messengers. They are called Hatta and Haigha. One is 'to come' and one is 'to go', a looking-glass image. Meanwhile the Lion and the Unicorn are having a fight that has already lasted eighty-seven rounds. Alice is given a dish, a carving-knife and a cake. The Unicorn criticises her for attempting to cut the prize cake before she hands it out. 'You don't know how to manage Looking-glass cakes . . . Hand it round first, and cut it afterwards!' Alice does as she is told. Sure enough, the cake divides as if by magic into three pieces. The Unicorn receives only one of the three pieces. The genial Lion receives two pieces, the Lion's share.

The Unicorn did not look like Disraeli. There is a portrait of Disraeli in the *Looking-glass* where Alice sits in the railway carriage before leaping the brook to the eighth square. It was the thrust of the Unicorn's horn and his impatience with Alice, rather than facial resemblance, that seemed like Gladstone in one of his more imperious moods. And the cake? Divided into three? Carroll and Gladstone? What possible real connection?

One connection was Oxford University. Like Carroll, Gladstone had been an undergraduate at Christ Church. He was twenty-three years Carroll's senior and of Dean Liddell's generation. He, like Carroll, took a First and had the honour of being made a Student (Fellow) of the College for a time, although he did not teach or reside there. As a politician he had been concerned with certain reforms in the University, attempts in the 1840s and 1850s to wrench it out of the eighteenth century and into the nineteenth. He was Member of Parliament for the University until the election of 1865, which was a three-way race for the two University seats under the prevailing legislation. For eighteen years, through four elections, Gladstone had been returned by the members of his *alma mater*. In 1865 Gladstone's political views on the importance of disestablishing the Church of Ireland as a part of the State were to fly in his face. A change of rules allowed the essentially Tory country clergy whom Oxford educated by the hundred to vote by post. These were the ones who supported the old High Church Canon Pusey, Carroll's father's friend. Gladstone himself, like many of these country clergy, was High Church on matters of doctrine and church ritual. His views on the Irish Church were political. He did not wish to attack the sanctity of

the Church of England, but he did feel that the political
grounds for Irish control of their own affairs were strong, his
mind evolving towards the idea of Home Rule. He had mis-
judged the Oxford University electorate. The Tories produced
an articulate second candidate, Gathorne Hardy, to add to the
already established Heathcote. Heathcote received 3236 votes,
Hardy 1904 and Gladstone 1724. Was the Lion who gets two
slices of Alice's looking-glass cake somehow the Tory party, or
Gathorne Hardy? If so, what was Carroll, whom we knew
mainly as a children's writer, doing parodying politics? What
was Mr Gladstone doing in the nursery?

In those days polling took place in different parts of the
country over a three week period, and having lost his Oxford
seat, Gladstone managed to transfer to South Lancashire, where
he won by a narrow margin. He was Chancellor of the
Exchequer under Lord Palmerston, who died before the year
was out. In swift changes of government, Gladstone also lost the
Lancashire seat and was returned as M.P. for Greenwich to
become Prime Minister in November 1868.

St Deiniol's Library was closed on Sunday, but on Monday
we crossed the threshold once more. In the back of the annexe,
beyond the books about Carroll, were stacked beige boxes containing Gladstone's pamphlet collection. Pamphlet 78/B/3 was
slim, only forty-eight pages long. *The Principles of Parliamentary
Representation* by Charles L. Dodgson. M.A. 'Student and Late
Mathematical Lecturer of Ch. Ch. Oxford'. It was given away
by its author – 'With the Author's compliments' being printed
on the outside. Its preface suggested that:

> A system of Parliamentary Representation, and of the con-
> duct of Elections, which shall secure, for the majority and the
> minority, a due share in the government of the country, is a
> great *desideratum* of the day . . .

The argument was for a complex but logical system of proportional representation, laid out in long equations. At first it was
hard to take seriously but on a closer look, it seemed to be
attacking the problem of how to improve representation in
Britain. A little of it in prose, most in algebraic form:

Let e = No. of electors in the district.

m = . . . members assigned to it,

v = . . . votes each Elector can give.

s = . . . seats it is desired to fill.

x = . . . Electors required.

This strange document is not in Carroll's *Collected Works*. Could that be because it is rare? There are long-out-of-print 'squibs' of Carroll's in the *Collected Works*, strange satirical attacks on Oxford colleagues. Could its exclusion be taken as reflecting a side to Carroll that others had missed? The franchise was constantly under debate in the nineteenth century. Politicians saw the issue of who should vote in terms of social standing. No mention of that in Carroll; but why should there be? Carroll did not appear to be interested in the 'common people' as they were called: he was concerned about numbers. Why not apply this to a theory of making elections fairer? In other words, taken on its own terms, the document was not so strange. Perhaps it was the politicians who were strange. Perhaps it was the political system that was illogical.

Working on this line, trying to take Carroll at face value, in other words trying to look beneath the surface of the Unicorn's character, facets of Carroll's odd relationship with politics caught the light.

The Unicorn's hands were drawn like those of a human, although the Lion had paws. The beast had a certain informality, had its hands in its pockets, as Gladstone often did. It combined this pose with sudden switches of attention. It had authority. The word the Victorians used of their heroes, 'mighty', came to mind when we saw a small bronze of Mr G in the library, hand raised in oratory.

At first the Unicorn is haughty towards Alice: 'Is it alive?' the Unicorn asks Haigha about her. At this point it is almost as if the real Alice Liddell enters the conversation. After all she would have known Gladstone when he visited the Deanery. Dean Liddell often consulted him. They met on vacation in North Wales when the Liddells built a holiday home on the coast. In St Deiniol's there is an account of the Liddell family

In case (a), the x Electors can give vx votes, which, divided among s Candidates, supply them with $\dfrac{vx}{s}$ votes apiece. Similarly, the $(e - x)$ Electors can give $v \cdot (e - x)$ votes, which, divided among $(m + 1 - s)$ Candidates, supply them with $\dfrac{v \cdot (e - x)}{m + 1 - s}$ votes apiece. Hence we must have

$$\frac{vx}{s} > \frac{v \cdot (e - x)}{m + 1 - s},$$

where v divides out;

$$\therefore\ x \cdot (m + 1 - s) > se - sx;$$
$$\therefore\ x \cdot (m + 1) > se;$$
$$\therefore\ x > \frac{se}{m + 1}.$$

In case (b), each of the x Electors can only use s of his v votes, since he can only give *one* to each Candidate: hence the x Electors can only give sx votes, thus supplying s Candidates with x votes apiece. But the $(e - x)$ Electors can, as in case (a), supply $(m + 1 - s)$ Candidates with $\dfrac{v \cdot (e - x)}{m + 1 - s}$ votes apiece. Hence we must have

$$x > \frac{v \cdot (e - x)}{m + 1 - s};$$
$$\therefore\ x \cdot (m + 1 - s) > ve - vx;$$
$$\therefore\ x \cdot (m + 1 - s + v) > ve;$$
$$\therefore\ x > \frac{ve}{m + 1 - s + v}.$$

PAGE 43 FROM CARROLL'S (DODGSON'S) PAMPHLET
'PRINCIPLES OF PARLIAMENTARY REPRESENTATION'

taking Mr G for a walk on a route that led down some cliffs. He became so terrified that he closed his eyes. The Dean had to take his hand and the others formed a kind of barrier to seaward. This took place at exactly the time that the 'Alice' stories were being told. Alice Liddell must have been well aware of the fallibilities of great men. In the stories Alice is forthright, not afraid of adults, and the real Alice had that same character. Her father thought her the best company, the sharpest of his girls. So did Carroll. The Unicorn met his measure. When the Unicorn asks if 'it' is alive . . .

'It can talk,' said Haigha solemnly.
The Unicorn looked dreamily at Alice, and said 'Talk, child.'
Alice could not help her lips curling up into a smile as she began: 'Do you know, I always thought Unicorns were fabulous monsters, too? I never saw one alive before!'
'Well, now that we *have* seen each other, if you'll believe in me, I'll believe in you. Is that a bargain?'
'Yes, if you like,' said Alice.

The 'yes, if you like . . . ' sounded just like Alice Liddell – at least, like a logical child who is not particularly in awe of an apparently frightening grown-up with a large horn in his head, one whom she had brought down to the level of striking a bargain. The bargain – 'if you believe in me, I'll believe in you' – sounded right for Gladstone, one moment on his high horse, and in the next down to the nitty-gritty of politics.

Gladstone lost the Oxford election over his campaign to cut the ties which linked the Irish Church with the English Church – a matter on which Carroll was vigorously opposed to Gladstone. In his diaries Carroll described going to listen to a later debate in the House of Commons on the disestablishment of the Church in Ireland. He had sent his card to his M.P., by then Gathorne Hardy (later Home Secretary in the Tory government), so that he could be sent a permit to sit in the Strangers' Gallery at the House. Hardy, the Tory Lion, failed to produce the ticket, but eventually a colleague of Hardy's obliged. There Carroll heard Disraeli and Gladstone debate with passion, both becoming Prime Minister in quick

IS THIS THE VILLAIN? TENNIEL'S *PUNCH* CARTOON SHOWING
GLADSTONE (RIGHT) HOLDING OUT FOR IRISH CHURCH
DISESTABLISHMENT.

succession in the two general elections of 1868.

In November 1868, Carroll was deeply worried that Tenniel,
secretly a Tory despite working for the Liberal *Punch*, would
refuse to illustrate the second 'Alice' book, *Through the Looking-
glass*. He was also exercised about the unsporting way in which
Oxford Liberals, among them the Bishop of Oxford, lamented
their loss of political influence at the University.

The day after he had heard Gladstone speak in the
Commons, Carroll wrote a letter, 'which I thought of lying
awake the other night'. In the letter, he included an anagram he
had devised in the night – he often slept badly – and sent it to
the paper, the *Standard*, which published the anagram:

William Ewart Gladstone; Wilt tear down *all* images?

Wilt tear down all images? It was a Victorian word game to
take names and turn each letter into a new combination which
had relevant meaning. The game of charades works by means of
a similar disguise. The individual scenes suggest words, which,
when added up to a whole, reveal the meaning of the parts.

Carroll noted at this time a Gladstone anagram made up by someone else: 'I, wise Mr G. want to lead all!' The letters, unscrambled, spell the Liberal leader's name – William Ewart Gladstone. Ingeniously, the Tory who produced the second anagram also devised a reply anagram based on the increasingly popular Disraeli's name. 'I lead, Sir!'

Roger Lancelyn Green, the editor of Carroll's published *Diaries*, pointed out that Carroll, who shared the Liberal Prime Minister's religious but not his political views, then wrote a third Gladstone anagram:

'Wild Agitator! Means well!'

The more we thought about it, the more we realised that the swaggering Unicorn Alice saw driven out of town was a portrait of the real Mr Gladstone, seen from the point of view of both a self-confident little girl handing him a slice of plum cake and of an Oxford don who had campaigned against him.

Confirmation came in a strange, mocking letter Carroll wrote later. He had signed it: 'A Liberal of the Liberals'. The letter itself is almost incomprehensible because it is a looking-glass joke. It says that he is appalled about the lack of violence by the Conservatives: 'Else what are fists meant for in "Merrie England"?' It spoofs 'Tory tricks, aristocratic art and the brute force of numerical superiority'. The Liberal candidate whom Carroll mocked was a University reformer who pretended he was received by the Conservatives 'with enthusiastic cheering and listened to in perfect silence'. In Carroll's looking-glass letter the Tory Party is (as the Unicorn calls Alice) a 'monster'. When the Lion asks her if she is animal, vegetable or mineral, the first question in nursery quiz games, the Unicorn, like a spoilt child who does not want to play the game, cries out: 'It's a fabulous monster.' In Alice's world it is the other creatures who are monsters, the rude and self-aggrandising grown-ups who do not play by the rules but with whom she deals patiently and firmly. That is what both the 'Alice' books are about.

In St Deiniol's were two anthologies of articles written about 'Alice' over the years. In two of these papers the investigators thought they had seen signs of real people in 'Alice', but they had laid only the vaguest groundwork. Both were educated at Cambridge. In 1934, Sir Shane Leslie (Winston Churchill's cousin), an Irish patriot, had written an investigative biography of Cardinal Manning, and he suggested that some of Carroll's nonsense characters were based on nineteenth-century theologians. He thought the message of *Looking-glass* was that Alice was converted to Catholicism by the Red and White Queens, and that this contained a coded message about Carroll's secret leanings.

Then in 1935 William Empson, a literary critic and sinologist (thereby used to dealing with ideograms) pointed out certain allusions to Darwinism in *Alice*. He connected her getting bigger and smaller with evolutionary theory. He even suggested – though Darwin had not arrived at the concept by 1865 when *Wonderland* was published – that the Pool of Tears in which Alice fell was the primordial fluid from which life emerged.

Empson's view of *Alice* is laced with Freudian analysis, and he did not identify individual characters. Leslie, caught up as he was in English Roman Catholic history in the nineteenth century, did name names and he did so with considerable tenacity. Reading him, we felt we must look more carefully at our discovery about the Unicorn. We also remembered that Carroll portrayed himself as the Dodo who accompanies Alice in the early part of the tale. Carroll himself admitted as much when he gave a copy of the book to his friend Robinson Duckworth, who used to accompany him and the Liddell sisters on rowing expeditions on the river Thames. 'From the Dodo to the Duck' he inscribed the little red-covered volume. Dodo was a mockery of Dodgson, the don who habitually stammered his name - Do-Do-Do-Do-Dodgson to his Common Room colleagues in days when men hardly ever addressed each other by Christian names. There was a political side to this, too. The Dodo is the extinct flightless bird from Mauritius. When Dean Liddell came to Christ Church, he changed the rules so that older Students (dons), such as Carroll, were members of the Old Foundation, to all intents and purposes an extinct cohort.

Surely all this amounted to more than just a game. The

portrait of the Unicorn seemed to catch Gladstone, to make him real, the brilliant man with thrusting rhetoric who threw a few insults around after getting a small slice of the electoral cake, but then did the political thing and struck a bargain with a little girl who stood up to him. If Mr Gladstone was there, what about others mentioned in Carroll's diaries, the Pre-Raphaelite painters for example, the poet Tennyson, or John Ruskin?

The answer was to appear when our work in Public Television took us three thousand miles *away* from the apparent source of our quest. With hindsight it was a move that had a looking-glass logic to it.

DO-DO-DODGSON

CHAPTER TWO

Denizen of
the Stacks

THE FAMILY arrived in Boston, settled down and made what it could of a barely furnished apartment. The English winter clothes we had purchased were inadequate, too warm for American central heating and no protection against the piercing sub-zero outdoor cold of the Boston winter. In a city with twenty-two universities, a child-minder was not difficult to find. He appeared, a Ph.D. student working on Mongol magic. He had a long drooping moustache and a sad face. The children loved him, perhaps because he was more interested in our fridge than in them. One Boston privilege attached to our work in Public Television was a limited right to visit collections at Harvard University which stayed open until late into the night.

The huge Widener Library at Harvard had been built of New England granite and established in memory of a graduate who was heir to a fortune but who was killed in the First World War. Up the icy granite steps to the library ran wooden duckboards. The architecture was American and yet our first impression of Harvard, with its extensive collections of English literature, theatre, art and politics made the university appear in many respects more English than England. In particular the Victorian critic, maverick, and seeker of socialism in art, John Ruskin, had made close friends with Charles Eliot Norton, the first Professor of the History of Art at Harvard, who taught under Ruskin's Oxford influence. Harvard was rewarded with a beautiful collection of Ruskin drawings and books. Perhaps Ruskin, a friend of Gladstone's, and Carroll would intersect, along with Rossetti and Millais and the other artists.

This library was a Wonderland on a different scale to St Deiniol's. From the main door the way to the books led up through marbled and gilded halls, then past rows of wooden card files, bruised with use. From curiosity we looked out the file card with Henry Kissinger's dissertation on Machiavelli, complete with annotations. There was card after card on Ruskin, edition after edition of *Modern Painters*, *The Stones of Venice*, other works distributed through the libraries of the university, some restricted and valuable editions, some reference copies. From the card files, the route to the particular Ruskin editions we wanted to see led through a tiny fire-proof door and into the stacks then down seven levels in a cramped grey metal elevator, a disconcerting experience because it was hard to know at any time whether one was above or below ground. The steel shelves of the stacks were lit by only a few low-power lights. There, in a deep recess, seeming to have been little touched, were three yards of Ruskin's *Collected Works*, bound in shiny russet-coloured cloth, an edition produced just after his death, a homage to a man who was arrogant and quirky but original enough to have influenced both Tolstoy and Gandhi deeply. When we took out one of the volumes of Ruskin's *Modern Painters*, it opened at some of his strange drawings, etched on copper-plate, of lions with eagle heads, 'Griffins' as Ruskin spelled them in the more usual way. Around the illustrations was a long pedagogical section on griffins which Ruskin had written, and in which he praised the medieval carving tradition and attacked earlier classical carving.

The thought came suddenly: could Carroll be mocking Ruskin as the Gryphon in 'Alice'? Ruskin was so fastidious about his Griffins. If Carroll had tried secretly to prick the pompous side of Gladstone, perhaps he did the same with Ruskin.

On the right-hand page was the delicate, densely engraved sepia illustration, on the left the interleaving tissue that had protected it for so long. Far away there were footsteps. Through the thick walls of Widener Library the plaintive wail of an emergency vehicle just penetrated from Massachusetts Avenue outside. Although the Griffin pages of this essay of Ruskin's fell open, many other pages in the volume were still unseparated.

In *Alice's Adventures in Wonderland*, Alice meets a Gryphon on the beach. Leaving the croquet party, the Queen of Hearts breaks off from the executions she is ordering and takes Alice there to meet the Gryphon.

> They very soon came upon a Gryphon lying fast asleep in the sun. (If you don't know what a Gryphon is, look at the picture.)

That is what Carroll said to his reader. As drawn by Tenniel, the picture Carroll referred to certainly looked like one of the griffins Ruskin had drawn for *Modern Painters*. In the first version of *Alice*, the handwritten one called *Alice's Adventures Under Ground*, illustrated by Carroll himself and on which *Wonderland* was based, the drawings were wilder and more frightening. Having unmasked the Unicorn, the sense that Ruskin might be the Gryphon convinced us that we were on to something important.

'You sound just like the people who are always trying to prove Shakespeare was Bacon,' Steve Wilson, the moustachioed child-minder told us. He had majored in English before taking up Mongolian studies. He refused to read *Alice* to our children. He said it was spooky. If sounding like the people who try to prove that Shakespeare was Bacon meant that our idea about real people hidden in 'Alice' was flimsy, we certainly needed more evidence about the Gryphon.

Ruskin was a Christ Church man, and of the same generation as Gladstone and Liddell. In 1855 Carroll read Ruskin's *Stones of Venice*, but did not pass comment. When Carroll met Tennyson in 1856, Tennyson made derogatory remarks about Ruskin, saying he had 'profound contempt for Ruskin as a critic', though he admired his writing. Shortly after this Carroll met Ruskin in the Christ Church Common Room:

> I had a little conversation with him, but not enough to bring out anything characteristic or striking in him. His appearance was rather disappointing – a general feebleness of expression,

with no commanding air . . . as one would have expected to see in such a man.

Paradoxically he added '*Dies notabilis*' at the bottom of the entry. Could one see in Carroll's remark a kind of envy of great men that had to do with his being rather humble himself? Why, after all, should Ruskin bother to impress Carroll who was only twenty-five and low on the college pecking order?

We felt the need for a guide. Deep in those stacks we found John Clive, a large, rumpled, tweed-coated man whose clothes seemed either too big or too small. He was Professor of English History at Harvard, and he kept a door open to visitors providing they could find somewhere to sit, or even stand, in an office overflowing with books and unbound journals sent to him for review. To our surprise, he seemed to welcome our ideas. There were too many books saying the same things about the Victorians who needed dusting off, he said. He urged us to look more into Oxford.

Did he have any ideas? He gazed at the ceiling, then squeezed his eyes shut and navigated deftly around the piles of books. He pulled from low in a pile, without disturbing its equilibrium, a book by E. G. W. Bill and J. F. A. Mason called *Christ Church and Reform*, on the dust-jacket of which was the photograph of Lewis Carroll taken by Oscar Rejlander. Carroll was wearing a white bow tie, the uniform of dons, and held a lens and lens cloth in his hands, his diffident face looking away from the camera.

Christ Church and Reform was based on access to college records and covered Liddell's early years. Its text was dense and full of unfamiliar names but from it emerged a sense of how Carroll really might have built looking-glass images. It was surprising to find Carroll, the anti-reformer, pictured on the dust jacket of a book about reform at Oxford. In a debate over arguments about Christ Church's constitution, this ancient college, it turned out, did not have one and required special acts of Parliament to make significant changes. Carroll and another don, Thomas Jones Prout, were among Dean Liddell's chief antagonists. They attacked his novel building plans, and his attempts to defend an archaic system of kickbacks in the running of the college kitchens. Where Liddell's ideas for syllabus reform and the times of college chapel involved change, Prout, Carroll and others in the Senior Common Room were the conservatives. On issues of power, such as giving the Students some control over what they taught, the Dean and Canons were the conservatives, while Carroll and Prout became the radicals. Liddell often ignored memoranda, so the Carroll faction took to other weapons of attack, circulating anonymous but vitriolic squibs sometimes in Latin, sometimes in English. As in *Alice*, individuals were parodied as strange beasts. The anger behind these squibs seemed to be a clear reflection of the violence in *Alice*.

Outside his own college, Christ Church, Carroll fired off more squibs about plans to turn university parkland into cricket pitches. Carroll, who was to write about a little girl's adventures in an often arcadian wonderland, loathed the male athleticism of organised sport. Our research intersected with Ruskin again over the issue of the newly constructed Natural History Museum. Carroll railed against the overspend on the new Natural History Museum which involved raiding the money that had entered the university coffers from the profits on the Bibles Oxford published. Ruskin and the Professor of Medicine, Henry Acland, were instrumental in the plans for this temple to science built in high gothic style.

Two weeks after Carroll's first encounter with Ruskin in the Common Room (which took place at the time of the building of the Natural History Museum) Carroll wrote a mocking poem called 'Hiawatha's Photographing'. Written in the metre of Longfellow's original, this Hiawatha has a commission to make portrait photographs of an enormously vain middle-class family whom the photographer scorns for taking up 'Ruskinian' poses. We had the same sense of Carroll being preoccupied with someone about whom he is uneasy and then producing a satire, as he did the Gladstone anagram, while lying awake at night.

On our next visit John Clive produced another gem from his stacks. He opened what we saw was a copy of Ruskin's fictionalised autobiography, *Praeterita*, looked at it hard, peered at it

33

THE POSTURING YOUNG MAN STRIKING
ABSURD 'RUSKINIAN' POSES, AS DRAWN BY A. B. FROST AND
DESCRIBED BY CARROLL IN *HIAWATHA'S PHOTOGRAPHING*

again closer to his face, and then handed it to us. It was an
account of Alice Liddell and Ruskin arranging a secret meeting
in the Deanery at Christ Church when Alice knew the Liddell
parents were going out. After the parents had set off in their carriage for dinner with the Duke and Duchess of Marlborough
Alice sent a servant to fetch Ruskin. When he arrived, Alice
and her sisters entertained him with tea and songs. Ruskin
referred to her as 'Alice in Wonderland'.

Alas for Ruskin, the parents intervened, having turned back

in a snowstorm. Mrs Liddell was outraged to find a bachelor with her daughters, despite the fact that Ruskin had taught the girls drawing. The Dean failed to back his wife and shuffled off, embarrassed at the admonition addressed to his friend, and went to eat supper. The entrance to Carroll's rooms was less than a hundred yards away. On the night of the snowstorm he would, presumably, have walked to dine in Hall, a black clad figure on the snowy quadrangle. Carroll's reason for depicting Alice as disgusted by the Gryphon began to make more sense.

> ... she [the executing Queen] walked off, leaving Alice alone with the Gryphon. Alice did not quite like the look of the creature, but on the whole she thought it would be quite as safe to stay with it as to go after that savage Queen so she waited.

As Alice Liddell knew how to deal with Gladstone from having met him at the seaside and at the Deanery, so she was confident she could handle Ruskin. Indeed the scene sounded like a mocking version of Alice's own drawing lessons with Ruskin. There was talk with the Gryphon and the Mock Turtle of what Alice learns, 'Reeling and Writhing . . . and Uglification'.

> 'Never heard of uglifying!' [the Gryphon] exclaimed. 'You know what to beautify is, I suppose?'

This led us back to looking more closely at the real Alice and Carroll's child photographs. When he posed them, as when he spun out his fantastical stories, it was Alice who was the central character, her sisters taking minor roles.

The years of the friendship were those between 1856 and 1863. Visits to Carroll's rooms were frequent, so were walks. There were inadequately chaperoned rowing expeditions on the river, Carroll telling Alice stories all the while. In these years Alice grew up from four to eleven. Then Mrs Liddell cut Carroll off, telling him to stay away from her children. He suffered in larger measure than had Ruskin on that night at the Deanery, for Carroll was closer to Alice than was Ruskin. Contact thereafter was reduced to polite greetings. The precise reason for the separation has never been made clear. In books about Carroll there has been much speculation over whether he had proposed to Alice or shown any intention of doing so. Her mother, Lorina Liddell, is said to have hoped for an eventual royal wedding for Alice. Carroll was right outside the socially privileged box that contained the Liddells' luxurious and well-connected world.

It seemed to us that he had only one weapon of revenge, his pen. His beloved Alice became 'Alice', her parents the vacillating King and the tyrannical Queen of Hearts in *Wonderland*. The King in 'Alice' plays second fiddle to his wife, Liddell rhyming with 'fiddle' in a contemporary Oxford lampoon on the Dean's subordination to his wife. There were also echoes of the Liddell of *Christ Church and Reform* in the King of Hearts – imperious, intelligent, capable of letting his attention wander, concerned with his own rewards and status as well as his role at the centre of affairs. Telling the jury to make their verdict before hearing the evidence, mumbling 'Guilty, not guilty' as if it did not matter which – this was the King at the trial of the Knave of Hearts. Here was Liddell as seen by Carroll, ignoring his and Prout's memoranda, making up his mind regardless of what others said, content that his Queen should get on with her own profession of executing people.

In some ways it might be thought that here was a clearer connection than we had managed to make between Ruskin and the Gryphon. We were still circling round Ruskin for clues that might reinforce our sense that he was the Gryphon.

'Have you thought of the Ruskin drawing collections at Harvard?' John Clive asked. 'See if they help. Above all, remember Victorian anti-science. It is misunderstood.'

*

In the Fogg Art Museum at Harvard was an extensive collection of Ruskin's drawings and watercolours. Their vividness was astonishing in someone we thought of as an art critic rather than an artist.

Clive and some of his students of Victorian history stood by and watched as carefully we examined the first work we were allowed to remove from the folio drawers. It was of a twig of barely-opened peach blossom painted in watercolour and set against a bright turquoise, jewelled sky – the colour of the cravat Ruskin used to wear when lecturing on Art to packed audiences in his prime. Nature fascinated Ruskin and this unforgettable painting showed it. He hated 'science' and he squirmed physically at the idea of nature dissected. Ruskin even refused to look down a microscope. He said that the sound of geological hammers in the High Alps rang in his ears like the death-knell of Mountain Glory.

Then we came across what appeared to be images hidden inside images. First there was a Ruskin drawing of a necklace of pearls, innocent enough and again delicately done. At the end of the thread, the pearls became the face of a girl, the same girl repeated again and again, except that these faces turned along the string of pearls into devilish heads, though still of the same girl. The name he had written under the drawing was that of 'Lily Armstrong'. Also the word 'Winnington' was on the paper.

Another, a drawing in pencil touched with charcoal, was of the tumbled rocks in an Alpine torrent, and the river was named neatly in pencil by Ruskin. At first sight this was a landscape drawing of the Alps, but on looking more closely, it was possible to see human profiles hidden in the boulders at unstable angles. Twisting round the drawing was the largest of these profiles, Ruskin's own. It showed the scar over his left lip which he hid from photographers so that the viewer only saw his 'good' profile. He had been savaged by a dog as a child.

With a copy of *Alice* in front of us, we showed the students how we thought Gladstone was hidden as the Unicorn and how Ruskin's personality might somehow be visible behind the Gryphon's odd antics. Some of the students took to the idea of secrecy as displayed in the Ruskin pencil sketch, and perhaps through Carroll's pen. That led to a discussion of how difficult it had been for certain Victorians to face different aspects of the new science. Ruskin had become quite unhinged by the thought of God's nature being knocked down into component parts. John Clive reminded us that Carroll and Ruskin each virulently opposed vivisection when it was introduced into the

Oxford laboratories. The Chairman of the decisive debate was Dean Liddell.

Later, another link appeared in a photograph of Ruskin by Carroll. In a secondhand book store we found the red-bound 'colonial edition' of the rare *Life and Letters of Lewis Carroll* by his nephew Stuart Dodgson Collingwood. Originally published at the end of 1898, the year in which Carroll died, this edition was dated 1899. It contained a fine studio portrait of Ruskin, one of Carroll's best. As we were to discover, it is unlisted in the catalogues of the Carroll photographic collections at the Universities of Princeton and Texas. Because one or two volumes of Ruskin's *Collected Works* had been borrowed from Widener Library we had missed the fact that this photograph was also in there. What was not there was a truly odd anecdote told by Collingwood, who stated that people often asked Carroll for copies of this handsome *carte de visite* photograph of Ruskin. Carroll therefore wrote to Ruskin to ask his permission to distribute it. Ruskin replied saying he could hand out copies of it if he first bought a back-number of a magazine he had recently launched for 'Working Men', including those he taught in London. It expressed Ruskin's latest views on the British economy. The magazine was called *Fors Clavigera*.

Carroll, a conservative in politics, who almost certainly did not approve of Ruskin's editorial position on working men, wrote back to say he could not afford the ten pence to buy it. By then Carroll had published *Alice* and his impecunious days as a young Christ Church Student were behind him. He could at least have been courteous to the great critic in his reply.

Perhaps this was an important indication of real and secretive sniping between the two men, a relationship as distorted as Ruskin's 'mad' drawing of himself in the rock. The particular issue of *Fors Clavigera* to which Ruskin referred also contained Ruskin's attack on the art of photography. If Carroll, the photographer, wanted to make jokes about Ruskin, he clearly knew exactly how to go about it.

CHAPTER THREE
Mirror Images

OUR DISCOVERY of the Ruskin photograph persuaded us that the time had come to look more carefully at Carroll's photographs, not just the famous ones of little girls, but those that were lesser known of adults, of which only a few have ever been published. At his death, Carroll's extensive collection of albums had been auctioned for a pittance. Of those that were still known about, there were two in Christ Church. Two other important collections were in the United States, three albums in Princeton University in New Jersey and five in the University of Texas at Austin. The Princeton collection had been preserved by Morris L. Parrish, the millionaire head of the Victor Gramophone Company, who had suggested in the 1930s that a building to house his Carroll collection should be created at Guildford where Carroll died and where his spinster sisters lived. In the depth of the Depression no English money was forthcoming and the collection remained in America.

We went first to see Princeton albums. There were Carroll's beautiful little photographs of Alice Liddell and other young girls in front of our eyes in the original for the first time. Blacker and whiter and much smaller than reproductions suggested, they were stuck into modest albums, their covers tied with a simple black lace. Often the top of the photograph was trimmed with scissors by Carroll, slightly clumsily, into an arch. If the sitter was identified, it was in his steady hand and mauve ink.

Among the children were several of Carroll's portraits of adults, including one of the distinguished Victorian physicist and inventor, Michael Faraday. This puzzled us. Unlike the case of Ruskin, Faraday had no known connection with Carroll. As far as we knew, Carroll's camera was not for hire. He only rarely requested payment for making copies, or if he photographed a specimen for a scientist, as he had done for the Professor of Medicine, Dr Acland, or a painting for an artist, as he did for the Pre-Raphaelite Rossetti. So what made him choose the subjects who were not little girls? There was no clear answer to this question, except that Carroll, often insomniac, hatched his plans privately, then stalked people who interested him.

In these albums a question about Carroll's sexuality emerged again. Dons at Oxford, except for Heads of Colleges and certain other senior appointees, were bound by law to remain celibate. Carroll was a man who spent as much time as he could in the company of little girls, and often invited them to stay with him on summer holidays in Eastbourne. In the back of one of the Princeton albums were other puzzling, disturbing items – some loose prints, haunting images of rickety little girls, apparently the sullen, neglected, bare-foot children such as might be found in a badly-run Victorian workhouse. The prints were uncaptioned and uncatalogued, not the kind of subject that he photographed. Yet it would appear that they would have been there when he lived in Christ Church, surrounded by these treasured albums. They gave a sense of how private Carroll was, of how one grown man or another, one little girl or another, might be enticed to sit for him, not for commercial purposes – he rarely exhibited – but for him to watch. These people did not meet one another. The moments of opening the shutter were private moments, requiring intense concentration if a natural effect was to be gained under long exposures. Could those he photographed also be those he parodied? John Clive's original advice had been to dig deeper into the adult Carroll. That now meant going further from the target in order to hit it. Texas beckoned.

*

The Texas collection, the largest single collection in the world, includes five albums, some single photographs and a few negatives. It had been assembled by Helmut Gernsheim who came to England as a refugee before the Second World War, rediscovered the Victorian photographer, Julia Margaret Cameron, and in the process of research recognised albums as being Carroll's work when a London dealer offered them as an unattributed property. The availability of Texas oil money and the desire to start a cultural research institute led to the Gernsheim collection being established in Austin, the state capital.

Although Shane Leslie and William Empson had begun to delve into the relations between 'Alice' and Carroll's wider world, Gernsheim approached the real people in Carroll's life in a different way, carefully identifying and listing those whom Carroll photographed and, by tracing the remaining diaries back to his family, others whom he had tried to photograph. He did not connect the adults with the 'Alice' stories, nor did he show an awareness of having read Empson or Leslie.

Forms filled in, brief-cases set aside, a promise made to use only pencil, the assistant archivist at the Ransom Institute in Austin, Texas, brought us the first Carroll album. Like those at Princeton, it was modest, about twelve inches wide by nine high, the kind of album covered with a mottled imitation-leather material that anyone might have bought in a Victorian stationers. There were two dark green velvet cushions, no bigger than a wood engraver's leather pad, on which we were shown how to rest the album cover so that the spine would not break. The archivist handed us white cotton gloves, a size that would better fit a child but of the kind used for film-editing. One's hands very soon became sweaty inside them but they protected Carroll's own prints which were small, delicate and fragile, generally no more than three by five inches, their backs again perfectly black.

The first photograph was of Carroll's father, wearing clergyman's cloth. He was square-jawed and rather rumpled, with a kindly face. Carroll had placed the old clergyman in profile and there was a sheen of light on the leather armchair in which he sat. The pose was not unlike the one Whistler chose for his painting of his mother, also dressed in black. Carroll's light source was different. It came softly from an unseen window on the left, as if God given. The picture conveyed respect as well as affection by the photographer for his subject.

How strange that this devout and scholarly man should have fathered eleven living children and brought up half of them alone. There were several pictures of Carroll's sisters, one showing them in their hooped skirts in a garden. The girls were grouped under a Catalpa tree with a chess-board set out on a cake-stand beside them. The corners of these pictures were trimmed to an arch at the top and looked quite different from reproductions of Carroll's work. He had controlled with consummate skill the contrast between blacks and whites. Divinity of light! Early photography, so technically cumbersome, placed the great photographers close to their subjects, drawing the modern viewer close to them in time as well.

There were several pictures of Carroll himself, one by Rejlander, his photographic mentor in the 1860s. In no photograph of himself does Carroll give anything away. He never seemed to age, but posed impassively, gazing with a mask-like expression into some secret distance. The pose reminded us of how much the Victorians liked to ponder the boundary between dream and reality. Alfred Lord Tennyson was fond of exploring the theme in his poetry.

Most of the photographs were of little girls, very few of boys. Some pictures of Alice Liddell showed her loitering dangerously, with her shoes off. In some poses she was tiny, five years old or even younger. Some of the little girls were draped on *chaises-longues*. Such poses were characteristic of early French erotic photographs of nudes, but Carroll completely transformed the impact of the *mise-en-scène* by peopling it with his 'child-friends' holding hairbrushes, some in night-dresses and pretending to be asleep. A few had signed their names underneath in the awkward hand of a child who was just starting to read and write, one of his favourite ages for a child model.

We came upon the famous photograph of Alice in her father's garden, sitting in profile in a chair, fringed and intent. It was a strange, still image beautifully focused on the face. It posed questions about Carroll's relationship with his photographic subject and the girl to whom he first told the 'Alice' stories. There was a copy of this photograph framed on our wall at home in Wales, but our copy was larger and greyer than the original.

There were other Alices, Alice Westmacott in dancing shoes sitting on stone steps, Alice Donkin climbing out of a window in a posed photograph called *The Elopement*, a strange concept since the subject was under twelve years old and probably under ten. There was tiny, podgy Alice Murdoch sitting on a table and holding her expression with courage but difficulty. She was wearing a gingham dress fringed with lace. There were, as in the Princeton albums, a number of famous Victorians, artists, scientists and churchmen. There was Archbishop Longley and the painter Dante Gabriel Rossetti, every other living member of the Rossetti family, the Crown Prince of Denmark in an Oxford mortar-board and gown. He did not give the impression, however, of having read many books. There was the Oxford scientist John Phillips with his little hammer. He was the ablest crystallographer of the age. Some of these Carroll had posed with their own daughters. The fathers looked self-effacing and the little daughters looked happy, as if the fathers were the price Carroll was prepared to pay for a relaxed photograph of their little daughters.

Xie Kitchin succeeded Alice Liddell as Carroll's favourite model, and was a friend of hers in later life. In one picture Xie (Alexandra) was standing in a white dress, wearing a crown and looking at the camera. She was on the right of the image. On the left was a boy with a huge sword on a rocking horse. This he pointed at another little boy – Xie's tiny brother draped in a tiger-skin rug. Carroll called the photograph 'St George and the Dragon'. There was something so incompetent about the way he had set it up that it reminded us of the White Knight in *Through the Looking-glass*. He was always falling off his horse and having to be helped up again by Alice.

The afternoon moved by fast and the archivist put her head round the door to say that they would be closing soon. We were looking at what the catalogue described as the 'Weld Album'. It had been the property of the Weld family who were, it appeared, friends of the poet Tennyson. We turned the page and saw Carroll's early photograph of the two Tennyson boys whom he had posed awkwardly on either side of Julia Marshall, their companion. In another photograph Carroll had posed them wrapped tightly in a Paisley shawl, no doubt to keep them still while giving his photographic plate a long exposure. They were handsome little boys with sly and mischievous expressions on their faces.

Quite suddenly the idea came to the surface that Carroll might have used the Tennyson boys as models for the mirror image children, Tweedledum and Tweedledee. We were looking at a photograph of Hallam and Lionel Tennyson both dressed up in similar striped costumes. Although they were very young when they sat for Carroll – apparently unwillingly – they had a bumptious, knowing look of the kind often associated with spoilt boys, though not usually when they are under five years old.

ALICE WITH
TWEEDLEDUM
AND TWEEDLEDEE
(by Tenniel)

Could we be right? At that moment the archivist returned to put the album back into safe-keeping for the night. We knew there were other photographs of the boys in these Carroll albums. The best we could do for the moment was to go to the main University Library and cross-check Carroll's diaries. At the desk we were given back our brief-cases and then we waited for what seemed like several minutes for the elevator to come. The only other passenger was a man in a raincoat who might have been a famous English historian, but his identity eluded us.

In the library we found Carroll's *Diaries*, published in two volumes in the 1950s, and looked for a reference to Carroll photographing the Tennyson boys. And there it was. He had travelled to the Lake District with his brother and his camera cases from the Croft on the other side of England. He had sent his brother off for a walk and then gone to the house the Tennysons were renting. There he had sent in his card, saying that he was the photographer of 'Little Red Riding-Hood' – in other words, Agnes Weld. An hour or so before we had seen Carroll's photograph of her in her cape, but had not taken particular notice of it. She was cousin to the Tennysons, and the connection worked as an introduction. Emily Tennyson invited Carroll in and before long he was photographing the boys – though, of course, Tennyson himself was the real quarry.

We were beginning to get a better sense of the way in which Carroll crept up on people he wished to have as his subjects. The library also yielded another useful confirmation in *The Tennyson Album*, a book published in England with an introduction by Sir John Betjeman when he was Poet Laureate. It was a kind of Tennyson scrapbook, full of photographs of the family, among them several of the boys, always together as if they were twins, and dressed as twins. That in itself reinforced the idea that they were models for Tweedledum and Tweedledee. In one by Julia Margaret Cameron they looked distinctly Tweedledum and Tweedledee-ish, dressed exactly alike, wearing white lace collars like the doilies around a birthday cake. In another by Oscar Rejlander they were older and Lionel looked thinner in the face than Hallam. They had the same white collars, the same felt or tweed tunics, the same disdainful, self-confident look.

The next morning we saw that particular photograph in the archive. This was in an album of pictures partly by Carroll, partly by photographers he admired and whose work was interspersed with his own, making identification of the photographer not always easy. On a number of pictures, Gernsheim had left room for doubt. There was one photograph, undoubtedly by Carroll, of Hallam Tennyson standing on a chair with a carved back. Hallam was holding a whip and looking sultry.

Then we saw another photograph of the pair together in this guise attributed to Rejlander, but possibly by Carroll. Once again we were reminded that he had all these photographs in his rooms when he wrote *Alice*.

There was also a photograph of Mr Gladstone which Gernsheim had attributed to Carroll. We showed it to Roy Fulkinger, the head of the Department, who agreed that it did not look like a Carroll print. It was larger than most, lacked the characteristic arch at the top and was in sepia. Carroll, however, did not always print his own work. Could it be by Carroll? It was not a Gladstone photograph we had seen before. He was standing in the centre of the room, more in profile than most of Carroll's photographs. Still, the fact that it was in Carroll's album meant that he had had it close to him. He could study the Unicorn. A tantalising note written in Gernsheim's hand referred to a photograph of Ruskin with Rossetti that was not in the main albums. The archivist thought it might have been a copy print used for an exhibition. Then, in trying to cross-reference Carroll with Gladstone, we discovered that Carroll also photographed Gathorne Hardy. He was stalking people with his camera. The reward was the satisfaction of having these portraits close to him at all times.

If nothing new on Ruskin came to light, the experience of seeing Carroll's photographs had certainly increased our belief that those whom he photographed were those whom he wrote about in his diaries, often in an uncomplimentary way. Could more of these real people be hidden in 'Alice'? Was it possible to spot further visual masking that Victorian cartoonists like Tenniel published but that cryptic satirists such as Lewis Carroll and John Ruskin tried to disguise? Tucked away in our mind was the drawing Ruskin did of the girl on the necklace, the one who became a devil. As it happened, it was she, a contemporary of Alice Liddell, who was to provide the next clue.

Carroll) Lewis]

CHAPTER FOUR

Children of Cheshire

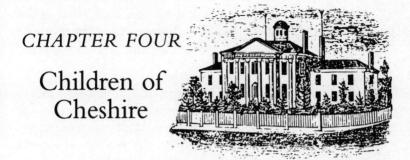

IT WAS Isla Crum, a neighbour of ours in North Wales, who provided the next clue when we returned to Britain. We were discussing with her the Ruskin connection and the social ambitions of the Liddells when she remembered seeing a photograph of Alice as a rather dumpy old lady in a straw-hat stepping off a liner in New York. It had appeared, she thought, in the *Illustrated London News* on the occasion of Carroll's centenary in 1932. She told us that two of Alice's three sons had been killed in the First World War and Alice had crossed the Atlantic to receive an honorary degree from Columbia University.

'Georgiana!' Isla said suddenly, as if out of the blue. Despite her eighty years and a recent operation on her ankle, she scrambled up on to a chair, refusing help from us, and took down from a perilously high glass-fronted bookshelf a copy of Georgiana Burne-Jones' *Memorials* – of her husband. It had been given to Isla by her grandmother when, as an art student, she had volunteered in the First World War for technical drawing and had spent her time shading in the mechanisms of naval guns.

Ruskin first appears in *Memorials* at Lucerne in Switzerland. Georgiana wrote:

> We rowed out on the lake and the two men [Ruskin and Edward Burne-Jones] talked all the time of scientific discoveries, the formation of the earth and the gradual development upon it of animal life . . .

How frightened we were when the spirit of the mountaineer showed itself in our beloved companion [Ruskin] and made him skip about the steep slopes of the Cathedral roof until each moment we thought to see him fall into the piazza below . . .

The Gryphon in 'Alice' never stands still. Then he took to dancing. Could this roof-top caper possibly be the origin of the Lobster Quadrille which the Gryphon dances so terrifyingly? Were we close to proof that Ruskin was the model for the Gryphon? Later in the book, Georgiana described Ruskin at a girls' school where she and her husband and Ruskin had all taught art.

. . . girls were taught to play cricket. To dancing also Miss Bell gave an important place, and a pretty sight it was to see the long schoolroom or the gallery filled with white-frocked, light-hearted girls dancing together. Mr Ruskin paid his tribute of admiration both in words and by taking his place occasionally in a quadrille or country dance.

Even more exciting, the school was called Winnington Hall. The word 'Winnington' had been inscribed in the Harvard collection in the Fogg Art Museum by Ruskin below his obsessive drawing of Lily Armstrong. Isla said she thought she knew Winnington, that it was a house in Cheshire, not far away.

She had the idea that it had been taken over as offices and absorbed into a factory. We found Winnington on the road atlas, but it was too late – on Friday afternoon – to make enquiries before the weekend.

It lay close to the M56 between our home and Manchester and ten miles from Carroll's birthplace at Daresbury. The Ordnance Survey map showed it as a suburb of Northwich, which is where the Cheshire salt-mines are located. On Monday an official of the local council said the hall belonged to ICI and was run as a staff club. Philip Martin, its manager, was not at all surprised when we said we wanted to see the building because we had an interest in Ruskin and the progressive girls' boarding-school that he had founded there. From a bookseller in Chester, who had been helping us collect memoirs of the Carroll period, we learned that an American book had been published about the school and he had tracked down a copy, remaindered by the Harvard University Press. It was called *The Winnington Letters: John Ruskin's correspondence with Margaret Alexis Bell and the Children at Winnington Hall.*

The Winnington Letters ran to seven hundred pages and was based on the long correspondence between Ruskin who supported the school, the Misses Bell who ran it, and the girls, his 'Birdies', of whom Lily Armstrong was one of the favoured few. Ruskin's attachment to her began when she was eleven – 'a pretty Irish Lily'. He compared her to his love of those years, the young and slender Anglo-Irish Rose La Touche. He continued to correspond with this particular Lily well into her married life. Part of the correspondence is marked by a sterner note, as when Ruskin wrote to her sharply about the death of a friend. Perhaps this was a period when he felt Lily was tempting him and, as his drawing from this period suggests, he became obsessed and turned the pearls on the end of her necklace into devils.

The Winnington letters had come to light among a bundle of old and decaying letters and papers discovered in a house in Brighton in 1962. Van Aken Burd, who found them, had written a history of Ruskin's tragic love affair with the very young Rose la Touche. (Rose eventually died of anorexia after repeatedly rejecting him.) The Winnington papers gave Van Aken Burd a completely new insight into Ruskin's radical educational activities in Cheshire while his suit to La Touche's delicate daughter began to founder. We had already discovered from Georgiana Burne-Jones, who taught at Winnington, that John Ruskin liked to dance the steps of the Quadrille at Winnington Hall. Ruskin was as fond of the Burne-Jones couple as he was of the Eliot Nortons from Harvard. Georgiana had gone to teach at Winnington at Ruskin's request. Her husband, Edward, whom Ruskin always called 'Ned' went with her and found the girls entrancing. In March 1864, when Georgie was teaching needlework and executing Arthurian tapestries with the girls at Winnington, Ruskin wrote to her:

My Dearest little narrow Georgie, Expand in mind as much
as you like, but don't get fat – or I shan't like you at all . . .
Love of loves to Ned.

Ever, Your affectionate Papa,
J Ruskin

Georgiana Burne-Jones, who had several children of her own
by this date, wrote of Ruskin when he was in residence:
'Ruskin joined the Quadrille looking very tall and thin, scarcely
more than a black line amongst . . . the white girls in his
evening dress.' Ruskin claimed to have danced with reluctance,
but this sounded far from reluctant.

Ruskin, a school governor, transposed a devil on to the picture of the head of a young boarding-school girl on whom he
doted at a time his relationship with Rose – who was too delicate to be sent to boarding-school – was collapsing. Carroll transposed a Gryphon, a lazy Gryphon, on to Ruskin who, unlike
Carroll, was rich enough never to need to work for a living.

★

Van Akin Burd noted that 'Winnington Hall was admirably
located to attract the daughters of the Cheshire gentry, clerics,
and Cottontot (to rhyme with Hottentot) *grandees* of
Manchester, as the Stanleys dubbed the Manchester Cotton
Magnates'.

Winnington School was opened in 1851. The house was
converted to a school because Lady Stanley found it too cold
and moved away to another Stanley residence in Cheshire. The
Misses Bell who ran it were bad at sums. Ruskin had met them
through Bishop Samuel Wilberforce of Oxford, who ordained
Carroll as a deacon.

Ruskin first came to Winnington on 9th or 10th March,
1859 after a tour of Yorkshire taken in his father's coach. He
persuaded his father to pay considerable sums into the school
account, which he did unwillingly until his death in 1864. To
claim her funds, Miss Bell used to arrive at the Ruskins' mansion in south-west London with girls aged from eight to as
much as twenty years old in tow. The burden of Miss Bell's

fund-raising visits fell on Ruskin's old mother, who lived in 'constant dread of falls and fever' when the girls came to visit. It was noted that when she provided a bed for each girl and Miss Bell, one of them preferred to share with someone else: '4 beds, 3 full', Ruskin's father noted in his diary on 7th August 1862.

By March 1867 the Ruskins had invested a total of £1,130 15s 4d in Winnington, and Ruskin himself went on funding Miss Bell until 1869. Then the venture collapsed. According to Van Aken Burd, Ruskin taught an odd blend of art and geology and drama to the girls at the Hall during his brief periods of residence there between 1859 to 1861.

One way to the school was to follow Ruskin's roundabout route. He had said that his eyes would be offended by the factories, grime and poverty of Northwich. So, instead of taking the direct line to the station hardly a mile from Winnington, he would go via the pretty Cheshire village of Hartford. Thereafter he was driven by carriage and could approach Winnington from its country direction and see it in its parkland setting, in the manner of the Picturesque. We followed Ruskin's route into the valley of the Weaver, drove over a wide canal bridge where the picturesque came to an abrupt end, and made our way through a forest of high chimneys and pipes, factory buildings and large signs for Brunner Mond, part of ICI.

Suddenly in front of us stood the facade of a Georgian stone building. On the lawn was a man who looked like a retired ICI executive, playing croquet with his wife. In the photographs from Ruskin's time, the mansion at Winnington was visible across lush shrubberies and a much larger lawn. Here the girls played croquet in their long hooped dresses. Now between lawn and house runs a tarmac drive with yellow 'no parking' lines on it. One wing, overlooking the old lawns, has been converted into *Winstone's Brasserie*. Direction signs give the old house an air of having been sanitised.

No ghosts here: but inside it was different. We found the Hall empty, polished, sparse and dim. In the entrance were metal-banded chests that must have been there in Ruskin's day. We were politely given the run of the place by an off-duty receptionist. There was no one about except the couple who came in from playing croquet and ignored us. It was an odd labyrinth of a house, the floors connected by various stairs from various building periods. At the back and upstairs were the girls' rooms and where Ruskin had played chasing games with them in the attic when they were tired of the garden. He ventured this to his mother.

The octagonal room used by Ruskin as a study still existed and was the most stylish space in the Georgian part of the house. Here he taught the Winnington girls drawing, when he had the strength, and took notes about conversations they were having with one another. These he put into exaggerated dialogue in his book *Ethics of the Dust*, a series of dotty conversations between these girls about minerals, set at Winnington Hall and written when Carroll was composing *Alice*. He also coerced the Winnington girls into making an index to his *Modern Painters*, in which he included the long diatribe we had seen in Harvard against 'false' and in favour of 'true griffins', as if all the world were meant to understand the distinction. In one chapter, called 'Of the True Ideal', Ruskin belittled a griffin from a Roman Temple for being too mechanically conceived. His favourite griffins were medieval ones from Lombardy. With

TRUE AND FALSE GRIFFINS, from RUSKIN'S 'MODERN PAINTERS'

these he was, to say the least, obsessed. To one holding up a pillar of the porch of the cathedral of Verona he attached particular importance. It was as though its mythical identity were almost part of his own psyche:

> The difference [between the true and the false Grotesque Beast] is that the Lombard workman really did see a griffin in his imagination, and carved it from the life, meaning to declare to all ages that he had verily seen with his immortal eyes such a griffin as that; but the classical workman never saw a griffin at all, nor anything else; but put the whole thing together by line and rule . . .
> What more? Having both lion and eagle in him, it is probable that the real griffin would have an infinite look of repose as well as power of activity. One of the notablest things about a lion is his magnificent *indolence* . . . Through every separate part and action of the [Lombardic] creature, the imagination is always right. It cannot err. The honest imagination has its griffinism, and grace, and usefulness all at once: but the false composer, caring for nothing but himself and his rules, loses everything, – griffinism, grace, and all.

Like Alice's Gryphon, the real griffin was a lazy griffin and often did not have the strength to do any of these things. On Tuesday, 20th August 1861, Ruskin wrote:

> Dear Miss Bell,
> I've left . . . for a run into Wales and Ireland: I am so pressed for time I cannot venture to Winnington – I shall run straight from Ireland [where he was courting Rose La Touche] to Switzerland, for the fall of the leaf . . . I never write nor read anything now but geology – my poor birdies must bear with me till I get well for I was really very ill this summer. My address will be Poste Restante, Bangor.
> Ever affectionately Yours,
> JR

Eventually he went on holiday to the beach at Bonneville where Turner had sketched. At the same time that he wrote to

Miss Bell he told his friend Charles Eliot Norton at Harvard that 'the present healthy feature of my character is intense indolence'. The Gryphon was indeed lying asleep in the sun when the Queen and Alice met it.

The arrangement of the staircases and linoleum-lined passages at Winnington made it easy to imagine this building as a boarding-school. It was a house made of bits. The dancing had taken place in the Long Gallery of the Wyatt Wing, and Sir Charles Hallé had conducted the ballroom music to which Ruskin and the girls would dance.

This gallery had pilastered walls interspersed with alcoves and a domed, plaster decorated ceiling. By coincidence its high frieze was plastered with 'False griffins'. Pair by pair, these griffins were arranged right round the room, facing each other in perfect symmetry of exactly the kind Ruskin taught the Winnington girls to disapprove.

The hall was hushed and polished, lit by a grey Mancunian sky. The ghosts of the 'birdies' danced silently in front of us, and Ruskin twisted among them. He wrote of these schoolgirls, to whose acne and gawkiness he seemed to be immune:

> Owing to their cricket, and the large park they have to run in, they dance like Dryads. I never saw any dancing at once so finished and so full of life. Old Captain Leslie did a step or two; Mr. Cooke [an old Christ Church friend of Ruskin's, then a Cheshire parson] and his sister danced in nearly all the merry dances. I kept resolvedly to the wall for a long time; but at last a beautiful girl of sixteen . . . pulled me out into the middle of the floor; and I find that henceforth I acquitted myself with satisfaction and that of the fair public; more especially in the course of a jig with little Dr. Acland which followed . . .

In fact, Acland was not little. He was Professor of Medicine at Oxford, a key figure in the public health of the city and the medical officer in charge each time cholera broke out. Dean Liddell helped him. He was known to Carroll, who photographed specimens of bones for him and told what happened at the Hatter's Tea-party to *his* children rather than the Liddells'.

Did Acland appear as a real figure in *Alice*? He had master-minded the building of the Natural History Museum at Oxford which cost more than it should have and involved digging into the university chest, so infuriating the careful Carroll, raised in the habit of parsimony necessary to impoverished clergymen's families. We added Acland to our list as one of the members of the Liddell, Gladstone, Ruskin coterie of Christ Church grandees who might have provided material for a character in *Alice*, but we needed to know more about Acland.

Meanwhile there was John Ruskin transposing the identity of his physician friend on to a Winnington pupil; information that had come from a footnote in Ruskin's *Collected Works*. The 'little Dr. Acland' with whom Ruskin had enjoyed dancing Winnington jigs and lively quadrilles was ' . . . a wild little Irish girl of eleven . . . as like Dr. Acland as a little girl *can* be to a middle-aged gentleman, which means that the face is very bright, open, and vigorous . . . '.

CARROLL'S GRYPHON DANCE IN 'UNDER GROUND'

Ruskin also adapted songs, to which the girls at Winnington School danced. One of these was 'Twist Ye, Twine Ye!' The words were by Sir Walter Scott. Ruskin, however, was not content with Scott's 'Passions wild, and follies vain, Pleasures soon exchanged for pain . . . ', which he replaced with his own more reticent lines: 'Passion's force, by Patience knit, Doubtful Reason reined by Wit . . . ' Carroll's dance under the sea was jollier:

'Will you, won't you, will you, won't you,
  will you join the dance?
Will you, won't you, will you, won't you,
  won't you join the dance?'

If Ruskin was the Gryphon in *Alice*, how had Carroll known what went on at Winnington? It was not easy to connect Georgiana Burne-Jones to any of Carroll's networks. To judge from his diaries and her *Memorials* over the same period, she did not seem to know the same Pre-Raphaelites that he did. She was a central figure in the William Morris circle and later became a Socialist local government councillor. She never appeared in Carroll's diaries, nor did he write to her, nor she to him. Ruskin adulated her, but that did not connect her to Carroll.

The only clue came from Ruskin's Winnington letters which included one to Alice Jane Donkin, written in 1859 when she was eight years old. She was a drawing pupil of Ruskin's. She was also, as a child, pursued by the second of Carroll's three younger brothers, Wilfred Longley Dodgson – named Longley after the future Archbishop of Canterbury, a friend of Carroll's father who was photographed by Carroll. Wilfred Dodgson wanted to marry Alice Donkin as soon as he could. She was the niece of the Savillian Professor of Astronomy at Oxford, whose own daughter was also called Alice, and both girls sat for Carroll, together and apart. Two years before, on 9th October 1862, Carroll took the photograph of Alice Donkin with a cloak over her night-dress at Barnby Moor, in Yorkshire. This was the photograph which we had seen in Texas, called 'The Elopement'.

Alice Donkin was thus one eyewitness who could have reported Ruskin's antics at Winnington and added them to the information Carroll had from Ruskin's books in order to portray him as the Gryphon in *Wonderland*. Indeed Alice Donkin was mentioned more than eight times in Carroll's diaries during the period when he was writing *Alice*. He booked her to be photographed by him the day after he had first met her. Thereafter she came to tea-parties and photographic sessions in Oxfordshire and in Yorkshire from the autumn of 1862.

This is how Carroll described the particular Alice about whom Wilfred was so serious. He went to stay with her family, and having spent the day photographing Alice, Carroll had had time to think about her manner. It was more lady-like in his opinion than the manners of the men in her family, manners being a matter of concern to him.

> A party of the Donkins came over to York . . . Mrs Donkin I decidedly liked and thought Alice very charming both in look and manner. The Donkins are very pleasant people to stay with, though the father and boys are quite farmer-like in tone and manner.

Normally 'lionising', seeking out the great, was done in the company of adults, but Carroll did it in the company of little girls, his significant friends. So he 'lionised' Alice Donkin round Oxford, taking her to meet the Bishop and other figures, and in 1868 holding a dinner-party for her with two friends, Bayne and Liddon, both Christ Church dons.

Alice Jane Donkin married Carroll's brother on 9th August, 1871, and became Carroll's sister-in-law, Alice Dodgson. She had nine children. Wilfred, her husband, found work as a land agent in the employment of an Anglo-Irish landowning family in Shropshire and by this means won her hand. Like Carroll's mother, Alice had seven daughters, some of whom lived until the 1960s, partly dependent on royalties from the 'Alice' books. It was one of her daughters, Menella, Carroll's great-niece, whom Helmut Gernsheim tracked down when he was looking for material associated with Carroll's photographic albums. Gernsheim did not connect the girl from Barnby in 'The Elopement' photograph in the Texas Album with the Menella who had custody of Carroll's surviving private diaries and she did not tell him of the connection. Alice Donkin was her mother.

Carroll's diaries are now in the British Library and we obtained a microfilm copy to check what had been edited out by Roger Lancelyn Green when he prepared a two-volume edition for publication after the Second World War. The years

1858 to 1862, however, had been lost altogether, or perhaps they were deliberately destroyed by Carroll's nephew. A new edition for publication is being put together volume by volume so that eventually the whole text of Carroll's surviving diaries will be generally available to the public.

Lancelyn Green claimed that cuts he had made of one third of the diary entries were not necessary to an understanding of Carroll. These, he said, consisted of 'the times of trains, the weather, the temperature of his rooms', and so forth, but there turned out to be more important items than this in the original and the ommissions were not all trivial. Among the sensitive sections left out were several meetings between Carroll and his uncle, Skeffington Lutwidge, in Oxford, and several accounts of unsuccessful intervention with Wilfred from the autumn of 1865. The two bachelors, maternal uncle Skeffington, a lawyer, and his eldest nephew, Carroll, met on several consecutive days to discuss Wilfred's infatuation for Alice Donkin. Carroll at that time also aired his feelings for Alice Liddell. 'On each occasion we had a good deal of conversation about Wilfred and about A. L . . . It is a very anxious subject.'

No wonder Carroll made the prancing, shrieking Gryphon such a vivid character. The Gryphon suffered the same pangs of unrequited love as Carroll and Wilfred.

This violence that pervades the 'Alice' stories has not received much comment from those who have concerned themselves with Carroll's legacy. Carroll himself refused to talk about 'Alice' and was capable of treating intruders on his privacy rudely. Victorian critics did not seek to interpret children's books and when Carroll died his mild-mannered nephew took on the task of creating the friendly and informative biography. At the centennial of Carroll's birth in 1932 there was a small flutter of criticism, but it was overshadowed by anecdotes from those who still remembered nineteenth-century Oxford. Lancelyn Green, who worked closely with Carroll's great nieces, openly, despised those who thought the stories any deeper than innocent tales told to children. And Carroll's diaries are master-pieces of understatement, so that when Liddell arrived at Christ Church he said, simply but snootily:

The Times announces that Liddell of Westminster [school] is to be the new Dean: the selection does not seem to have given much satisfaction in the college.

By the time we left the Hall we realised that the girls at Winnington Hall were not all quite as happy there as Ruskin supposed. In ICI's brochure about the house, their archivist drew attention to a window-pane in the girls' wing of the school on which was still scratched: 'Mary Summers. My last term. Thank God.'

We took one more look at the shiny-floored gallery. The space was immaculately painted now, but as we left we could just discern the bumps under the new paint, the kind of bumps that woodwork suffers when a lot of rowdy children use a public room for dances and other activities.

★

The map showed Daresbury as a tiny village caught in a notch between the M56 and the older A56. Carroll was born in the Rectory here, four miles south of Warrington. Both *Wonderland* and the *Looking-glass* are set in rural havens, and we wondered whether Daresbury would be nudging the modern world as Winnington had done. Below the A56 the view stretched out, a sweep of farm-land, then the silver and black pipes of the chemical factories at Runcorn, then the tide-covered mud-flats of the Mersey.

Daresbury was in the opposite direction, the small turning across from a road-house, the Lord Daresbury, white painted and set in tarmac, surrounded by salesmen's cars. The village was at the end of a high-hedged lane, built of russet Cheshire sandstone and hidden under limes and evergreens, a cluster of buildings around a T-junction, most noticeably the church, and the 'Ring O' Bells' public house. An old and solemn red sand-stone courthouse had a plaque laid into it saying that it was to be *The Lewis Carroll Centre*. It was closed.

A lone boy of about seven was circling around on his bi-cycle, across the road and in and out of the driveways of the houses opposite, caught up in his own world of a small English village, as if Warrington and its worries did not exist outside this little hidden haven.

'You can go in if you like,' he said cheerfully as we stood looking into the graveyard.

We walked around the old Victorianised church, altered considerably since Carroll's father had given many sermons there, often two on a single Sunday.

There were cows munching thick grass in the field below the churchyard, defined as belonging to the 90s by its uniform and EEC fertilised greenness. Otherwise it was all similar to what Carroll would have seen when he came to the village or to church from the outlying rectory, not on a bicycle but with the internal exuberance of the boy who was still doing figures of eight in the lane.

Daresbury had an enveloped, dark feeling to it. The rectory where Carroll was born had been knocked down by 1870. Carroll had come back to photograph it before its demolition. Inside the church there was a foxed and faded copy of this print framed. The print was mounted in an oblong oval shape, which somehow made the house look further away, as if seen through the wrong end of a telescope. The small picture showed a two-storey house with a room on either side of the front door. The house stood out in a field. In the foreground was a muddy lane and an untidy stile next to an old rough-hewn five-bar gate. Charles Dodgson, Carroll's father, had been the son of a bishop, had graduated from Christ Church with first class degrees in mathematics and classics but had chosen to get married. That meant he could not stay on to teach and instead took on the Daresbury parish and the small rectory on Morphaney Lane. The parish was in the gift of the Dean of Christ Church. Carroll and his father were enveloped by Christ Church, by a tradition which, from the Reformation, gave Oxford colleges control over large numbers of country parishes.

Clever families like the Dodgsons never quite fitted with the squirearchy, nor with labouring people. If they did have professional friends these came from the church hierarchy. In this sort of isolation, Dodgsons and Lutwidges often remained unmarried, but when they did marry they tended to do so with a high

degree of consanguinity. On both sides of Carroll's family, first
cousins had married first cousins over several generations, and
some brothers and sisters had married into the same lines. In
this Ruskin and Carroll did have something in common. Each
was the offspring of a first cousin marriage where secrets could
be kept in secret cupboards and behind doors. In Carroll's case,
when he was quite young, a strange and wonderful sense of
humour developed in the recesses of an old house in an old
village.

We saw, in the faded image Carroll had decided to perpetu-
ate of the old rectory at Daresbury, the starting place for a mind
that wandered easily into secret Wonderlands. It was a rather
dark place. There was little spare money, but there was spare
space.

Carroll's father had had a strange sense of humour which was
alternatively deadpan and slapstick. If he had stayed at Christ
Church he would have had a Common Room audience for his
banter. Here he had his tall, pale, timid, precocious eldest son
who listened attentively, started to write verse and drew slapstick figures with a strange contorted line. The games Carroll
played and the humour he developed were not different to
those of other children of his age and background, but early on
he was a creator of new ideas and absurdities and somehow, as
he grew into an adult, he was always able to reach straight into
the cabinet of his childhood mind.

Outside the little boy still whirled around on his bike on the
flint gravel of the house opposite the church. He was clear-eyed
and friendly and able to occupy himself, the kind of boy that
Alice was a girl. He was interested in us and wanted to help us
but he was puzzled about what we wanted. He was full of the
curiosity of childhood that Carroll depended on for his success
as a puzzle-maker and story-teller. All his work for children
depended on the child being curious. He must have been the
most curious of all children himself.

Carroll was born on 27th January, 1832. It was now 8th
February, and the mild west wind was coming up off the
Mersey mud-flats, blowing home-going seagulls around above
the church tower. It was just possible to hear the main line

railway below the ridge. The light was dying. Under the sulphurous glow of street lamps we walked along a lane by the main electric line that connected London and Crewe, Warrington and the north. There was a canal next to it, which linked Warrington and the heartland of England and connected at Nottingham and the Trent. This was where Carroll's father brought down the silver chalice and his vestments and conducted communion services for navvies and forgave their sins on what was known as the 'mission barge' that plied the network of canals joining east and west.

Carroll never forgot Daresbury, and unlike many people who are glad not to be children any more, he wrote about his childhood as though it were the only hallowed state. He was fixated on it. At the age of twenty-one, Carroll wrote:

> I'd give all wealth that years have piled,
> The slow result of Life's decay,
> To be once more a little child
> For one bright summer-day.

This was at a time when many people look forward, caught in the excitement of 'coming of age'. Six years later, he wrote again with an unusual nostalgia for Daresbury and expressing his misery at being an adult.

> An island-farm – broad seas of corn
> Stirred by the wandering breath of morn –
> The happy spot where I was born . . .

> The pictures, with their ruddy light,
> Are changed to dust and ashes white,
> And I am left alone with night.

Was this why he did not like his child friends to grow up, why he had hated the whole experience himself? This poem was called 'Faces in the Fire'. In it he contrasted the bright colours of infancy with the dreary greys and blacks of adulthood.

In *Alice*, the child was bright and pert. The Dormouse was sympathetic because it was a child's pet. The Flowers in the Garden of Live Flowers bickered and spat. They gave the impression of being teenagers. The Dog was a puppy and the Lory and the Eaglet were children, Alice's sisters. Tweedledum and Tweedledee were boys, but obnoxious.

The rest of the figures were adults. The old Sheep whom Alice rowed with was placid, if petulant. The White Rabbit was flustered, determined and brusque. Some characters seemed like transvestites, Pantomime Queens. The Ugly Duchess and the Red and White Queens gave the impression of having something male about them. All the rest were knowing. Most were more stubborn and ruder than any nursery child in Carroll's day would dare to have been. The Hatter was imperious until he grew apologetic at the trial. The Hare behaved in a similar way. The Red King could never make up his mind, and allowed himself to be manipulated by the officious White Rabbit. The Queen behaved worst of all. The White Knight talked about inventions and fell on his head. The Cheshire Cat was sly and elusive. Lion, Unicorn and Gryphon were portrayed in anything but a flattering light. These were all adult figures. They suggested that Carroll, by and large, took a dim view of the adult world.

CHAPTER FIVE

Hat Without
a Head

ÆDES CHRISTI
in Academia Oxoniensi

THE FOCAL POINT of all Carroll's world was Christ Church.
If we were to find more people who were on Carroll's
mind while he was writing 'Alice', there was the most likely
place to track some of them down. We took the train to
Oxford, then walked, as Carroll would do, through Carfax, the
old city centre and down St Aldates.

About a quarter of a mile down from Carfax on the left was
the facade of Christ Church with Tom Tower in the centre,
designed by Christoper Wren, domed and pinnacled. It was in
the smaller corner tower before this that Carroll had the suite
of rooms he occupied for most of his career. They had a view
which we now saw under the cobble-paved archway of Tom
Tower, we saw as though through a small tunnel into the grassy
quadrangle with low, stone buildings beyond. They were glow-
ing in the sunlight, an Italian ochre. The low proportions were
such that, seen through the short tunnel of the arch, the place
appeared like the perspective of a secret theatre set. We were
stepping into the island of Carroll's Oxford, from the world of
town to the world of gown.

Christ Church had been founded as a university college by
Cardinal Wolsey around the Cathedral of Oxford and a monastic settlement. The Cardinal's head was cut off, not by an axe-
wielding Queen – they lost theirs too in that period – but by
Henry VIII. The Cardinal's hat was still the college emblem, a
flat-brimmed piece of headgear, rather like Buster Keaton's,
with a triangular arrangement of tassels hanging down. It was

an appropriate symbol for a college that still has Oxford Cathedral in its midst as its chapel; and still has a Dean as its head, rather than a secular president. Its theatricality was not an inappropriate symbol for Carroll, a heraldic banner of the type the White Rabbit had on his trumpet at the trial of the Hatter. The Cardinal's hat is on Christ Church ties and notice-boards at the entrance; it was also engraved in the walls near to Carroll's rooms, which were to our left. Carroll and Alice lived less than a hundred yards apart. We could almost hear the tinkle of silverware as scouts took breakfast on salvers around to Carroll and his colleagues or the slapping of the harness and squeaking of the wheels on Mrs Liddell's coach.

A procession of activity and royal grandees crossed this quadrangle in the nineteenth century. Christ Church was not – and is not – quite the richest of the Oxford colleges, but it probably aroused – and still arouses the most jealousy. It still calls itself 'The House', with 'The' underlined, The House of God. In the nineteenth century, particularly, it was intensely powerful through its connections with government. Gladstone is perhaps the best known of the Prime Ministers it has produced. The Liddells were connected to the Royal Family and Gladstone, and entertained Disraeli. Ruskin was connected with the College, as were the Prime Ministers Lord Salisbury and Lord Derby. Salisbury so admired 'Alice' that he invited Carroll to read the books to his children at Hatfield House – much to Mrs Liddell's chagrin – and befriended him.

While we stood by Carroll's rooms in Tom Quadrangle, the world seemed strangely still. The buildings masked the sound of traffic and the scale was such that even footsteps in the quadrangle sounded muffled.

To the right was Canon Pusey's house where Carroll came for his first interview. Beyond was the Senior Common Room, where Carroll chatted when he felt inclined and worked on squibs and paradoxes. Then there was the pinnacled Dining-Hall built by Wolsey. At the far end stood the heavy castellated bell-tower which Dean Liddell built and Carroll hated. Then there was the entrance to the Cathedral, with its spire visible, where Carroll prayed each day and, at the end of his life, led services for the Oxford servants. Further round on this third side was the entrance to the Deanery.

The paved walkways round Tom Quad were raised. Carroll's rooms have been remodelled, we were told, but it was where we stood that he came and went with his child friends to a now demolished glasshouse that was his roof-top studio. We stood in the corner from where he watched the world, watched Ruskin, Gladstone, Liddell and many others who came and went to the Deanery where Alice lived. Undergraduates, men and women, the odd porter in a bowler hat and suit went by. The fountain around the naked statue of Mercury played in the centre of the quadrangle. Around the walkway were the vestiges of the arches Wolsey intended to build, for this was to have been a closed cloister.

Our destination was the Library. This meant passing through Tom Quad, near to the Deanery door, under an arch where there was a statue of Dean Liddell, looking down from on high, rather snootily we thought. The next quadrangle was Peckwater, where Carroll had rooms as an undergraduate, among the aristocrats who used to dominate it. It was different from the mainly sixteenth century Tom Quad, aristocratic in structure, three sides of a Palladian building of honey-coloured stone. The fourth side of the quadrangle was taken up by the library. This building is so grand that its pillared façade over-shadowed even Peckwater.

We entered through a huge oak door with a brass handle that required two hands to turn it. Inside was a black and white tiled floor and a couple of desks and computer terminals, sitting rather shyly in the gloom, as if this place were not quite built for day-to-day learning or for the librarian and assistant sitting at desks with computer terminals. There was something temporary about their presence in such a formal space. It was as though they had come to camp out there for a couple of centuries.

On either side of the entrance were two large rooms and we could see into one of them, full of dust-jacketed and modern books used by the undergraduates who were working studiously, backpacks on the table.

Having distinguished himself in mathematics as an under-graduate, Carroll was offered further tenure as a Student, the Christ Church equivalent of a Fellow in other colleges, and began to prepare himself to follow his father and grandfather into Anglican Holy Orders. A Student's stipend was minimal, so he found a job in the library that would help to keep body and soul together. Each day he would come through the large door, cross this hall and go upstairs to a small office.

The wide staircase arched upwards and away from the sound of the telephone, the walls painted in a strange orange colour that looked like the eighteenth century gone a bit wrong. At the top was a huge but sombre panelled room, lined with cream vellum and brown leather-bound books. So large was it that we were tempted to pace it. We reckoned it to be 155 feet long. The huge shiny-floored space was occupied only by a few tables and chairs and glass cases in the middle of the room where Carroll's photographs, some letters and some special editions of his work were laid out. Among them were stories by him illus-trated by Salvador Dalí and Ralph Steadman.

In one there was an untidy amateurish-looking paste-up that Carroll had made of the print which got smaller and smaller for the Mouse's Tale, the story the Mouse tells Alice and the Dodo and the assembled company when they are drying off from their swim in the Pool of Tears.

'Mine is a long and sad tale!' said the Mouse, turning to Alice, and sighing.

'It *is* a long tail, certainly,' said Alice, looking down with wonder at the Mouse's tail; 'but why do you call it sad?'

Carroll had painstakingly laid out the tail for the printers with the words of his verse squiggling down the page, and had pasted it up.

Who was the Mouse? What was sad about his Tale? We did not know, but took a closer look; Fury met the mouse in the house.

The House was where we had arrived. This was exciting. '*The* House' was mentioned several times in 'Alice'.

This part of Christ Church was built in the eighteenth-century, and we were sitting in a room dominated by books written at that time or earlier. By the fourth decade of the nineteenth the earlier tradition was growing a bit thin and Dean Liddell was brought in to overhaul the structure.

Carroll saw the matter differently. As a Student at the House at the time of the reform crisis, he was badly paid and his diaries show that he worked intensely hard. The Students requested the Dean to address their working conditions, but he had other priorities. Even though Carroll may not have been the most effective of tutors in a subject that is far from everyone's favourite, he seemed to work assiduously at tutorials, college and university discipline and marking.

A young woman of about twenty-five in a light-coloured raincoat came up into the Library, puffing slightly, and glanced at us. She took her bag into a room with a door which was not obviously visible in the panelling at the back of the library. A moment or two later she came out again, without her coat and handbag. She introduced herself as Linda Homphray, the assistant archivist.

We pointed to the concealed door. 'Is that the archivist's office?'

'Yes. These are our offices,' she said, clearly wondering why we asked.

That hidden room must have been where Carroll worked. He would have come up the same flight of stairs, in less of a rush than is the twentieth-century norm, wearing not a light-coloured raincoat against the threat of Oxford drizzle but his regulation black coat, and perhaps carrying an umbrella. She let us look into the office. We had made another discovery, not quite like that of Winnington Hall, but one where real geography gave us an insight into Carroll.

On one long side of the Library were the windows looking down over Peckwater, through which a large yellow crane could be seen fiddling about with bits of Oxford stonework, like a fisherman with a long pole. On the panelled side was the small narrow room which the archivist showed us. On the table stood an electric kettle and some plastic cups, instant coffee, photocopies and some stationery, the impedimenta of office life.

This was Carroll's office, just as it must have been when he worked here with library cards and an ink pen – worked and day-dreamed, and looked out of the window.

Through the window was a view of the Deanery Garden which is a very private space. This garden was hidden because it was flanked by the Deanery on one side, the Cathedral on another, the Library on the third and other gardens beyond. It symbolised the Dean's privilege to live almost the life of a country gentleman, married, with children and a large garden in a college where the working Students had a communal garden but were celibate by law.

THE DEANERY GARDEN – CARROLL'S DRAWING OF THE KING
AND QUEEN OF HEARTS FROM 'UNDER GROUND'

We had with us Carroll's diaries and found a series of entries for 1856 of which this was the first. He was twenty-four at the time:

April 25. (F). Went over with Southey in the afternoon to the Deanery, to try and take a photograph of the Cathedral: both attempts proved failures. The three little girls were in the garden most of the time, and we became excellent friends: we tried to group them in the foreground of the picture, but they were not patient sitters. I mark this day with a white stone.

Alice was still not four years old. Carroll could have seen her on occasion in Tom Quad, but the Deanery had no large window that looked out on the quadrangle. If she went into the quad it would have been to go through it, either in her parents' carriage or perhaps in the pram with her governess, Miss Prickett. She would not have lingered or played in the Tom Quad, but in the garden she was free to wander and occupy herself as best she could.

The garden was empty of people, but there were blackbirds and thrushes singing in it: its trees were in full bright leaf and its roses in first bloom. The lack of people somehow emphasised the sense that it was secret. With his job in the library from 1856 onwards, Carroll was almost the only person who could look down on what, in his eyes, was Alice's private garden.

April 28. (M). Deanery again in the afternoon. Southey tried the view of Merton [college] from the walk before the house, a much more promising view as far as the light goes – however all failed. The children were with us a good deal of the time. Boat races began.

April 29. (Tu). Went over again with Southey to the Deanery about 4, but all failed. Harry [who was Alice's brother] was with us most of the time, and Lorina just at the end.

April 30. (W). We went for the last time to the Deanery, and brought everything away, to wait for chemicals before trying again. We saw none of the family this time.

The next entry, that for 1st May, recorded his own camera arriving. Chemicals came on 8th May.

May 10. (Sat.) Spent the greater part of the day photographing with Southey, or rather looking on. He took Faussett, Hewitt, Harrington and myself, etc: as it was a good day for it, I went over to the Library and called to Harry Liddell from the window, and got him to come over to Southey's room. We had great difficulty in getting him to sit still long enough: he succeeded at last, by placing him in a bright light, in getting a fair profile.

By finding this room inadvertently, we could see that Carroll had a private view down on the Liddell children at play. This was where they played croquet. This was where royalty were entertained. Did we hear the White Rabbit's trumpet? Or was it the Cathedral organ?

The question in our minds was whether Carroll would have had access to the Deanery had it not been for his photography. The social pretensions of the Liddells would suggest that the answer was no: he would not have been invited except to the larger receptions when all the Students came. Or, if he was invited in small groups, it would have been on a duty basis as the head of the college shared out responsibility to see his juniors socially. The Liddells were grand, and Carroll was not. Moreover, because Liddell was a Liberal, connected to Gladstone and Ruskin, Carroll was grudging about his appointment from the start.

The Liddells danced with royalty. When the Prince of Wales came to Oxford to study, Dean Liddell was put in charge of him. Their great friend, Arthur Penrhyn Stanley (of the family who had owned Winnington Hall before it became a school) became Dean of Westminster and a royal chaplain. Their other friend – and doctor – Henry Acland, the Professor of Medicine, was on the royal panel of doctors. Carroll was the poor but able son of a poor but able son of Christ Church. Carroll came as a commoner to a college where the aristocrats wore gold-tassled mortar-boards and were not obliged to take examinations.

The idea kept nagging in our minds that photography was Carroll's entrée to the Deanery. We still could not identify Tennyson in *Alice*, but the way Carroll had ingratiated himself with Tennyson by photographing his children, the fact that he had photographed Ruskin and now the fact that his key to the secret world of the Deanery garden was with his camera all suggested that his brass-encased lens and trays of developing fluid were the implements that got him close to company from which he otherwise would have been excluded.

We were trying to discern how Carroll, his outside world, Alice Liddell and the 'Alice' stories interacted. Alice herself said in later life that Carroll told stories to the children to establish a mood when photographing them, and that the telling of them on the river was in keeping with that.

She claimed, as an old lady in 1932, the centenary of Carroll's birth, that the story which became *Wonderland* was most completely told on a river expedition in the summer of 1863. But she also recalled that other fragments of the tale were lost to memory during photographic sessions.

Alice wanted the stories told while she was being photographed and relished the chance he gave her after each sitting was over to see the plates turning into positive prints in the developing fluid. In this early period of his photography, Alice was his outstanding model. To her he addressed the stories rather than to any other child. But he photographed many other people at this time and some of them seem to have drifted into the stories, like the Gryphon, Tweedledum and Tweedledee and the Unicorn.

To our surprise, we found many more of them in Alice's own photographic album, the one presented to her by Carroll.

CHAPTER SIX
Alice's Album

CAREFULLY, we opened the album on a shiny table. The atmosphere in Christ Church Library was more casual than at Austin, but perhaps that was appropriate. There were no white gloves here.

It was from a later period than the Texas albums. Most of the photographs were taken in about 1860, when Carroll was on intimate terms with Alice Liddell, photographing her and telling her stories, the period of his life for which the diaries are lost. This was the album that Carroll had actually given to Alice. It had recently been lent to Christ Church, along with editions of *Alice* and other papers, by her grand-daughter.

Inside the front cover was a note in Alice's strong handwriting dedicating it to her youngest son, Caryl Hargreaves. It was written on the kind of notepaper that might have been ordered through the 'Army & Navy Stores', or a quality Bond Street stationers, at about the time that Alice gave up her Rolls-Royce. Alice had married Reggie Hargreaves, not one of the royal family as her mother had hoped. She had married late for one of her background and generation. Reggie had spent most of his life shooting, fishing and playing cricket for Hampshire. He was a beneficiary of a cotton fortune from Lancashire, and was therefore in the world of the even grander Stanleys, a North Country 'Cottontot'.

Although Carroll and Alice inhabited worlds far apart from one another, he had written to Alice when she was thirty-nine and he fifty-nine.

My dear Mrs. Hargreaves,

I should be so glad if you could, quite conveniently to yourself, look in for tea any day. You would probably prefer to bring a companion; but I must leave the choice to you, only remarking that if your husband is here he would be very welcome . . . I met him in our Common Room not long ago. It was hard to realise that he was the husband of one I can scarcely picture to myself, even now, as more than 7 years old!

The opening photograph in the book reflected the importance to Alice of royalty. It was of the heir to the Danish throne whom we had seen in the Texas album, and whom Carroll had tracked down when he failed with English royalty. Next there was one of Pen Morfa, the large stone villa Dean Liddell had built on a beautiful piece of North Wales coastline near the Great Orme's Head.

There were one or two that seemed to be of Rome. Carroll's only trip abroad had been with Henry Parry Liddon, when he went to Cologne and then to Russia on an Anglican diplomatic mission to meet senior members of the Russian Orthodox Church. He had obviously purchased these photographs of Rome for Alice. This was interesting only because it suggested he might have purchased the photographs of Pen Morfa too. If Carroll had taken them, it would mean he had been invited there. This implied that Carroll could have counted on a greater degree of social intimacy with the Liddells than we believed he had ever been granted.

If the authorship of this photograph, and two others of the Great Orme's Head, were in doubt, that of the rest was not.

One was of the Deanery garden, showing the perfect flat plane of the trimmed lawn and two twisted hawthorns that had grown around each other like gnarled companions.

Abutting this garden was the rear face of the library building and the window from which we had looked down, the window where Carroll called out to Alice's brother when he was trying to master the qualities of light and shade that showed themselves in his fragile print of the garden.

Another library, a new angle on *Wonderland*: we were looking at this old photograph of a view just behind the panelled door fifty feet from where we sat, one hundred and thirty years after the picture was taken. That view was over our left shoulder. In front of us were the roof-tops of Tom Quadrangle, the backs of the Canons' houses at the end of which was the place where Carroll had his studio and developed his pictures.

Alice as an old woman testified to the pleasure of being told stories as a little child on Carroll's sofa up there. Other children, including Julia Arnold, later the mother of Aldous and Julian Huxley, gave similar accounts. Alice recalled the stories were 'slowly enunciated in his quiet voice with its curious stutter . . . Occasionally he pretended to fall asleep, to our great dismay. Sometimes he said "that's all till next time", only to resume on being told it was already next time.' The greatest treat was to be allowed to see the pictures emerging.

> What could be more thrilling than to see the negative gradually take shape, as he gently rocked it to and fro in the acid bath? Besides, the dark room was so mysterious, and we felt that any adventure might happen there! There were all the joys of preparation, anticipation and realisation, beside the feeling that we were assisting at some secret rite usually reserved for grown-ups! Then there was the additional excitement . . . of seeing what we looked like in the photograph.

The print of the Deanery garden we were looking at must have been made up there, perhaps with Alice watching, and it expressed well the delicacy with which Carroll saw natural places, Victorian garden scenes and the lovely countryside that is the setting for much of the 'Alice' books.

Following this in the little leather-bound album was a print of the site that was most important to Carroll and Alice Liddell beyond the Deanery garden – the walkway from Christ Church to the river. The camera was placed in the middle of the avenue and the light shone through from above. The result was a strange mystery that captures the antiquity of the avenue better than colour could ever do. In spite of being a tiny print, it conveys the scale the walk actually had, due to the symphonic proportion Carroll had given it, an eerie skill in such a tiny photograph.

There were a number of pictures of Alice Liddell, and these showed her evolving confidence as a model from the age of three to the age of ten. One showed Alice and her sisters, Ina (Lorina) and Edith standing by a door. The door was built like a barn-door, and the bottom half was shut, throwing off some light. To the left was a wall of Cotswold stone, encrusted with acidified grime – just like the Deanery garden wall we had looked out on. The three girls were in matching white cotton dresses, each fringed with little balls of satin stuff of the type used along the edges of an upholstered *chaise-longue*. Each had black shoes and short white socks and held a small ukulele.

Edith, the smallest on the right, was obeying directions, but she was looking at Ina, the oldest, with a false expression. Ina in the middle acted the playing of the ukulele well, delicate fingers on the strings, head bowed to the instrument.

The pose went with the minstrel song, 'My girl, Sally!' Alice, holding her ukulele, was looking directly into the camera. She looked quite natural, the most natural of the three, the least contrived. She had a fringe, and her face was round and rather wise. This may have been an early photograph, taken perhaps a year after the diary entries we had read, when Carroll was twenty-five and Alice five. It was possible to sense her brightness from the picture, which made her so special to Carroll.

In another portrait of Alice she appeared as a beggar-maid. She wore a torn white shift which exposed both shoulders and much of her chest. Her skirt was a wrapped-round version of what a beggar-child might wear in a pantomime, but not a real torn, grime-encrusted garment. Her feet were bare and she wore no stockings. She was again standing up against the Christ Church Deanery wall, in this case with some vegetation behind her. Her left fist was on her hip, her right hand cupped, but it was quite clear that this child was not used to collecting alms. Her hair was a little less precise than in other photographs, but Alice's fringe and short straight locks, cut to the neck, were hard to disrupt.

In contrast to the ukulele photograph, Carroll had caught an intelligent child looking quizzical about what she was intended to do, but skilled enough to look charming and convincing.

Not much child modelling reaches this level of conviction. Alice's beauty came less from strong features than from the intelligence of the eyes and the straight, firm mouth.

Because she was in costume, because we could feel Carroll dressing her up or watching her change, his eyes on her feet or undraped chest, she seemed to be more the real Alice. And the more we thought about this the more we realised that the real Alice demonstrated the intelligence, good humour and ability to accommodate others that was the hallmark of the literary Alice.

At first we did not think this album so surprising. Then it struck us that the majority of the pictures were portraits, and portraits of men, a number of them from Christ Church, having names with which we had become familiar. But what a strange gift from an older man to a little girl! How could they possibly have interested her? Whether or not these real people Carroll photographed were hidden in the 'Alice' text, they were certainly part of the experience of people at or visiting Oxford that Alice Liddell and Lewis Carroll had in common.

Their names were indexed neatly at the front of the album in Carroll's hallmark mauve ink. They were also named under the portraits in pencil in Alice's hand. For many of these men little Alice sang, perhaps danced, took up poses in *tableaux vivants*, and, if they were not too shy, she probably joked with them. (Carroll disliked little girls who were too shy to speak.)

Here, for example, was Henry Parry Liddon, a classic of Carroll's portrait photography. He was a handsome, square-jawed man of Carroll's age who exuded character and who was almost smiling, an achievement in the days of long exposure and wet collodion plates which Carroll used. 'Liddon': could Liddon be the Mock Turtle, a Turtle because he had a lid on?

Quite close to him in the album was Bishop Wilberforce who had sacked Liddon from his job as Vice Principal at Cuddesdon Theological College, a fact that was difficult to extract from the published record. Liddon had been unjustly suspected of steering too close to Roman waters, of turning budding Anglican teachers over to Rome, because he was the only teacher at Oxford to whom many troubled High Church students felt they could turn when racked with religious doubt.

Certainly his unfair dismissal from Cuddesdon could explain why Carroll might portray his best friend Liddon as the sobbing Mock Turtle. Mock Turtle soup itself was not made from turtle but from calves-feet. It was a soup served at Victorian civic banquets where money was short but illusions of grandeur high. So was there a real person hidden in the soup?

'Once I was a real Turtle', the Mock Turtle said to Alice. The Mock Turtle could sing better than he danced – as befitted a High Anglican clergyman.

At the core of the joke was a series of Carroll puns on Tortoise and 'taught us'. It brought to mind what the Duchess said to Alice as part of their interchange on the Queen's croquet ground: 'Take care of the sense and the sounds will take care of themselves.' This, as Martin Gardner pointed out, was the Ugly Duchess's spoof on the proverb: 'Take care of the pence and the pounds will take care of themselves.'

CARROLL'S ORIGINAL
DRAWING OF THE
MOCK TURTLE

The Duchess's advice to Alice to listen to words was not just verbal fun. It was a Carrollian clue. Certain puns in *Alice* can only be detected by listening to the sounds, not by looking at the spelling of words – 'little' for 'Liddell', for instance, or 'paw' for 'Pa' (father) – jokes requiring an ear for American English, to which Alice Liddell was accustomed from the minstrel songs she and her sisters sang for visitors to the Deanery.

Among other men in Alice's album at the Christ Church Library was Canon Arthur Penrhyn Stanley. There was Reginald Southey who taught Carroll photography in the Deanery garden before he put himself in the care of Oscar Rejlander, the most professional of all his photographic mentors. There was Thomas Jones Prout, the crucial figure in the opposition to Dean Liddell

Then there was Quintin Twiss, another colleague and don, who was dressed up as a shanty-singing sailor in Alice's album. Elsewhere we had seen him posing in character, dressed as the Artful Dodger from *Oliver Twist*. No one other than Twiss was acting in character. Several actual Christ Church dons in the album were close to Carroll. Osborne Gordon and Thomas Vere Bayne, like Henry P. Liddon, posed for Carroll with more genial expressions than the undergraduates would have encountered at their tutorials with them.

Then came a surprise. William Empson had pointed out how steeped in evolutionary theory Carroll's *Wonderland* and *Looking-glass* worlds appear to be, and as if to prove that Empson was right, there in Alice Liddell's album, and in no other album of Carroll's as far as we knew, was a three-quarter length photographic portrait by Carroll of the young Thomas Henry Huxley, evolutionist. Huxley had come to Oxford – it had been a last minute decision taken at Charles Darwin's request in 1860 – to defend the evolutionary hypothesis against Bishop Wilberforce, Carroll's bishop. The bishop, wearing his gaiters and looking irritated, was also in the album, on the very next page in fact.

Here were two arch-enemies only three pages from each other in the album given to Alice. Wilberforce, the Bishop of Oxford, whom Alice would have known, appeared to have more important matters than Carroll's photograph on his mind. He looks as if he could barely keep his hands still and his legs crossed or hold his pose for the camera. Huxley, Darwin's 'Bulldog', was leaning forward and making a well-intentioned effort to understand what Carroll required of him.

Carroll's photographs of Huxley and Wilberforce at the time of the so-called 'Monkey Debate' during the British Association Meeting at Oxford have never been particularly noticed, and there are few portraits of the great biologist and science educator dating back this far.

Carroll photographed Huxley standing against a huge sheet

of dark paper which had bagged and reflected the light unevenly. Huxley was looking just off-camera, slightly to the right and below the eye-line. He was wearing a tail-coat that barely fitted him. His waistcoat was a plain and common affair, crumpled from much wear when lecturing and travelling in trains. It was a waistcoat that did not divide at the bottom like the waistcoat of an Oxford dandy. He was a trifle stooped over, clutching his gloves and top-hat, as though he needed to concentrate on not dropping the unaccustomed fine accessories. His hair was shiny and trimly parted and his often pugnacious expression was mellowed in Carroll's presence almost into a smile. He had on a high collar and a large tie with which he looked uncomfortable. He was a man of modest means, and a former assistant sea-surgeon, who possibly hired this finery just for the debate and the photograph. Yet he was the winner in the debate in the heart of Oxford, and he looked as if he knew it, modest, quiet, pensive and looking confidently to a future where evolutionary theory might no longer be derided.

It was extraordinary that Carroll had presented this album containing such a rare collection of personalities of note to Alice, a child. It had in it photographs of herself and her sisters, her mother in a gigantic hooped dress, her dark hair done in a bun, Carroll himself, and older men, some from Christ Church, some from the wider world beyond, like Huxley.

We put the album away and, as we did so, noticed in another album a small *carte de visite* photograph of Dean Liddell himself. Like the photograph of Gladstone in Texas, there was nothing to indicate whether it was taken by Carroll or not. Carroll's backgrounds were usually sparser, but he did on occasion photograph the Dean and we had been unable to trace those photographs. So perhaps he had gone over to the Deanery and done as he was asked.

Most noticeably the Dean was sitting on a throne-like chair which might have been designed by Pugin, looking disdainfully away from everyone. Aloof and patrician, he looked like the King of Hearts trying but failing to find out who at Christ Church had stolen the tarts, which were there in front of his eyes on a plate in the well of the court.

Carroll chose the scene of the King of Hearts sitting in judgement at the end of *Wonderland* as the frontispiece of the book. What if the King of Hearts were also the Dog that crushed the Mice early in the story? After all, one real person can have more than one disguise. Carroll made his own rules.

CHAPTER SEVEN

American Telegrams

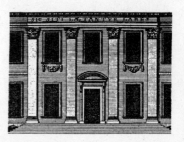

RAIN SPLATTERED DOWN on the flat sills of the Library and the occasional undergraduate ran from the doorways on Peckwater Quad hunched and holding a rain hood at the chin. By one of these doorways there was a chalked-up Cardinal's hat with the victories of a college team beside it, water dripping over faded white lettering on yellow stone. Brighter yellow, as if oblivious to a disappearing past, the high crane silently angled itself round, carrying the cut stone for some new or restored building. In front of us on the shiny table were two different versions of the poem Carroll wrote called 'The Mouse's Tale'.

First we noticed that *The* House was where the Mouse lived in the *Wonderland* tale. It did not state whether it lived there or not in the *Under Ground* version, but by the time Carroll published *Wonderland* in 1865, college politics and his personal involvement in them had intensified.

The *Under Ground* tale of 1864 described how the Mice were killed under the Mat by a Cat and a Dog which hunted them down. They told the short and brutal story of their own extermination. Oddly, they survived to tell the tale. It is as though they had been through the experience of being killed, but this did not really happen. This first and simpler tale ends: 'Think of *that!*'

The second, more elaborate tale of 1865 was built up in a dialogue between an unnamed Mouse and a brutal autocratic Cur called Fury. Fury did not kill the Mice in the House. I threatened to take them to law and doom them by its legal judgement. 'I'll be judge, I'll be jury!' it told the Mouse.

In both versions, that of 1864 and 1865, beside the Pool of Tears the Mouse told its tale to 'a queer-looking party assembled on the bank'. They were flustered and wet and shocked every time the word 'Cat' or 'Dog' was mentioned. Alice, who kept forgetting how sensitive this matter was for them, listened to the tale with the Dodo, the Duck, the Lory, the Eaglet, the Owl and the Magpie beside her as well as a number of other curious creatures.

The Lory was her elder sister, Lorina, and the Lory refused to tell its age. The Eaglet was a small child's mispronunciation of Alice's little sister's name, Edith.

Also present, though some were not in the picture, were other creatures with speaking parts. And some of the animals, such as the Monkey, are seen but not heard. The old Magpie was added for the 1865 version.

The Dodo, the largest and clumsiest of all the creatures on the bank, stood behind the Mouse as it told its tale. At times, ridiculed by the Duck and the Eaglet, it tried to clarify the agenda or organise a game, for the animals were all drenched. This was the kind of thing Carroll did on public occasions. His actions were an over-organised substitute for chat and conventional sociability, well-meant but over-particular. As we had realised in the Gladstone library, the Dodo was Carroll. The Dodo was an extinct bird and Carroll was an extinct member of the 'Old Foundation' of Christ Church, which Dean Liddell had replaced with the New Foundation. Carroll stammered when he pronounced his real surname, Do-do-Dodgson.

The Duck was Duckworth, a singing clergyman from Trinity College not at all involved, as Carroll was, in Christ Church politics. The key question is, if the Dodo is Carroll by his real name, do other members of the 'queer-looking party' have real names and Christ Church connections as he does, grown-up ones, Common Room ones, political ones? Are they, too, involved in the alignments of interest that were taking place in the matter of Christ Church reform while 'Alice' was being written? If so, could their names be found hidden in the text? Would their actions in each case match the individual suggested in the animal skit, as in the case of the Unicorn and the Gryphon?

We had with us *Christ Church and Reform*, which John Clive at Harvard had suggested we read as a way of seeing Carroll in his neglected political guise. Being a history of a reform, for some people it told a sad tale. It was certainly a long tale and it had a twist in it.

On the cover was Oscar Rejlander's portrait of Lewis Carroll. He was thirty-one and developing 'Alice' when he commissioned it. Was Carroll so reticent? This was by no means the only photograph he had taken or took of himself, or distributed. And this apparently shy man was in the thick of college politics. That was the first twist in the tale. It was a twisted tale too, because for three centuries the College had been without a Constitution, although it seemed to have muddled along without one.

Then Dean Liddell, who had already played a part in the reform of the university and its syllabus, supported by Gladstone and others, was brought to Christ Church as a reformer. By this time a climate of thought had been established whereby the old professorships in religion had begun to seem archaic. The undergraduates were not performing well and the College was not attracting outsiders as Students. Understanding nineteenth-century Christ Church – and thereby Carroll's role – meant understanding a mix of university and college bodies, the Christ Church mix of Canons' powers and privileges and its role as a secular college. It also meant untangling Christ Church's power over university professorships, salaries, emoluments, treasuries and privileges.

Canons Jelf, Heurtley and Stanley, Dean Liddell, Prout, Osborne Gordon, Dodgson, Vere Bayne, Pusey: these were the names of some of the important players in the reform era at Christ Church, and they were a very individualistic bunch of animals.

The Mouse told its 'long and sad tale'. Alice sat on the ground in front of it, still wet from the Pool of Tears, her legs stretched out in front of her. She imagined the tale written out in the air in front of her while the Mouse spoke it. Important points in the twisting structure she visualised were clustered at the bends in the tale. This was similar to the way Carroll, a nervous speaker, visualised the text of a sermon he was to deliver as he stepped into the pulpit. It would appear that he saw the sermon stretched out in front of him from start to finish, and always hoped to read the lines off pat without many hitches.

Alice questioned the Mouse on what was sad about its tale. (Liking Cats and Dogs as she did, she saw no harm in their mousing activities.) When the Mouse accused her of failing to attend to its story, she made it clear that, on the contrary, she was attending closely, but she was concentrating on those parts of the tale which had bends in it.

> 'I beg your pardon,' said Alice very humbly: 'You had got to the fifth bend, I think?'
> 'I had *not*!' cried the Mouse, sharply and very angrily.
> 'A knot!' said Alice . . . 'Oh, do let me help to undo it!'

The knot seemed like a deliberate Carroll plant, as if something had to be untied at the locus he had indicated through Alice's clues. Perhaps it was a matrix.

Then we noticed that the Mouse described how the Dog tried to prosecute it in 'The House'. If **D** stood not for Dog but

" Fury said to
a mouse, That
he met in the
house, 'Let

We lived beneath the mat

us both go

Warm and snug and fat

to law: I

But one woe, & that

will prose-

Was the cat!

cute *you*.—

To our joys

Come, I'll

a clog, In

take no de-

our eyes a

nial: We

fog, On our

must have

hearts a log

the trial ;

Was the dog!

For really

When the

this morn-

cat's away,

ing I've

Then

nothing

the mice

to do.'

will

Said the

play,

mouse to

But, alas!

the cur,

one day, (So they say)

'Such a

Came the dog and

trial, dear

cat, Hunting

sir, With

for a

no jury

rat,

or judge,

Crushed

w o u l d

the mice

be wast-

all flat,

ing our

Each

breath.'

one

'I'll be

as

judge,

he

I'll be

sat

jury,'

Underneath the mat Warm a snug & fat.—Think of that.

said
cun-
ning
old
Fury:
'I ' l l
t r y
t h e
whole
cause,
and
con-
demn
you to
death.'

86

for Dean, this put a new twist in the tale. In that case, the Mouse was complaining about changes at Christ Church that affected every Mouse's standing, a consideration which the Dean was deliberately brushing under the carpet. If so, Carroll's Mouse's Tale presented an on-the-spot report to other endangered Christ Church animals not from Dean Liddell's point of view but from Carroll's. Indeed the Mouse's Tale might well contain a message in a bottle from Carroll's faction in the Christ Church reform controversy. Who else could have been involved?

Carroll set out the TAIL with five bends, built up of simple words and letters which grew smaller and smaller until they vanished. Then we noticed, just before she asked the Mouse to tell the tale, Alice reminded it to tell her 'why it is you hate – C and D'.

From Carroll's point of view, the central issue was one of privilege. A New Foundation had been created at Christ Church altering the terms and conditions of employment for the Students, apparently to make the college work more effectively. In his autocratic way, the Dean had drawn the reins of power more tightly around himself and the Canons. At least, that is how the Mice saw matters. The initial letters 'C' and 'D' are specially abhorrent to the Mouse because they stand for 'Cat' and 'Dog'.

They are also the initials of the name 'Charles Darwin', whose theories William Empson had interpreted as a 'pervading bad smell' among High Church members of Oxford Common Rooms like Carroll and Liddon at this time. In the contest for the survival of the fittest at Christ Church, the Dean and Canons fought to remain supreme. The Mice were angry.

The *Wonderland* version of the Mouse's Tale ends with a death threat from the Dog: 'I'll try the whole cause and condemn you to death!'

The type-face in which this phrase is set is tiny, so it is possible to imagine a child reading it as if it contained in Alice's own words, 'some secret rite usually reserved for grown-ups'. It was this bend that Alice (in real life used to finding Carroll's hidden anagrams on her *own* name) found most interesting.

We decided to look at this end of the tail first, the thin end, and to try to see what names we could extract from the letters. We found:

'CHRIST CHURCH', 'DEAN', 'CANONS', 'STUDENTS'.

These were short, easy words to find in such a long sentence, but we could not find, for example, Dodgson, or the name of his ally against the Dean and Canons, Prout. We could, however, find the names of the two reformers at Christ Church of whose religious and political views Carroll most strongly disapproved. They were two prominent, patrician Oxford Reformers and their names were: 'DEAN HENRY LIDDELL' and 'CANON ARTHUR STANLEY'.

Professor Arthur P. Stanley's portrait was among those stuck into the album given to Alice. Carroll photographed him in 1863, when Rejlander photographed Carroll. It was the year when Stanley left Christ Church and was promoted to be Dean of Westminster. Stanley looked young, informal and handsome as he unselfconsciously contemplated a large open book in front of him, his legs neatly crossed and the starched collar of his dicky-front slightly adrift from its moorings. He was a lithe figure with a studious, aquiline face and sensitive expression, Queen Victoria's 'little Dean'. He was well-travelled, spending a lot of time away from Christ Church, particularly in the Holy Land and Egypt. He wrote about ecclesiastical and travel matters. He was the Prince of Wales's favoured travelling companion and everything he wrote went straight into print. His regular disappearances from Oxford, like those of the Dean, were a subject of rancour among the Students who had heavy teaching loads.

Stanley was a close ally of the Dean's and of Benjamin Jowett, much satirised by Carroll, later Master of Balliol and later still Vice-Chancellor of the University. We seemed to be in a thicket of reformers. We thought about the other Cat in 'Alice', the Cheshire Cat. The Stanleys came from Cheshire and had been the owners of Winnington Hall before it became a school. They were a Cheshire family – to Stanley family members, *the* Cheshire family.

Prout was also in the Christ Church album. He was someone

whom Alice Liddell would have seen regularly around the quads, but he was very much a Mouse, not at all part of the Liddell and Stanley milieu. For his tenacity in sending memoranda to the Dean and proposing Common Room motions, he eventually picked up the sobriquet, 'the man who slew the Canons'. The only sign of the letters of his name in the tale was the Dog's first warning, 'I'll prosecute you!'

In Carroll's photograph Prout is facing the opposite way to Stanley, and there is no drift on his starched collar or tie. A twinkle about the eye illuminates an otherwise set and stolid face, head down like a gentle bull in a china shop.

At the time of the struggle for recognition of the Students, Prout was a well-built, sturdy-looking man who appeared to have his feet planted firmly on the ground, whereas Stanley wore the air of an intellectual. Prout looked like a man who would wait and wait doggedly for his chance, if he engaged in a cause, and then close in effectively. And so he did. He was a Junior Censor of the College from 1857 to 1861 and, although not well-liked at The House, he was unflappable. He appears to have been, like the Mouse, sceptical of what others were saying to him. Prout was the Canons' toughest adversary – with the Dodo looking over his shoulder and egging him on meticulously with memoranda.

There was something taciturn in the way Prout sat for the camera, as if he had plonked himself down on the chair, not wanting to hurt Carroll, but taking a donnish, bachelor's view that there were better things to do than have his image reproduced. It seemed that when he was not taking on the Canons and Dean, Prout was a sturdy mountain-climber, as familiar with Snowdonia as the Jones that was his middle name suggests.

Stanley in his album photograph by Carroll looks pleased to pose, and purposeful, while Prout looks as if he is used to working behind the scenes, beneath the carpet, or around the wainscoting.

We re-examined a noticeable difference in wording between the first and second tales. In the second version of the tale, the Mice, led by the Mouse, are more in charge. They are fighting back.

Indeed they were. By 1865 the Students were on the way to having more say in college affairs and the beginning of a break with the old tradition of canonical dominance was in sight. Ironically, for all the memoranda Carroll and Prout sent and the Dean sat on, it was the undergraduates who forced the pace. An arcane controversy over the back-handers taken by the autonomous Butler and Manciple of Christ Church found its way under various young aristocratic signatures into the columns of *The Times*. It was the 'Bread and Butter Row' at Christ Church, not the Tutors' (Students') Revolt which finally forced Liddell to confront the wider issues.

The character of Prout seems appropriate for the Mouse, someone not very visible, but who gnawed away. Perhaps it was coincidence, but we were finding that we could penetrate Carroll's intense secretiveness by exploring his clues as though they were laid out in a muddled knot of strings, or string of knots. One would unthread one of them in a certain way and then get stuck. The lesson was to try another thread, to be gentle with the problem, not to pull too hard, but to see whether any other little untied part helped reveal the whole length of string.

This particular thread led to our remembering that the Mouse was an experimental animal and that dissection, and worse, vivisection were flash-point issues at the University's new Natural History Museum, which was built as a result of pressure from Acland and Ruskin. On 25th March 1858, Carroll wrote:

> Called on Mrs. Harrington to ask her to bring over the children tomorrow to be photographed. In these last few days I have begun reading physiology by Dr. Rolleston's advice. To Kirk's *Handbook*. I have found it necessary to add Knox's *Handbook of Anatomy*. I find Prout is also much interested in the subject, and talks of us doing a dissection together next winter.

Was the Mouse Prout, with whom Carroll thought of sharing the experience of dissection? And would they have been dissecting their first mouse? Be that as it may, the dissecting session was summarily cancelled and Carroll remained an ardent and outspoken anti-vivisectionist for the rest of his life and opposed the funding of laboratories where animal experiments were practised. However, we had learned that one clue to Carroll's characters was that he tended to make the animals he chose for his disguises suit the original. Thus Ruskin and Gladstone, Honorary Students, were both mighty heraldic Beasts. The lesser creatures were harder to spot because they were less visible – though that did not mean they could not be found. For there they were, as in the text of *Alice*, as large as life, just biding their time.

Carroll's second entry concerning Prout was dated 17th March 1882 (Friday). Even this much later entry revealed odd, disparate, but connected threads. The whole knot that we were untying was, after all, called 'Alice'. The entry began: 'Took Julia Arnold for a walk, ending in my rooms.'

She was to become the mother of Julian and Aldous Huxley and grandmother of among others Francis Huxley, the anthropologist. He has written a book entirely devoted to an analysis of the unanswered riddle Alice was asked at the mad Tea-party: 'Why is a raven like a writing-desk?' Once again this suggested that Carroll believed the old religious Oxford was being dismantled and did all he could with his pen to stop this trend.

Carroll's 1882 diary entry continued: 'Called on Mrs Hatch.' She was the mother of the child-actress, Beatrice, and gave her permission for Carroll to photograph her little daughter in the nude close to the end of his career as a Victorian child photographer. Finally, in the evening, he got round to seeing Prout:

> . . . took to Prout's room the Ms book Bayne has lent me (record of meetings of Students etc. in the days when we negotiated with the Chapter etc. about our position) and we looked through the letters he had on the subject.
>
> I contemplate printing, for private circulation, a history of the whole affair.

He never circulated this. All the same, we were convinced that he had already given his own account of it in coded form as the nonsense verse of the Mouse's Tale. At least, we were convinced enough to go on turning over the lines of the verse and twisting them into this light and that. The third knot we chose to untangle was located on the second bend. There we found more words relating to the Students' campaign to extend their rights. The Cur, Old Fury, notified the Mouse:

> I'll take no denial;
> We must have the trial;
> For really this morning
> I've nothing to do.

Among the scrambled letters planted here it is possible to discern the headlines and targets of the agitation:

UNIVERSITY REFORM, DEAN HENRY GEORGE
LIDDELL, OLD FOUNDATION, NEW FOUNDATION.

Again there are a number of letters here in which anagrams of names can be found – C. Lutwidge Dodgson, for example, although Prout is not present. Further, if it is taken as a *characterisation* of Liddell from the Students' point of view, the spoof has bite. 'I'll take no denial / We must have a trial / I've nothing to do / this morning . . . ' has the ingredients of the determined counter-attack of the Mouse and the Dodo on the indolent 'D' and arbitrary 'C's like Stanley. The spoof also reveals Carroll's hand in the evolutionary debate. The doctrine of the overpowering of weaker species by the stronger should not prevail.

We found the surnames of five of the Christ Church Canons along the bends in the tail. Their names and the stalls they occupied in the Cathedral were:

> JELF (Canon of the VIII Stall)
> JACOBSON (Canon of the V Stall)
> HEURTLEY (Canon of the II Stall)
> STANLEY (Canon of the III Stall)
> PUSEY (Canon of the VI Stall)

Carroll, a meticulous record-keeper as well as a spoof writer, photographed every one of them.

One other person we thought might have been cast in the tale. Osborne Gordon and Carroll liked one another from Carroll's days as an undergraduate. At that time Osborne Gordon had been Carroll's classics tutor, and they continued to enjoy each other's company when Carroll in turn became a tutor and they took long walks together between 1858 and 1862. Carroll photographed Osborne Gordon twice, once in 1858 and then again in 1860.

John Ruskin, who had not been a good student of classics at Christ Church, specialising more in oratory, described Osborne Gordon patronisingly as 'an entirely right-minded and accomplished scholar'. He forgot to mention that he was a notable after-dinner speaker and the most adept punster in Greek, Latin and English who ever took Carroll, at a formative age, under his wing.

We found another description of Gordon by Dean Kitchin, father of the beautiful Xie. Kitchin's Gordon sounded more like Carroll's photograph in the Christ Church Album than Ruskin's:

> Lean and haggard, with bright eyes, a long reddish nose, untidy hair, odd voice and uncertain aspirates. Of quaint appearance with exquisite scholarly tastes, extraordinary mathematical gifts, he had a very kind heart.

Alice exclaimed to the assembled creatures of her little cat, Dinah: 'Dinah's our cat. And she's such a capital one for catching mice, you can't think! And oh, I wish you could see her after the birds! Why, she'll eat a little bird as soon as look at it!'

At this point in the *Wonderland* story an old Magpie, who is not in the illustrations, comes forward. (It is not in the *Under Ground* Tale.) Could the old bird be Gordon, easily imaginable in real magpie trim – black and white feathers as a bib and tucker – characterised in a thumb-nail sketch by his friend and fellow-punster? Gordon had a wry face and posture, full of character which became more exaggerated as he aged. Carroll captured these in his photograph, as well as the kindness of the old don from a passing generation.

93

One old Magpie began wrapping itself up very carefully, remarking 'I really must be getting home; The night-air doesn't suit my throat!'

The phrase 'One old magpie began wrapping itself' hides, in loose form, letters making up the name and office of: OSBORNE GORDON, MODERATOR.

The expression 'one old' rather than 'an old' suggested that Carroll needed an 'O' to complete the anagram.

As with the Unicorn's remarks to Alice, the magpie skit depicts not only Carroll's view of the character but also his political attitude. Gordon's gait and appearance, his capacity to seize on little points, like a Magpie, and build sonorous jokes and sermons on them were reflected in the choice of bird for this sketch. The evasive tactic Gordon took during the dispute between the Students and the Dean was reflected in the Magpie's behaviour in its short, sharp scene. Carroll's drawing of the animals fleeing when trouble was in the offing was deeply felt. Protest was not Osborne Gordon's way of resolving the mounting problems at Christ Church if they concerned his Dean. Nor was it Carroll's other close friend Liddon's practice to be disloyal in this particular respect. Carroll and Prout it was who came into the open to confront the hierarchy which had abolished the Foundation under which they held their college appointments.

To confirm that Carroll's portrait of Gordon, the Magpie, was compatible with this sketch of him drawn at the time of the Reform crisis, we checked Carroll's diaries. Carroll was certainly close to Gordon, the first don to supply him with maths pupils when he became a tutor. Gordon had been a demanding teacher, as a letter Carroll wrote to his sister from Oxford before his finals reveals. 'I believe 25 hours *hard* work a day *may* get me through all I have to do but I am not certain.' But he helped Carroll to shelve the new books that came into the library where we sat working on the jokes in 'Alice'. In the rough and tumble of university life, Carroll mutely admired Gordon, as he did also Pusey and Liddon, but this did not mean he refrained from spoofing them:

Watched Gordon turn several men of Hall for unruly behaviour. The noise was tremendous.

Another entry in Carroll's diaries shows that Gordon had Gladstone to dine in Hall (at High Table, of course) and then afterwards brought him to meet the Students, including Carroll, in the Common Room. This was at the end of January in 1857 and reconfirmed that Carroll had seen and heard Gladstone and his condescension at close hand – useful material for the Unicorn sketch.

Gordon's instinct for loyalty made him a passive ally of the Dean. Nervous about the way that the Mice were gnawing away at tradition, the Magpie made an abrupt departure, pleading frailty. Still, he was a witty member of the Common Room whose company Carroll relished. And the cat Alice commended for its skill at pouncing on birds was the Deanery cat.

*

Linda Homphray had with her a battered scrapbook. 'You were asking about Vere Bayne . . .' she said. We had enquired about the roles of one or two Christ Church people photographed in Alice's album. Once again being at a location had helped us to discover material related to Carroll that we never would have found in a card index. Vere Bayne, she explained, had held the Archivist's position here.

The Bayne scrapbook contained a rare piece of Carrolliana. It was reproduced in *Christ Church and Reform* but it had not been included in the collected editions of Carroll's work. This squib was a direct example of how Carroll satirised real people anonymously elsewhere and helped us to ask, rhetorically, if he did so elsewhere at the same period of his life as a writer of squibs, why ever not in 'Alice'?

The Vere Bayne album was a collection of cartoons and squibs, by Carroll and others, and in addition included a sheaf of letters to *The Times* about Dean Liddell. Carroll called the squib his 'American Telegrams'. Only Christ Church's own historian, the knowledgeable Dr Mason, had published it and we had never seen it elsewhere.

The false 'telegrams' were printed on a double sheet and were of an obscure nature. They concerned the American Civil War, then raging. In fact it was an attack on the Dean of Christ Church and his financial ally, Mr Blott, the Under Treasurer of the College. It attacked the College Butler in a spoof that was an ingredient of the Bread and Butter Row taken further by Christ Church undergraduates in the national press. It scorned the mathematical qualifications of the College Examiner, Mr Marshall, and recommended that Junior Students like Carroll should replace him. For good measure Carroll raised the question of piety. He attacked the Dean for changing the hour of College prayer from 7 a.m. to the lenient hour of eight o'clock.

When Carroll had the document printed in Oxford and circulated by messenger to all the Common Rooms around the University, as was his practice with university squibs he wrote at the time he was writing *Alice*, the names were not spelt out. Everyone in the Common Rooms in Oxford knew, however, that Liddell was President L[incoln], and the cheating College Butler sometimes General Grant but otherwise General Butler. Liddell was leader of the spoofed Federal side in the Christ Church Civil War 'telegrams' and the document drew up a series of proposals by the Confederates among whom Carroll numbered himself. The telegram alluded to 'dictatorial powers' and 'enormities perpetrated' by the College Butler, Mr Grant. It demanded in martial tones, from a Southern point of view (which was Carroll's), that Federal forces leave Confederate territory: 'We can discuss no terms of peace . . . with an armed foe . . . '

'Martial' law was a name joke against Mr Marshall, the examiner Carroll wished to depose. In the copy in front of us, Vere Bayne had filled in the names that Carroll had deliberately left blank when the time came to post his squib round the university. These were Bayne's solutions to Carroll's political game, written in his handwriting. They had remained in the Christ Church Archive unnoticed until they were dug out of the files for the writing of *Christ Church and Reform*. We turned over the pages of the album to look at Carroll's picture of Bayne, his translator and code-breaker, holding his mortar-board, a long-faced man with an amused, intelligent smile, big eyes, a high forehead and a bushy beard cut away from his chin.

The Confederates in Carroll's telegram were Carroll's party, the slave-owners, High Church country Tories. Indeed he had been interested to meet a Southern planter within weeks of composing this squib at the Canon's house occupied by Stanley and commented favourably on this planter's views in his diaries. 'The Federals' were Liddell and Stanley's party, Broad Church Whigs, many of them Liberal Conservatives, whose religious, educational and political opinions dominated the College. These were anathema to Carroll, at levels well beyond college politics. The rift between them was unbridgeable as far as Carroll was concerned, but only he and a few Common Room spoof-breakers knew it.

The date was 17th February 1865, when Carroll had put the finishing touches to *Wonderland*. There was a sense of consistency between what he did in these squibs and the nature of the jokes hidden in 'Alice'. The album, or scrap-book, also gave us a strong sense of consistency between Carroll's preoccupations with, particularly, Liddell and Jowett, and those of people around him. Was Jowett in 'Alice', we wondered?

One series of letters attacked the Dean for being away from the College too much, dallying with royalty and letting examination results at Christ Church deteriorate. A squib reported:

Mr Wombell begs leave to announce the arrival of his splendid Menagerie in Oxford. Among other curious animals, the following, he trusts, will merit particular admiration. For the accommodation of visitors, Mr. W. has assigned to each beast its respective keeper . . . '

Against a sketch of a 'shaggy and voracious Bear' were letters and blanks referring the reader to 'the D--N OF C--- C---'. A footnote added that: 'This animal is fed at least three times a day, but the more he eats the more he wants which renders him so expensive to the Menagerie, that they think of disposing of him.'

'A well-fed and laughing Hippopotamus' was labelled unmistakably 'the B--SH--P OF OXF--D', and there were in the menagerie a Pelican, a Chameleon and a Baboon, representing other members of the Oxford and Christ Church communities.

Unlike the Mouse's Tale in *Alice*, this document did not have the mysterious imprint of a Carroll spoof. Nevertheless, the joke about the Dean being 'expensive to the Menagerie' was exactly what Carroll and his colleague Prout, felt about Dean Liddell's very considerable salary. The sub-text of these reform spoofs expressed a deep anger over the attempt to consolidate power around the Dean and the Canons at the expense of those who did the day-to-day teaching.

There was also in the Vere Bayne album a *Punch* drawing that looked very like Carroll's for the Pool of Tears. It is known that Tenniel sourced some of his drawings for 'Alice' from existing English *Punch* and French *Charivari* cartoons which he and the great French satirist, Grandville, had already devised. These Carroll himself kept in a sketch-book which Alice Liddell remembered. For instance, Tenniel's Alice is a little girl character he had used before in a cover cartoon putting wreaths of roses round the neck of the Lions in Trafalgar Square, just erected. Hence the long-haired Alice of the published book. This little *Punch* drawing of creatures round a pool was a reminder of how closely Carroll followed *Punch* humour when working on 'Alice'.

What this album showed was that just as Darwinism produced a 'pervading bad smell' in Carroll's Oxford, so visual and verbal satire of this kind had, by 1860, become an ubiquitous weapon of attack nationally in the Liberal-tending *Punch*, in Oxford and in some of the printed squibs Carroll secreted in 'Alice'. Carroll was neither the ablest nor the most outspoken of those who wrote squibs, though we were beginning to think him the most surreptitious. Squibs were part of his life, his defence mechanism, the only effective way he could bring himself to express what he thought about the adult world at the time. Perhaps we were wrong about the specifics of the hidden names, but in the library where Carroll spent so many hours, we were sure we had identified a new facet of 'Alice'.

CHAPTER EIGHT

The Velvet-
cushioned Boat

WE WENT OUT into the fresh air and walked across Christ Church. We were puzzling about the extent to which Liddell was a model for the King of Hearts and for the Red King. We walked under Liddell's statue and past his house, then under the Bell-Tower for which he was so unpopular with Carroll. Liddell shared many characteristics with the King of Hearts, his taking second place to his wife, his dithering in court, his regal character. Both he and the Red King were so lightly sketched, to the point that the Red King – while always present in *Through the Looking-glass* – was almost a dream-figure, enigmatic, and yet landed so firmly in the reader's lap at the end of the story. Finally, Alice talks to her cat about who was in whose dream. Was Alice in the Red King's dream, or was he in hers? Whose dream was it? Was this a clue that there was an overt child's and hidden adult level in the story?

Finally Carroll himself addresses the reader and asks: 'Which do *you* think it was?'

If Liddell were a model for the Red King, that would suggest that marionettes ('grotesques' in Carroll's word) from Liddell's bad dream were playing on the whole 'Alice' stage. Liddell was there as the central figure in the dream. He was the central figure in the lives of his daughter Alice, and of Carroll himself. From Carroll's perspective, Liddell was the figure who dominated their lives – lives of innocents who could escape into children's dreams.

Certainly this was the way that Carroll saw dreaming and

turned it over in his mind as a theme from at least 1856 when he began to publish his early verse. Certainly there is the strange conundrum with which Tweedledum and Tweedledee threaten Alice. They warn her that, if she wakes the Red King from his dreams, she will cease to exist. This is the only piece of spite Alice encounters in the *Looking-glass* story which reduces her to tears.

Continuing through Christ Church, we realised that today it is still more Dean Liddell's Christ Church than anyone's since the eighteenth-century additions of Peckwater Quad and the Library. Beyond the small Cathedral cloister were Meadow Buildings, Liddell's greatest legacy, a huge residential Victorian block, gothic-windowed, with balconies from which no one gave speeches, and odd Islamic decorations. It was an overpowering edifice for which Carroll had no good words, and few people have had any since. Liddell was notorious for doodling in meetings and we had seen his little dotted drawings preserved in Alice's archives. The King of Hearts said 'Guilty' at the trial one moment, 'Not Guilty' the next, as if he did not care about the outcome. He would still be king. Under this overshadowing set of high rooms, out of proportion with all this end of the College, it was very possible to imagine the anger Liddell aroused in the poor old mice when he played, as he often did, the strongest trick in the power game. He ignored them, their memos and pleas. He just ignored them and very often did exactly what he wanted, whatever their objections.

Meadow Buildings dominated one side of Christ Church. They also faced over the open space of Christ Church Meadow and the gravel-covered Broad Walk which ran down to the river. We wanted to see the river where Carroll and his companion nursed along their boat, with small, delighted girls sitting in bow and stern. By turning round, we turned our backs on a view dominated by this Victorian institutional facade to see one of those English places that seem to have been there for ever, the route Alice and Carroll took to the river. We wanted to see more of Alice's dream, of the places where it was developed.

The Broad Walk was a wide gravel driveway, lined with

poplar trees, that runs straight down to the river. Alongside it
was an expanse of rough pastured meadow. The leaves of the
poplars were silvered and the extent of the meadow stretched
out with plump, chomping cows spread across it. There were
Japanese tourists on the Broad Walk and a group of small
Oxford schoolgirls in crimplene and tights. Some were on bicycles which had white tyres and small white wicker baskets.

Recently we had seen Carroll's mysterious view of this
place in Alice's album. Then it was lined with elm trees, but the
character of the avenue was little changed, a strange piece
of formality alongside the rough meadow.

At the river we turned left. All the college barges which used
to be moored here have gone now. They were like highly decorated houseboats, each with its college emblems and from
which each college's supporters would watch the boat races.
They were popular from Carroll's time, when competitive rowing was beginning under the auspices of such Cambridge
'Muscular Christians' as Charles Kingsley and, later, Leslie
Stephen, Virginia Woolf's father. Their Oxford equivalents
included Dr Benjamin Jowett and the Dean.

We walked along the front of the Meadows to the modern
Christ Church boathouse, where undergraduates, women as
well as men, were taking a rowing shell out to the water under
the guidance of the tutor in engineering, equipped with his
stop watch. The Cardinal's hat was there, incongruously Tudor
on this plain 1940s brick building, as utilitarian as the old college barges had been elegant. Dean Liddell was particularly
keen on the Christ Church Boat Club and its part in competition. It was seen as a way of dissipating the sexual energies of
rowdy undergraduates.

Then we walked back in the other direction to where
Carroll, Alice, Duckworth and Alice's sisters went rowing. The
old barges have gone but Salter Brothers has not. Their
boathouse, where Carroll almost certainly rented his pair-oared
craft, was still there. Among the fibreglass boats were still some
wooden 'gigs', as they were known, clinker-built, probably of
American cedar, and varnished, with iron outriggers, ironwork
seat backs and green velvet cushions.

In her reminiscence of Carroll, Alice Liddell (by then Mrs Hargreaves) wrote:

Unfortunately my mother tore up all the letters Mr. Dodgson wrote to me when I was a small girl. I cannot remember what any of them were like, but it is an awful thought to remember what may have perished in the Deanery waste-paper basket. Mr. Dodgson always wore black clergyman's clothes in Oxford, but, when he took us out on the river, he used to wear white flannel trousers. He also replaced his black top-hat with a white straw hat on these occasions, but of course retained his black boots, because in those days white tennis shoes had never been heard of. He always carried himself upright, almost more than upright, as if he had swallowed a poker.

She continued:

The party usually consisted of five – one of Mr. Dodgson's men as well as himself and us three. His brother [probably Wilfred, who had been an undergraduate at Christ Church and was in love with and later married Alice Donkin] occasionally took an oar in the merry party, but our most usual fifth was Mr. Duckworth, who sang well. On the way back we usually sang songs popular at the time, such as,
   'Star of the evening, beautiful star!'
and
   'Twinkle, twinkle, little star!'
and
   'Will you walk into my parlour? said the spider to the fly'
all of which are parodied in *Alice*.
   On one occasion two of Mr. Dodgson's sisters joined the party, making seven of us, all in one boat. They seemed to us rather stout, and one might have expected that, with such a load in it, the boat would have been swamped. However it was not the river that swamped us but the rain. It came on to pour so hard that we had to land at Iffley, and after trying to dry the Misses Dodgson at a fire, we drove home. This was a serious party, no stories or singing: we were awed by the 'old

ladies', for though they can only have been in their twenties, they appeared dreadfully old to us.

The old ladies in *Wonderland* are the Duchess and her Cook. Carroll watched Alice closely for what amused an alert and logically-minded child out on a river expedition. With the help of the only one of her three sons to survive the First World War, Caryl, Alice transcribed these recollections at the age of eighty in 1932, to help celebrate Carroll's centenary. She remembered a young girl – herself – with a physical presence that mirrors the Alice of the stories, alert, agile and focused on the posture, body weight and assured overview of the adults in the party. Alice Liddell was an able horse rider. She posed like an amateur model and danced. She remembered the fat sisters and she remembered Carroll – the Dodo – as a physical presence that was absurd in the eyes of a child. The more we developed a picture of the real Alice as a child, standing up to Gladstone, amused by Ruskin's pompous drawing lessons, loving jokes about grown up people, learning to row, taking pleasure in her own agility, and being squashed into a narrow space, the more we saw the Alice stories as full of characters she would know, like or be puzzled by. 'Alice' was real. Surely this was an important clue to understanding the origin of the grotesques who surrounded her.

Iffley, where they rowed the Dodgson sisters, was downstream, further beyond the Christ Church boathouse than we had walked. When they went this way and it did not rain they sometimes went through two locks, down as far as Nuneham Courtney where they stopped at the boathouse that belonged to Carroll's scientist colleague Vernon Harcourt's family. Most of the rowing expeditions were upstream, and we followed this route. We walked under the old tollbridge with its Georgian decoration, past the Folly House built on an island, a small castellated gothic building put there in 1849. For the next mile there were small houses backing on to the river, again much as they must have been in 1862.

The main railway line running north through Banbury to Birmingham and eventually Darlington and Carroll's home at

FOLLY BRIDGE, OXFORD

Croft – the line we had taken to Oxford – crossed the river. As
we walked along the towpath, a blue and white Sprinter train,
rumbled over the iron bridge, shaped like a half-moon.

In Alice's testimony, it happened like this:

After we had chosen our boat with great care, we three children were stowed away in the stern, and Mr. Dodgson took
the stroke oar. A pair of sculls was always laid in the boat for
us little girls to handle when being taught to row by our
indulgent host . . . I can remember what hard work it was
rowing upstream from Nuneham, but this was nothing if we
thought we were learning and getting on. It was a proud day
when we could 'feather our oars properly' . . . Sometimes
one of us was allowed to take the tiller ropes: and, if the
course was a little devious, little blame was accorded to the
small but inexperienced coxswain.

Nearly all of *Alice's Adventures Under Ground* was told on
that blazing summer afternoon with the heat haze shimmer-
ing over the meadows where the party landed to shelter for a
while in the shadow cast by the haycocks near Godstow. I

think the stories he told us that afternoon must have been better than usual, because . . . on the next day I started to pester him to write down the story for me, which I had never done before . . .

Shortly after the railway bridge, the river flows under the road leading to the A34 leaving the town behind. Everything changes. The river becomes narrow and runs through a wood of alders and brambles and some pink wild roses. When we were there a strong smell of wild garlic filled the air. Because it was near to the Oxford lock, there was not a ripple on the stream. Two women in a pair-oared boat came by, straining for pace.

It was rather like the way to the Eighth Square, where Alice 'was rambling on' until 'she reached the wood: it looked very cool and shady' and she forgot her name. 'Just then a Fawn came wandering by . . .'

'What do you call yourself?' the Fawn said at last.

'I wish I knew!' thought poor Alice.

Then, the talking Fawn realised, 'Dear me! you're a human child!' It ran off: 'Alice stood looking after it, almost ready to cry with vexation at having lost her dear little fellow-traveller so suddenly.' Almost ready to cry with *vexation* seemed right for a Liddell child.

Rather like coming out on quite a different square, we left the enclosure of the wood, trees arching over the river, and came to Bossoms' Boat Yard where there were cabin cruisers moored and one old college barge, a strange piece of architecture decaying among hurriedly put together modern plastic boats.

We crossed the river here and it became wider and more open. We were opposite Port Meadow, more than half a mile square of rough open pasture. This was probably where Carroll and Duckworth and the girls moored and Carroll sometimes brewed water for tea in the shelter of those old hayricks which were shaped like a bell. Alice Liddell in her old age had written:

> The verse at the beginning of 'Alice' describes our rowing. We thought it nearly as much fun as the stories. This was the poem:

> All in the golden afternoon
>   Full leisurely we glide;
> For both our oars, with little skill,
>   By little arms are plied . . .

> Ah, cruel Three! In such an hour,
>   Beneath such dreamy weather,
> To beg a tale of breath too weak
>   To stir the tiniest feather! . . .

> Imperious Prima flashes forth
>   Her edict 'to begin it':
> In gentler tones Secunda hopes
>   'There will be nonsense in it!'
> While Tertia interrupts the tale
>   Not *more* than once a minute . . .

> Alice! A childish story take,
>   And, with a gentle hand,
> Lay it where Childhood's dreams are twined
>   In Memory's mystic band . . .

Prima was Lorina, the eldest, Secunda, little Alice, and Tertia, Edith, then the youngest. 'Childhood's dreams': looking back across Port Meadow, the rabbits had vanished, the brown ones and the white one, but there were water rats' holes in the river-bank and a pair of mute swans gliding along, arching their necks and orange beaks down into the hair-like flow of water weed. In places the bank was broken down by the cows that fed on the meadow and two or three Charollais crosses were there now, in water up to their knees. Swallows and sand-martins darted and dashed over the river surface. The towers of Oxford clustered together in a way that made the city seem like a place from a fairy tale. Tom Tower and the Cathedral were among them, only a mile and a half away, their worries and real people in another world.

At the end of the first book, *Under Ground*, Alice woke up but her sister 'sat there some while longer, watching the setting sun, and thinking of little Alice and her Adventures, till she too began dreaming after a fashion, and this was her dream:'

> She saw an ancient city, and a quiet river winding near it along the plain, and up the stream went gliding a boat with a merry party of children on board . . . and among them was another little Alice . . .
>
> Then she thought, (in a dream within the dream, as it were,) how this same little Alice would, in the after-time, be herself a grown woman: and how she would keep, through her riper years, the simple and loving heart of her childhood: and how she would gather around her other little children, and make *their* eyes bright with many a wonderful tale . . . and how she would feel with all their simple sorrows, and find a pleasure in all their simple joys, remembering her own child-life, and the happy summer days.

This section of intense nostalgia for childhood, the dismissal of adulthood as 'riper years' in which someone can conjure up 'the simple and loving heart of childhood', reminded us of Carroll's poem about the loss of his own Daresbury rectory childhood. Alice's own testimony was that:

> The stories . . . owed their existence to the fact that Mr. Dodgson was one of the first amateur photographers, and took many photographs of us. When the time of year made picnics impossible, we used to go to his rooms . . . escorted by our nurse. When we got there, we used to sit on the big sofa on each side of him, while he told us stories, illustrating them by pencil or ink drawings as he went along. When we were thoroughly happy and amused by his stories, he used to pose us, and expose the plates before the right mood had

passed . . . We never went to tea with him, nor did he come to tea with us. In any case, five o'clock tea had not become an established practice in those days.

We walked on, still opposite Port Meadow, thinking that one item of real common currency between Alice and Carroll was the people they both knew, that the sharpness of the jokes came from the fact that the animals were not soft, cuddly creatures like the Fawn in the wood (which wore no clothes and did not have human hands) but more acerbic individuals such as the White Rabbit, who had a watch, a waistcoat, a pair of hands and kept demanding that Alice fetched its gloves, something servants normally did, causing the child Alice some 'vexation'.

We were not at all sure who the White Rabbit could be, but there was something familiar in the way it treated Alice, and something to do with science or medicine in the potions Alice found and tasted down in its warren.

The light was falling on the river and a cabin cruiser with a pale green hull, full of noisy people drinking white wine from a long stemmed bottle, came by. The boat was going fast and its wash splashed up against the bank and broke the spell of our thinking about Carroll and Alice's 'golden afternoon'. We crossed the old bridge at Godstow where there was a weir that Mavis Batey, the Carroll scholar, thought might have been used in Tenniel's drawing of Father William balancing the eel on the end of his nose. The eel nets were visible in the engraving.

Somewhere beyond here was the mill which Thomas Combe bought. He had made a fortune as printer to the University, particularly from the Oxford University Press's huge sale of Bibles. He collected Pre-Raphaelite paintings which he and his wife later gave to the Ashmolean Museum, and which Carroll took Alice to see. Mrs Combe was one of those who introduced Carroll to the members of the Pre-Raphaelite brotherhood when they came to paint the murals at the Oxford Union. Thomas Combe arranged the layouts of *Wonderland*. Carroll and Alice came here together to see him. But in the suburban development, and with only the Ordnance Survey map, we could not find the actual place where the mill stood.

This frustration turned our mind to practical matters. We reminded ourselves that, while some afternoons with the girls were 'golden', on other afternoons it rained and the logistics of dealing with wet little girls were not easy for Carroll and his companion. On one occasion he had described the story as 'interminable'.

Any uncle or aunt who takes a little party of children aged four to ten for a day out on the river, even in anoraks and sneakers, knows that talk of 'gentle hand' and 'mystic memories' covers a number of possible disasters which repressed clergymen must have found difficult to confront, such as going to pee behind the bushes, jamming a tiny finger between the rowlock and the oar, getting mud on your shoes and socks and then frock and petticoat and most of all – for this is the quintessence of all English children's stories – getting soaked and not being able to dry out again all day.

We turned back towards Oxford in the dusk. Headlights were visible on the bypass beyond Godstow and a big-bellied supply plane came over low, making for one of the Oxfordshire American bases. Either the thought of the mill and the eel trap, (an eel reminding us of slipperiness), or the recollection of Port Meadow's rough, unimproved landscape, so scarce now in England, made us recall Carroll's long satirical piece about 'improving' such a landscape. How infuriated Carroll had been at the turning over of the 'Parks' in North Oxford to playing fields for competitive sport, particularly cricket. A major force in instigating this had been Benjamin Jowett.

Could Father William possibly be based on Jowett? We were as yet unsure.

We walked back in the dark along the river towards Oxford, through the dark wood and then into the lights near the lock and the built up part of the river. The strange castellated building at Folly Bridge with its gothic windows shimmered in reflection in the river. The punts and rowing boats at Salters' Boat Yard rubbed alongside each other and tossed slightly in the wash of another cabin cruiser which splashed against the stone embankment. The Meadow was now closed and dark, so we walked back up St Aldate's to the entrance to Christ Church.

We looked into Tom Quad, now darkened except for pools of pale light from the globe shaped glass lanterns around the quad. To our right was the entrance to the Junior Common Room and Carroll's staircase, high up and above the emblem of the Cardinal's hat.

It was here, just before Christmas in 1891, that Carroll met Alice for the last recorded time. He had invited her to tea. The 'Alice' books, which he called 'your adventures', had sold more than a hundred thousand copies.

He noted in his most neutral voice that 'she could not' come to tea 'but, very kindly, came over with [her sister] Rhoda for a short time in the afternoon'. He gave her a 'Postage Stamp Case' inscribed: 'Mrs. Hargreaves, from the Inventor'.

Three years before this: 'Skene (Lorina's husband) brought as his guest, Mr. Hargreaves (the husband of Alice), who was a stranger to me, though we had met, years ago, as pupil and lecturer.'

Of Alice's grown-up presence on this occasion he said that:

> It was not easy to link in one's mind the new face with the olden memory – the stranger with the once-so-intimately known and loved 'Alice', whom I shall always remember best as an entirely fascinating seven-year-old maiden.

Alice and Carroll had grown far apart with only nostalgia and book sales to link them. Or rather Alice had become the affluent Mrs Hargreaves whose husband owned a large country house in Hampshire and sometimes moved to another one in the winter. Carroll was much the same, still doting on little girls.

A few months after the visit by the thirty-nine-year-old Alice Hargreaves, he reported in his diary in May 1892: 'Called on the Stevens', and found only Enid at home, with whom I stayed about two hours. She gave me tea: the youngest, and not the least charming hostess I have ever had!' Three weeks later he met, through Enid Stevens, her best friend whose mother 'gave leave for me to borrow Ruth in the afternoon – and a more delightful companion it would not be easy to find'. He was at this time in his sixtieth year.

Carroll was incorrigible and his appetite for the temporary companionship of young girls never dimmed. Up here in these rooms later in his life he even photographed them naked. There had been a real Carroll and a real Alice whom he took on the river, but then she simply passed out of his life. As a sign of how finally unsentimental she, Mrs Hargreaves, felt about him, when needing money to pay death-duties she sold the manuscript copy of *Wonderland* which he had written here and carried over to her, and which had lain on a prominent table in the Deanery even after Mrs Liddell had expressed her displeasure with Carroll's presence and he had expressed his displeasure at Alice 'reaching the usual awkward stage'.

At least the manuscript reached the highest price ever given at auction when an American outbid the Berkeley Square dealers Maggs.

As a sign of how unsentimental Carroll felt about the adult Alice, his present for her wedding was a share with another don in a watercolour. He did not attend the wedding. What triumphed was *Alice*: it was considered so important that an American fund was raised to buy back the manuscript after World War II and present it to the British Library as a gift of thanks for Britain's part in the war. The more we thought about the book's reality, stripped away the sentimentality surrounding its creation, the more we were sure we would find more real people.

It was dark, but the Porter allowed us into Tom Quad. We walked around the raised flagstones of the quadrangle and just paused at the Cathedral entrance. We stood in the shadow and could hear faint strains of the organ. Someone was practising Handel's 'Zadok the Priest'. Three undergraduates came by, two of them girls, arguing about whether Quentin Tarantino's new film *Pulp Fiction* contained an anti-drug warning.

The clock in Tom struck the half hour and the ghost of Carroll walked back from the Common Room, as incongruous and permanent as the Cardinal's tasselled flat hat.

CHAPTER NINE Playing Trains

IN 1843, when Lewis Carroll was eleven, the Dodgson family moved from Daresbury in Cheshire to a larger rectory at Croft in North Yorkshire. Croft village is set on the bank of the River Tees. The low, slightly crooked church stands in the centre of the village, as unimproved as that at Daresbury was 'improved' by the Victorians. It was here that Carroll first preached, first baptised and officiated at a funeral in the long vacation in 1863 when he was writing *Alice*. Croft was Carroll's home from home when he was at Rugby and then Christ Church, where the Oxford terms lasted only twenty-four weeks of the year.

We were beginning to find enough real people in *Alice* to move our research to a different dimension. We had begun to realise too that the rectory at Croft was more than just a boy-hood home to Carroll. It was the safe haven in which Carroll's imagination could begin to express itself.

Next to the Church the road turns right over the Tees on an old three-arched bridge. Beside the bridge once stood a hotel, now a health spa. Behind this houses are grouped round a green. Surrounding the church is a graveyard and next to this the river, rippling over small rapids. This village is northern and rather austere. It has a different light, more limpid and less cloudy than that of the Thames valley. Like Daresbury, its character has remained unchanged since the early nineteenth century. In spite of a few new bungalows it is still possible to connect this place to the old, stratified, rural England which sheltered High Church Anglicans such as Carroll's father in the 1860s. For him this remote country parish was the epicentre of a life devoted to the study of God's mysteries through close application to churchly ritual and duty.

We entered the churchyard.

Croft Church is low and ancient and part of the nave seems to have sunk slightly into the ground. Close by the east end of the nave, we found the grave of Carroll's parents, who had been cousins, like *their* parents in turn. It was near the vestry door in a spot reserved for rectors, as though the last resting place of Carroll's parents was the only privilege that had survived their earthly life. The inscriptions were hard to read under the splotches of grey and black lichen. Unlike most of the other graves, this one is protected by iron railings. Theirs remains a closed, protected world.

Carroll's mother had died in 1852 just as Carroll went up to Christ Church. Her death left his father, who was by then Archdeacon Dodgson, with the eleven children. There were seven girls and four boys. Carroll was the oldest boy and third in the family and he had to adjust to a new attention-seeking sibling when he was one, three, four, six, eight, nine, eleven and fourteen years old. Each of these required food, a bed, bedding, clothes – in the case of the girls the tailored day dresses in which Carroll later photographed them; in the case of the boys the tailored coats, school uniforms (and school fees) that went with a Rugby education. Listening to the river and the rooks, it was not hard to recall the fecund parson and his children.

Inside the church, the Milbank family pew stands raised even above the pulpit, like an ornate box at an Italian opera, roofed and curtained and set on huge classical wooden pillars, like the raised dais on which the King and Queen of Hearts sat in Carroll's court scene. The church is full of oddities, gargoyles, a fertility god and a Cromwellian army helmet atop a huge family tomb.

Carroll grew up among archaic symbols at Daresbury and Croft, but he turned them to his own use. As he began to construct his imagined world, his siblings were his audience. This was a very early Carroll railway game:

All passengers when upset are requested to lie still until picked up – as it is requisite that at least three trains should go over them, to entitle them to the attention of the doctor and assistants.

When a passenger has no money and still wants to go by train, he must stop at whatever station he happens to be at, and earn money – making tea for the Station Master (who drinks it at all hours of the day and night) and grinding sand for the company (what use they make of it they are not bound to explain).

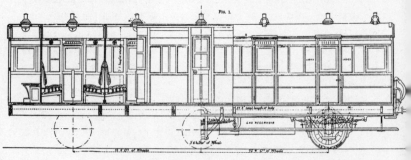

In the train scene in *Through the Looking-glass*, composed more than thirty years after the Croft railway game, Alice sat opposite Benjamin Disraeli:

> . . . the gentleman dressed in white paper leaned forwards and whispered in her ear, 'Never mind what they all say, my dear, but take a return ticket every time the train stops.'

Other passengers suggested that Alice should be sent like a letter, a telegram or a dray-horse. She:

> '. . . must go by post as she's got a head on her –' 'She must be sent as a message by the telegraph –' 'She must draw the train herself the rest of the way –'

Carroll took in realities – the expanding railway system, and the passengers and the newly efficient Penny Post – and made them a vehicle for a theatre which exploited the absurd, for children. Or was it for adults, as well? The more we looked, the more we saw that everything in Carroll's skits, even from an early date, was based on reality.

Dec: 15. (M) Dined with Uncle Skeffington [Carroll's solicitor uncle, Skeffington Lutwidge, who had introduced him to photography] in Brompton, who showed us a curious new French toy, the 'Orthoscope'.

In the evening to the Olympic – *Wives as they Were and Maids as they Are*, a stupid old comedy of Mrs. Inchbald's, but extremely well acted; and *Jones the Avenger*, in which Robson's acting was a perfect treat.

Dec: 16. (Tu). Visited Albert Smith [a writer who had contributed to a satirical magazine for which Carroll wrote, *The Train*] in the afternoon, and the Princess' in the evening – *A Midsummer Night's Dream*, the scenes in which were beautiful almost beyond description.

Dec: 17. (W). Returned to Oxford, my chief reason being that Rattle [a friend and mathematician] is going in for Honour Moderations on Saturday, and I wished to give him as much help as possible.

Dec: 18. (Th). Called at the Deanery and took Harry [Alice's brother] a Christmas box, a mechanical tortoise: (I gave Ina [Alice's sister] one the other day, *Mrs Rutherford's Children*. The Dean and Mrs. Liddell intend leaving on Saturday: they are going to Madeira.

Dec: 19. (F). Began the Common Room File-book, which turns out a much longer job than I expected.

Dec: 20. (Sat). Sent to Watkin and Hill, Charing Cross, to arrange to buy a Magic Lantern.

Dec: 24. (W). Was up till 5.30 packing, and as it was not then worthwhile going to bed, I spent the remainder of the night till 6.30 in an armchair. Left Oxford by the 8.15 train and arrived at Croft about 8 p.m.

Until 1868, Croft was home for Carroll. The rectory stood between the old school and the church. It was a dark house. The photograph of it in Texas caught its gloomy hidden-away character, the tall Georgian building with its low sloping roof shaded under large bare trees. The rectory faced east and was shaded from the south. It was built of brick with large rectangular windows and simply pedimented front door.

Anne Clark's biography of Carroll, published in 1979, had reported that the rectory still existed but had been turned over to flats. She stated that when the Church of England ended its days as a rectory and made the conversion, some tiny children's toys and conjuror's gloves were dug up from under the nursery floorboards. They may have been hidden there by Carroll.

Gloves were one of the items of clothing about which we knew Carroll to have been fastidious. They symbolised conjuring and trickery with the hands, a precise view of uniform and a phobic attitude to cleanliness.

There was a five-bar gate across the drive and we went in and knocked at the door. The rectory, it turned out, had been reconverted to a family house, purchased by a surgeon and his wife, Mr and Mrs Atkinson. Mr Atkinson had delicate and strong hands. His Victorian grandfather had been a distinguished local dialect collector, who had worked for the English Dialect Society in the Cleveland Hills and had written, besides a dictionary, *Tales of A Moorland Parson*.

While we were there jet aircraft passed overhead, but this house was thick-walled enough to be insulated against such sounds, its old flagstoned hall and leather-bound books right and fitting for the study of a nineteenth-century rector and scholar. There was no television visible or audible. Because of the trees surrounding the house, the light which shone through the large floor level Georgian windows was diffuse. Indeed it was a still place full of diffused light. At Croft and at Christ Church Carroll developed his uncanny understanding of light values. Here Carroll learned to catch the patina of indirect daylight when photographing his sisters with their patient, godfearing faces. Sadly, that gaggle of shy, clever Dodgson sisters of marriageable age had even plainer faces than their eldest brother.

Standing in Mr Atkinson's study, it was possible to imagine, as in the Texas photographs, the Dodgson girls sitting in their hooped skirts in this deep-windowed room, lit by pale and subtle natural light; or the old Archdeacon sitting in his leather chair, the light source not visible, illuminating the kind humanity in his face.

Outside in the garden was where Carroll had photographed three of his sisters leaning over one another. They were reading from a single book held open by Margaret, the eldest. In another group they were sitting on a garden bench under a hundreds-of-years-old oak tree, their croquet mallets standing neatly in a rack behind them by the sundial. This too was the setting for the picture of the sisters sitting under a tree with a chess-board set out. Here the people, the sisters, were large and the board small.

As we looked out into this family garden that he photographed so often, it was easy to see how Carroll could transpose its scale, so that the tiny chess-board became a landscape on which life played itself out, and people became tiny figures for him to push about in a series of child-like moves on the chess-board in *Alice*.

Carroll went out into the world, but he came back to a soft cushion at Croft. At the rectory his sisters, with no school to go to, were under his control. They were made the captive

audience for his marionette theatre performances or for playing charades which he wrote for them.

In this thick-walled, simple, spacious house it was possible to
see how the distinction between games of charades and people
who were their subject could seem to blur. This house, with its
old furniture, dim hallway and old prints, had a strong sense of
permanence. When Carroll began to invent one of his jokes
here – his railway jokes, his name jokes – he was never suspected of malice. His numerous sisters and girl cousins simply
passed around the cakes again and smiled, pouring him out a
second cup of tea. At the end of the day they all came together.
The old dark-suited Archdeacon would come in his gaiters and
all would kneel before a cross on the wall while bedtime prayers
were read, the servants there with the family in the room.

We thanked Mr Atkinson for letting us intrude.

Just down the lane and on the south side of the church is
what had been in Carroll's day the small, ecclesiastical-looking
National School. There had been a photograph of this in Texas.
The building is now a surveyor's office, complete in all its original features. Carroll's diary entry for the end of 1856 referred
to the show he gave at this school.

Dec: 31. (W). First exhibition of the Magic Lantern: the
largest audience I ever had, about eighty children, and a large
and miscellaneous party of friends, servants, etc.

I expected the whole thing to last about an hour and a
half, so as to be over soon after 3; as it turned out it did not
begin until 2, instead of 1.30, and lasted till nearly half past
four. I divided it into two parts, of twenty-four and twenty-
three pictures, with a rest of about half an hour in between.
I introduced thirteen songs in the course of the performance,
six for myself and seven for the children . . .

So, almost a decade before he wrote the first 'Alice' book,
Carroll was working on a programme for interspersing picture
and text and song and riddle.

The 'six for myself and seven for the children' was how
Carroll scripted his Magic Lantern performances. It suggested
that he was already experimenting with the tight organisation

he used to intersperse text and verse in *Alice*. He was particularly interested in the number 6, as he was in the number 42. Each of the 'Alice' books has twelve chapters.

The night that he gave the Magic Lantern show on the eve of 1857, Carroll wrote:

> 11.30 p.m. Now at the close of the Old Year, let me review the past and take counsel with myself for the future. I must with sorrow confess that my bad habits are almost unchanged. I am afraid lately I have been even more irregular than ever, and more adverse to exertion: though the labour of last term has been nearly as heavy as at any period in my life, it has been forced upon me by my position, rather than taken voluntarily.
>
> As to the future: – I may lay down as absolute necessities *Divinity Reading* and *Mathematical Reading*. I trust to do something this vacation, but most of the Long Vacation must be devoted to work . . . On other subjects I think there is no use in making resolutions. (I hope to make good progress in Photography in the Easter Vacation: it is my one recreation, and I think should be done well.)
>
> I do trust most sincerely to amend myself in those respects in which the past year has exhibited the most grievous shortcomings, and I hope the most merciful God may aid me in this and all other good undertakings. – Midnight is past: bless the New Year, oh heavenly Father, for thy dear Son Jesus Christ's sake!

He did not mention in his prayers his hopes to write 'for the children I love so well'. That desire welled from deep in his imagination. But he was gaining in experience from the special performances he put on for them throughout this time.

Rooks circled above the lime trees around the Croft graveyard. Driving back due west through the Yorkshire Dales, we stopped high on the moors on a single track hill road. There was a traffic blockage not far ahead of us where a number of cars were jostling for parking space in the places set aside for passing.

The sun was half out. It was drizzling and there was a vivid rainbow. Men in raincoats were getting out of the cars and propping up video cameras against the dry-stone wall fronted by a ditch and they had to try to cling on to slippery surfaces in town shoes to be able to point their cameras over the wall. We managed to pass after a long wait, found a place to park and walked back. We heard the hiss of steam from an engine, a hiss and then a whistle, and then the juddering sound of a steam-engine, that emphatic repetitive rhythm of 'puff! puff! puff! puff!' as its wheels ground against the gradient.

A billowing old-fashioned steam-engine was on the opposite face of the hill, imposing old machine on older land and past on present.

The drizzle stopped, and the sun came out bright and warm. The echo of the train faded behind the hill. We crossed the heather with our old black dog and heard the call of a ring-ouzel. Further westwards, we saw a lolloping hare. Perhaps it was off to have tea with a Hatter.

CHAPTER TEN

The Vestry Cupboard

ONE CLUE was that the mad Tea-party did not take place in *Under Ground*. It was probably not told to Alice Liddell. The author, Mavis Batey, suggested that this part of the story was first told to Dr Acland's children. She was the wife of the ex-Treasurer of Christ Church. She had investigated many Oxford connections with Carroll's 'Alice' stories and learned about the possibility of the Acland children hearing the story from the Harcourt family. It was to the Harcourt boathouse at Nuneham that Carroll took the girls and his sisters for shelter when they rowed downstream and were caught in pelting rain. In any case, the mad Tea-party was a later set-piece than the Pool of Tears. This suggested that a discrete group of individuals may be hidden in the scene, or a group outside Alice's experience.

At the core of the puzzle was the Hatter's Riddle. That trail was not easy to follow, for so much interest has centred on it that any footprints Carroll may have left would have been trampled over many, many times. Trampling more passionately than anyone else had been Francis Huxley, the descendant of the scientist, T. H. Huxley (whose photograph we had found in Alice's album), and Carroll's child friend, Julia Arnold. He devoted his whole book to and named it after the riddle, *The Raven and the Writing-Desk*.

Alice had sat down at the Tea-party table. It was set out for many on the Hatter's lawn. The Hatter demanded:

'Why is a raven like a writing-desk?'

Delighted to try to answer a riddle she had not heard before, Alice exclaimed: 'Come, we shall have some fun now!' But the Hare and the Hatter put her down imperiously for attempting to solve the riddle, a preamble to further rudeness. Finally she walked away from them all, showing her mettle as Dean Liddell's daughter.

The Writing-Desk riddle has elicited ingenious and odd solutions. Francis Huxley, interested like ourselves in who dreamed the dream, noted that subtracting the words 'RED' and 'KING' from 'WRITING DESK' leaves you 'almost out of your WITS'. Martin Gardner quoted Sam Loyd, 'the American puzzle genius' for suggesting that the Raven and Writing-Desk were alike because 'the notes for which they are noted are not noted for being musical notes'.

Such an ingenious answer seems to throw more light on Loyd than on Carroll whose word games had about them an approximation, a mixture of sense and sounds, the quality of charades where actors act out one syllable and then another until a word or name is put together, and then they act that too. We saw the Hatter's 'Riddle' more as a charade in which something might be hidden, like a fishy word, rather than a riddle with a specific answer.

In Carroll's lifetime many people tried to find the answer. Opaquely he gave an answer to his riddle in a preface he wrote to the 1896 edition of *Looking-glass*, two years before his death. In his own mocking 'solution', he produced 'a fairly approximate answer, viz: Because it can produce a few notes, tho' they are *very* flat; and it is never put with the wrong end in front!' He added, however, that this was 'merely an afterthought'.

Surely Carroll did not expect his readers to believe this, yet he did not deny the idea that something was hidden. We wondered if he were suggesting that the raven and the writing-desk, viewed from the correct vantage point, could be seen as wedges, flat in front but pointed behind. The writing-desk was a wedge used for making notes. The raven was a wedge which sang them. A raven, like a bureau desk opening out, can emit a flat, flat note.

Carroll was interested in the geometry of the wedge. Using

it as a metaphor, he wrote a lengthy and subversive diatribe against teaching science at Oxford, which he sent to the *Pall Mall Gazette*. He called his attack on the institutionalisation of experimental physiology at Oxford: 'The Thin End of the Wedge'.

Francis Huxley and others pointed out that the Raven came into Carroll's mind because Alice knew the Liddell family connection with the family seat of Ravensworth – belonging to the earls of that name. That in itself, without reference to music or geometry, would be enough to explain an in-joke about a raven with any author other than Carroll. Besides, the writing-desk could have reminded Alice of her scholarly father, the Dean, who sat customarily at his high desk writing out the latest significations for Liddell and Scott's great Greek-English Lexicon. We concluded that he had reasons of his own for hiding away the real solution.

Then there was a literary raven. It croaked 'Nevermore!' at night in the poet's haunted study in Edgar Allan Poe's *The Raven*, a scene which the Pre-Raphaelites vied with one another to depict. Poe was a cryptographer and poet, and Carroll admired his work.

None of these ideas persuaded us. The Liddell family's earldom, its heraldic device and all the other solutions we had seen, were not enough to explain the Hatter's riddle. Carroll's endless delaying tactics and his temporising pseudo-solutions seemed an embellishment. The real solution, we concluded, was one that he had reasons of his own to hide away.

So we tried another tack and looked for a person. *Ravenshoe* was the title of an epic novel by Henry Kingsley. Two of the three Kingsley brothers were authors, Charles and Henry, (the third was a medical doctor). Charles, author of *The Water Babies* and already famous, had rebuffed Carroll when Carroll asked him for a contribution to *College Rhymes*. Henry, the lesser-known brother, was photographed by Carroll. Both were published by Macmillan. Henry claimed in a memoir that he saw the manuscript version of *Under Ground* in the Deanery at Christ Church and recommended it to Macmillan. True or not, Henry worked as a talent scout for Macmillan and liked Carroll.

Macmillan's success was due to such networks of contacts. In 1861 *Macmillan's Magazine* had serialised Henry's family epic, *Ravenshoe*, which was written, presumably, at a writing-desk.

Where did this take us? We remembered seeing on the book-shelf in Croft Rectory – had we seen?, we *thought* we had seen – the two volumes of *Charles Kingsley: His Letters and Memories of His Life*. It was compiled by Kingsley's widow, and we had a vague impression of his face as the frontispiece to one of the volumes. Could we claim from this brief glimpse that Kingsley looked like the Hatter, the 'mad' Hatter as he is known?

We tracked down a copy of Fanny Kingsley's book, bound in greyish-mauve with black mourning lines round the titling. The pages were uncut, which added to our sense that we had begun penetrating a secret of Carroll's concerning his rivalry with an Anglican parson quite different from himself. There was the frontispiece we remembered and two engravings of Charles Kingsley, one made from a photograph of a head-and-shoulders bust.

This bust had been sculpted by Thomas Woolner, who was a rival of Carroll's friend, Alexander Munro. Carroll met

Woolner twice at the Combes' house in Oxford and on one occasion Woolner criticised Carroll's own drawings for *Under Ground*. In the photograph of Woolner's bust, Kingsley had an eagle-like nose that made him look not unlike the Hatter as drawn by Tenniel. He had an arrogant and sardonic, almost disturbing smile: a smile that conveyed something supercilious, which reminded us of the Hatter. In Woolner's funeral portrait head, any illusion of madness had been eliminated, but Kingsley appeared powerful and strange in marble, his strong shoulders cut into a flat plane at the arms as if, like the Hatter's, his head had not quite belonged on his body.

We examined the plate of the bust and compared it with Tenniel's engravings. In both there was a sense that the eyes of the Hatter were in some way sightless, that this was an insensitive man. The likeness between the bust and the engraving was more to do with an impression, with something that emanated from the face, than with exact features, but we immediately felt a thrill of the kind we had had when we first connected Ruskin with the Gryphon.

Kingsley's base was Eversley in Hampshire, the parsonage as rough as Croft was smooth and ordered. Set in woods south of Finchampstead, Eversley was for a time also a rural home for Henry Kingsley. Was Henry, then, the Hare, the Hatter's rude associate at the Tea-party who appeared before the Red King at the trial in *Wonderland*? Certainly the relationship between the two brothers seemed right. Both were excitable, but Charles was the more so, and the more imperious.

Eversley was the focus of a hallowed Kingsley legend. It was here that he wrote the novels and children's books which bear his given name, Charles Kingsley. Here he wrote a series of passionate Christian Socialist tracts, which were widely read, especially in Cambridge, when Carroll was an undergraduate. For these Kingsley used the pen-name 'Parson Lot'. To inspire his followers and other Broad Church clergymen, he published his sermons under a second pen-name, the Parson of Eversley. It was Kingsley who had penned the famous phrase, 'Religion is the opium of the people' – not the sort of sentiment that would appeal to Carroll.

Kingsley's writing about the countryside was sonorous and lyrical. In his time, before the coming of the Southern Electric railway and its green trains speeding through heaths and fields, parts of the belt around London were home to a truly rural society. That was where the Parson of Eversley found his most enduring vocation as preacher, pastor, teacher, naturalist and church reformer.

We went in search of his ghost, afraid that the wildness of old Eversley would have gone for ever. As the road curled into Eversley village, we could see neither a church nor a sign to one. We passed Kingsley Drive. It was hard to stop on this road with salesmen and commuters hurrying home, and when we did we could not find anyone who knew the church. The mid-nineteenth century seemed a long way off. We asked at a brassy pub; we asked an older woman out riding; and we asked a younger woman driving a Vauxhall Astra. We crossed a small, clear-flowing Hampshire trout stream and recalled Charles Kingsley's passion for fishing. Then we saw a sign to a church. There was no church. Instead we found ourselves quite lost, outside the Charles Kingsley Primary School. A grey-haired man, stooped but tall, strong and athletically built, wearing a hunter-green T-shirt and cotton trousers was entering a door-way. We wondered if he was a parent; or perhaps the caretaker.

He turned out to hold Kingsley's position as Parson of Eversley. His name was Canon Graham Fuller and he told us with courtesy and a lively interest in Carroll and Kingsley that if we could wait at the church, which was half a mile outside the village, he would show us some Kingsley relics. He was coming to the church to rehearse a wedding later that evening.

We drove on for a mile, leaving behind the suburban part of Eversley, with its new buildings imposed on the landscape, and passed through scruffy bracken-lined woodland, with oak trees and papery-barked birch and scrubby wild cherries. It had rained earlier and above the bracken hung a silvery mist.

This was a place where it was possible to see Kingsley not as his critics saw him but as he liked to be seen – as the Robin Hood of the early Victorian era, stirring the conscience of the local gentry about poverty, enthusiastically addressing his novel about a poor tailor to the undergraduates of Cambridge when he was made Professor of Modern History there.

Graham Fuller himself suggested the very Christian side of Kingsley's character Carroll had chosen to forget, if indeed the complex portrait of the Hatter was based on him. Kingsley at his best was an active and generous parson with his sleeves rolled up for brisk Christian action. If Carroll wore a hat, Alice's evidence was that it would be either a top-hat or a straw-boater. Kingsley, in contrast, had the bohemian love of old worn clothes that was the fashion among Cambridge walkers and climbers of his and Leslie Stephen's generation. No fetish here about little girls' shoes, or indeed about little girls at all. It was Kingsley's friend Tom Hughes, a fellow Christian Socialist and a lawyer, who wrote *Tom Brown's Schooldays* and who opened up a lucrative market for Alexander Macmillan and his publishing house in boys' stories based on real boys' adventures.

We found Eversley Church. It stood away from the road, perhaps on the site of an earlier village, just beyond a brick house and a wooden-sided barn, the latter now 'Kingsley Antiques'. It was a red brick church, modest in materials with countrified Georgian lines and a little tower with a stubby spire on each corner, simple and English. There was a sense of architectural purity about it. Nothing gothic here: we had begun to understand more about 'improvement' of the kind that had been so widespread in England in the 1850s. We had observed it in Carroll's birthplace at Daresbury in Cheshire and in Liddell's efforts as an architectural improver on the river side of Christ Church.

This church was built a century before Kingsley became the incumbent. The architecture was just right for a man who was both rustic in temperament and a Christian Socialist.

The wicket-gate was under low, ancient yew trees. Kingsley's grave, where Fanny was buried too, was to the left of the narrow church pathway, indicated by a sign for Kingsley pilgrims. At the head of the grave was a slender white marble stone, a cross and a circle, the four arms of the cross linked in a circle, entwined with delicately carved sprigs of morning-glory. The stone was translucent and it seemed to shine in the summer evening light. We had sighted the ghost of Charles Kingsley.

On the pedestal of the tomb were two names and a year of death, 1875 in Kingsley's case. At the base was the simple Latin motto: *Amavimus, Amamus, Amabimus.* 'We loved, we love, we will love for eternity.' Fanny and Charles Kingsley must have chosen it together with the celebration of an adult, sexual love partly in mind – so different from Carroll's passing child-loves. Some of Kingsley's line drawings were of himself and Fanny ascending into heaven entwined and naked. In Carroll's drawings at the time he wrote 'Alice', the figures tended to wear their clothes, even if in some of the pictures the little girls were without shoes and socks.

We entered the church through the creaking oak door and found ourselves in a simple interior. To our right was a decorated screen in front of the altar with *Holy, Holy, Holy, Lord God Almighty* engraved in gilt on powdery blue and above the decoration of a cross and orb was a painting of flying angels, executed by Kingsley, himself an accomplished artist. The angels appeared rather squashed under the low ceiling.

Kingsley had been Parson of Eversley from May 1844 until 1875, when his close Broad Church ally, Dean Stanley, had come down from Westminster Abbey at the distraught Fanny's request to give the funeral address.

Later it was Stanley who, as Dean of Westminster, saw to it that the bust of Kingsley by Woolner was placed in the Abbey. It was sight of the engraving of this bust that set in mind the idea that Kingsley looked like the Hatter.

The name of Stanley kept appearing and reappearing in our journey and researches, like a face that came and went in the trees. Meanwhile we were trying to find the Hatter, and possibly his other Tea-party guests, in a slightly damp church on a cold evening, deep in the Hampshire woods. We hoped to find the Hare and the Dormouse, which was why any connection we could detect between like-minded individuals, any pattern of alliance was important to us. It might be a clue to more real people in *Alice*. Stanley was linked to Liddell, for he was his only really trusted friend among the Christ Church Canons. We knew from Carroll's 'American Telegrams', which we had

read in Christ Church Library, that the bread and butter consumed at the mad Tea-Party was at the very least a grown-up
anti-Liddell reference. That Oxford joke would fit with Stanley,
but Kingsley was heavily involved, not with Oxford, but with
Victorian Cambridge in its radical aspect. Carroll never went
there as far as we knew, not once in his life – St Petersburg and
Cologne yes, but Cambridge no. It was alien soil.

We noted the Stanley connection but could not see how it fitted. All we had was a glimpse of who the Hatter might be, as we
located Kingsley in the beautiful place where he had worked.
Any overlap between these identities needed establishing.

Early in the New Year of 1856, when he was twenty-two and
began to train himself in the several strands of his creative life
that fed into 'Alice', Carroll had written:

> Finished *Alton Locke*. It tells of the privations and miseries of
> the poor, but I wish he would propose some more definite
> remedy, and especially that he would tell us what he wishes
> to substitute for the iniquitous 'sweating' system in tailoring
> and other trades.
>
> If the book were a little more definite, it might stir up
> many fellow-workers in the same good field of social
> improvement. Oh that God . . . may make me hereafter such
> a worker! But, alas, what are the means?

Alton Locke was Kingsley's novel about a man who escaped the
sweating system of the garment trade and became a Cambridge
poet. It contained descriptions of the working conditions of
poor hatters, felters and garment makers.

A year later, also at the New Year, Carroll wrote:

> Finished *Hypatia*: it is powerful, like all that Kingsley writes
> – outrageous to taste in some parts, which is a new fault (to
> me): I mean especially the sneers at Christianity which he
> puts into the mouths of some of the heathen characters, and
> the undisguised horror of the gladiators' show in the theatre,
> and the death of Hypatia . . .

'Outrageous to taste': the effects of *Hypatia* reverberated in
High Church circles for some years. In 1863, when Carroll was

working on *Alice*, the Prince of Wales had come as an under-graduate from Cambridge to Oxford and was put in Dean Liddell's care. Carroll talked to him at a Deanery reception but could not persuade him to sit for a photograph: the Prince had just been to Canada with Dr Acland and Dr Stanley as his medical and spiritual guardians, where he had done enough sitting for photographs. At Cambridge, before the Prince went to Oxford, Kingsley had been his moral tutor and taught him an odd blend of Saxon history and Platonic philosophy. He had also been a respectful and tolerant friend. The royal family liked Kingsley because of his Broad Church views and respect for German protestant values, those of Prince Albert. The connection between an active Christian Socialist and royalty was surprising, but it was real.

To make a link between the two hostile universities, the Prince of Wales suggested that Oxford should honour Kingsley with an Honorary Degree of D.C.L. Canon Pusey, with Carroll and Liddon giving support, thought *Hypatia*, with its lurid descriptions of pagan Alexandria after the Fall of Rome, corrupting – even though it was widely known that the Princess Royal had relished the novel and recommended it highly to her royal mother, the Queen. Pusey let it be known that he would vote against the Prince's well-meant proposal. This was enough to threaten an embarrassment to the Prince. The idea was dropped. Thereafter Kingsley consistently refused to preach, though urged to do so by Stanley and by Benjamin Jowett, in an Oxford that had so conspicuously declined to honour him.

Where Pusey trod, Carroll trod also.

On the facing white plaster wall of Eversley Church was a sculpture of Kingsley's face, his long sideburns conspicuous in the waxy surface of the bas-relief. He was half-smiling through narrow lips. It was not a very successful portrait of Kingsley – too flat and prissy. This was not quite the Kingsley who went on wild fishing and climbing expeditions with Tom Hughes.

Next to the half-relief was a memorial to Mary Kingsley, Charles's niece, the neglected but talented daughter of the doctor of the Kingsley family, George. Mary was the African explorer in the family who had travelled in the Cameroons and taught in West Africa in the 1890s. She ended her courageous life nursing concentration camp prisoners during the Boer War in South Africa in 1900. There were no African explorers in the Dodgson family: after his father died and they all moved from Croft, his unmarried sisters lived together, mainly at his expense, in a respectable house in Guildford, and several of them seem to have scarcely ventured out at all.

This combination of memorials caused more evidence to click into place. The half-relief was such a thinned-down version of Kingsley that it was possible to take a more cynical view of him. We were looking at the Kingsley Carroll saw, the Kingsley who made a lot of noise about the conditions of the poor, yet to Carroll's business-like eye, reaped royalties from his writing on such themes. The Kingsley of the bas-relief on his church wall looked intelligent, focused, but sardonic, as if, given half a chance, he might show off at any minute, like the mad Hatter.

We were startled. The door opened with a clang and Graham Fuller came into the church. He had a few minutes before his group for the wedding rehearsal arrived, and he took us into the locked vestry at the back of the nave.

It was a cramped, scruffy place, full of ecclesiastical impedimenta, unsold videos of family worship, hymn boards and vestments, a desk and a fading painted notice, grey with age and its gilt muted, announcing the Cope bequest of £10 to the parish. Graham Fuller was still wearing the pair of old trousers that had a walkers' outfitters' trademark on them. In a cupboard which he opened was a full yard of Kingsley's works in various editions together with other small memorabilia, including a tattered book of trout flies.

There was also in the cupboard a photograph of Kingsley in a flat-topped black hat. It was pulled down at an odd angle over his eyes. He was walking intently, parallel with a waist-high hedge in the front of what Graham Fuller said had been the rectory garden at Eversley. Charles Kingsley, lurking in profile in the shadows behind the hedge in this rare outdoor photograph, was on the move. He looked quite dotty.

Along the shelf in front of us were faded copies of Kingsley's early tracts, which painted vivid pictures of the conditions of the poor in the 1840s. In this dim-lit vestibule to which Graham Fuller had guided us, we talked of his plan to use this space for a church meeting hall that would double as a Kingsley display area.

Graham Fuller's wedding party came in in a mixture of Barbour jackets and cotton frocks and corduroy trousers, and he left us to browse.

Charles Kingsley, F. D. Maurice and Tom Hughes, helped by Julius Hare, were founders of, or sympathetic to, Christian Socialist ideas and tenets from the period of the Chartist Movement. They were also active in Cambridge's most famous secret society of the period, 'The Apostles'. Carroll worried and fretted about the 'nostrums' by which the Christian Socialists proposed to cure society's ills, of which the Working Men's College in London was the cutting-edge. The mad Tea-party, seen in this light, was no more than a vicious parody of socialism, an early Orwellian dystopia, a Victorian *Animal Farm* written for the nursery, a portrait of the behaviour of an ostensibly sharing group whose members squabbled incessantly. They persecuted their weaker brethren, had none of the supplies they advertised – there was no wine, for example, even though they offered it – nor would they listen to the polite questions of an intelligent outsider, Alice. When Alice came to the Tea-party, the Hare and the Hatter turned any topic of conversation on another one and abused the Dormouse, a guest at the party, as they did Alice. In the mad Tea-party, the participants all move round: 'The Hatter was the only one who got any advantage from the change,' Carroll wrote. It was a wicked parody of socialism. Everybody is supposed to share. Only the strong get anything.

The abuse was physical and violent, for the Dormouse was pushed into the teapot. Once they had moved – leaving her hungry – Alice found herself 'a good deal worse off than before'.

Nor was this the last she saw of them. They reappear as witnesses at the trial in *Wonderland* and as the White King's mes-

sengers in *Through the Looking-glass*. The trial reduces the Hatter
to a pathetic figure who claims to be: 'a poor man, Your Majesty'.
'A *very* poor *speaker*,' the King corrects him.

Kingsley, like Carroll, had a speech impediment in the form
of a rather bad stammer. Unlike Carroll, Kingsley did not retreat
from his, speaking his sermons at a great rush once he had passed
the starting point. Through the glass pocked with little spots
of mould, we looked again at the faded sepia photograph of
Kingsley stalking along behind his parsonage hedge in his dark,
squashed-top hat. Kingsley had indeed been subject to bouts of
melancholia. Overwrought with work and family and parish and
the ills of society, on occasion he would just walk away from
Eversley and physically debilitating depression and disappear
deep into the English countryside like an old peasant with a pack
on his back, a stick in his hand and his old battered hat.

His books were 'mad', in a certain sense – written in an
emphatic, racy style – and peopled with characters as uncom-
promisingly prone to the physical expression of their feelings
as their author. In *The Water Babies*, which was about a poor
boy, not a well-to-do girl like Alice, real people came into
the narrative, in particular two prominent Victorian scientists,

OWEN AND HUXLEY — REAL PEOPLE IN KINGSLEY'S
'THE WATER BABIES'. CARROLL USED LESS OBVIOUS METHODS.

Thomas Henry Huxley and Richard Owen. Their portraits
appear engraved on wood in an illustration found in one of
the later editions of the story. These portraits, however, were
thrust into the narrative, not central to it as they are in 'Alice'.
These overlaps were intriguing.

Soon after *The Water Babies*, *Wonderland* was published by
Macmillan, with the same page size and cover, only *Alice* was
bound in red instead of green. Carroll, alert to all aspects of
publishing technique, would have watched Kingsley closely.
Kingsley, quite uninterested in a High Church Oxford don with
a penchant for odd verse, would probably not have noticed
Carroll. In discussion, Kingsley was capable of dominating any
conversation just as the Hatter did at the Tea-party. He was
well-known for his emphatic, overbearing manner when con-
fronted with some of the other teachers at the Working Men's
College such as Ruskin, himself renowned for being imperious.

We tiptoed out behind the group who were listening intently
to a talk about the Christian marriage service. They were
arranged below the arch decorated with angels by Kingsley.

Out in the churchyard was the delicate grave with its lively
twisting flowers. There was also a large Wellingtonia which
seemed out of place, larger than life next to the crooked English

yews. Graham Fuller had told us that the seed had been found in Kingsley's pocket when he died, brought back from his Canadian tour. His daughter had planted it and it had grown and grown. The grave expressed the lyrical, caring Kingsley; the great tree expressed the side of him that was unwieldy and larger than life – too big for his boots. Carroll aimed his arrow between the good and the too good.

We went to find the parsonage where Kingsley had stood with his hat and where, early one morning, he had spontaneously written out the text of *The Water Babies* in a great rush for his little son. It was on the other side of the church, a broad, low, overgrown old brick house, just as we had imagined it from early photographs.

Was this the setting for the mad Tea-party?

We walked down the lane beyond the rectory. It was a paved road, but rather muddy and no cars passed us. We were in the deep countryside of Kingsley's most successful prose. We found a small path that ran deep under holly and laurel and across a little stream, a tunnel that emerged by a field where a Shetland pony was munching hay. The barbed-wire looked as if it had been knocked up by an amateur. Two fat grey pigeons flapped away. We had seen the man who owned the rectory drive home in his Saab and eye us with suspicion. Now as we approached, he and his wife were drinking what looked like gin and vermouth on ice in tumblers, talking in the lane to a man with a shotgun.

Kingsley would not have approved. He wrote a ballad which lambasted landlords for keeping the exclusive right to shoot hares, thereby depriving the common people of this source of protein. Nor would he have appreciated the incongruity of a man and a woman having a drink in a road outside a fence where once the Kingsley brothers had reaped and scythed and mown, and sat down to read the newest draft of each other's novels for *Macmillan's Magazine* as the summer light faded under the overhanging boughs.

There might even have been a cat in the tree telling a little girl which way to go to meet a Hatter or a Hare. And of course she knew she was at the Hare's house because there were ears on the roof.

Charles Kingsley had a rural wildness about him. His brother, on the edge of penury when Carroll knew him, had more of the same, and also a perverse streak that had sent him down from Oxford before gaining his degree. The straws in the Hare's hair at the Tea-party were in keeping with Henry Kingsley's rough and tumble lifestyle. He was an insomniac, a heavy drinker of spirits who died only a year after his eldest brother, who always kept a sharp eye out for his welfare, in a Christian spirit of forgiveness. Charles *was* his brother's keeper. When Henry came back penniless from Australia, he worked for a time on the glebe lands at Eversley, harvesting to keep body and soul together. Even if Carroll did not see the lawn that we were looking at, he did later take tea with Henry and his wife at Wargrave, by the Thames, and probably in the garden.

We walked on up the muddy lane.

If Kingsley was the Hatter, there was a good case that Henry Kingsley was the Hare. But we had also discovered an odd Christ Church connection of Carroll's to the surname of a family called Hare.

At the time Carroll was writing *Alice*, A. J. C. Hare had a job working as a secretary for Canon Stanley. It was an unpaid post, given to Hare in an attempt to bring him back on the clerical rails after a profligate life as an undergraduate. A Common Room gossip, Hare told stories about Stanley writing his sermons with one hand and eating buns with the other, then walking off the effect in the Oxfordshire lanes. Here, when Stanley got particularly bound up in a reformulated Christian message he was to preach, he would forget his companion's presence and absent-mindedly force the wretched Hare into the ditch. He had Common Room dining privileges in Christ Church and in the Common Room Carroll listened more than Hare knew. He oiled his information before producing it in a literary form.

Part of this information was about two other Hare brothers, a generation older than A. J. C. Hare. These were part of that Cambridge, German theology, Christian Socialist leaning network to which Kingsley belonged. An obvious subject for parody as Hares, they wrote a wonderfully-entitled book called

Guesses at the Truth by Two Brothers, another bestseller on the theological network.

One of them, Augustus Hare, was always late, so late that when guests were invited to dinner, he would finish a sermon – he held the richest living in England – forget the guests and disappear into the Sussex countryside. Perhaps that was why the clock in the mad Tea-party was always set at six. Like Kingsley, Hare was imperious. His sermons at Matins were said to carry on into the winter dark, so long did he hold forth. He knew Kingsley, admired him and would, like the Hare in *Alice*, have taken second fiddle were Kingsley at the head of the table.

So perhaps the Hare was a composite character. We still did not know who the Dormouse could be, whether he was a mute friend of these socialists or an enemy. Did they dunk him in the teapot because they liked him but thought him feeble and disliked his falling asleep? Or did they do so because they despised him? We could not fit him into the Kingsley coterie.

Meanwhile we examined the scene of the Tea-party with Kingsley and Hare in mind.

Carroll, we were sure, hid real people by suggestion, by fragments of clues. It was not wise to depend only on the anagrams common in his other writing, which he developed into a new game like a precursor to *Scrabble*. The danger was to read more into any one of these than he planted there. Experience with the Mouse's Tale in 'Alice' had taught us that educated guesses over name jokes could lead to clues which otherwise would remain undetected. Walking along the lane near Kingsley's house this idea seemed to make sense.

The Hatter made excuses in court about the 'twinkling of the Tea'. That was a stammer joke, like Do-Do-(Dodgson): 'T-T-T-T'. Then we thought we spotted a college in the 'twinkle' of 'twinkling', a sound and sense joke about 'Kings' . . . the often radical London college to which Kingsley belonged for part of his undergraduate life and at which his admired mentor F. D. Maurice held two chairs as Professor.

Then we spotted a book title in a line that has always been supposed to be nonsense, but Carrollian nonsense. Supposing it was not nonsense at all but had the ingredients of an anagram?

'Two days wrong!' sighed the Hatter. 'I told you butter wouldn't suit the works!' he added, looking angrily at the March Hare.

'It was the *best* butter,' the March Hare meekly replied.

'It was the best butter' works as a loose anagram on the Macmillan children's book title, *The Water Babies*. The remaining letters of the sentence, (with an R shared), oddly, make up the word, 'Stutter'. Carroll and Kingsley shared a publisher and a stutter as Carroll was well aware when he wrote this scene. The phrase the 'best butter' suggests a slippery nostrum that obviously did not work. Carroll was remorselessly punctual. The Kingsley circle were not.

Kingsley's *Hypatia*, like Tennyson's 'Princess', raised the question of the intellectual liberation of young women, already a burning issue in the 1860s and 1870s. *Hypatia* gives an overheated account of the misadventures of an Alexandrian Platonist who was a beautiful young girl.

'If you knew Time as well as I do,' said the Hatter, 'you wouldn't talk about wasting it. It's *him*.'

'I don't know what you mean,' said Alice.

'Of course you don't,' said the Hatter, tossing his head contemptuously.

'Tossing his head contemptuously' was a gesture reminiscent of the way Kingsley described characters in his pot-boiling novels, *Yeast* and *Hypatia*. It reflects the over-blown defiance of Charles Kingsley himself, when he walked out of meetings, which he often did when he did not agree with the majority. Kingsley wrote *Cheap Clothes and Nasty*, a key Christian Socialist tract, describing the weekly living wages of clothing workers. One of these budgets corresponds to the 10/6 label which is always firmly fastened to Carroll's Hatter's hat.

'Why is a raven like a writing-desk?' could also be seen as a matrix from which the letters of Henry Kingsley's name and his best-selling book title, *Ravenshoe*, can be extracted, except that the 'O' in *Ravenshoe* was missing. So can the word 'Eversley'. As if all the words, phrases, riddles, likes and dislikes, twists of expression and puzzles, floated around, connecting and inter-connecting in Carroll's mind, Carroll took up the theme of the writing-desk again in his logic text book, *Symbolic Logic, Part I, Elementary*. Never shy to advertise himself, he described this as 'the very first attempt that has been made to popularise this very fascinating subject'.

It was pioneering work, ingeniously designed to teach even amateur logicians to recognise syllogisms and to beware of falling into the errors of logic they engendered. It was the Carroll scholar, Edward Wakeling, who commented on Carroll's fascination with the number 42, to which he was as attached as he was to 'wedges'. This was Carroll's proposition 'number 42' in *Symbolic Logic* – a startling one.

1. There is no box of mine here that I dare open.
2. My writing-desk is made of rosewood.
3. All my boxes are painted except what are here.
4. There is no box of mine that I dare not open, unless it is full of live scorpions.
5. All my rosewood boxes are unpainted.

Carroll did own painted boxes, prop boxes. We had seen Alice Liddell, Xie Kitchin and Julia Arnold among others, pos-ing in Mandarin costume sitting in front of them. But what were the scorpions? Why were they not ravens? They were also symbols of tribulation and doom. Carroll set the answer at the end of the questionnaire for amateur logicians and by elimina-tion it is as follows:

Answer: My writing-desk is full of live scorpions.

We walked back along the lane and then up to a small wood above the church where, Graham Fuller had said, Kingsley had wanted to build a new rectory. It did not happen. The landlord would never part with a piece of land that was on the edge of a pheasant covert. Kingsley had to stay in the rectory; but up on this hill Kingsley's daughter had planted a second seed on the day of his death and there, still, stands a second mighty Well-ingtonia to mark her foresight. We moved on, southwards.

CHAPTER
ELEVEN

In and Out
of Focus

THE FERRY from Lymington to the Isle of Wight grumbled slowly down the narrow estuary between salt mud-flats, engines curtailed. It made no wash, slid past yachts, mostly of fibreglass, some wooden, out into the silky open water. In front was the low-lying pale green and misty island which had about it some strange promise, a sense of a far-off land. It was a grey August Friday with the suggestion of sun behind a hangover of morning mist. There were only a few yachts sailing. One came past the ferry under motor power with a large balding man at the wheel. He called out in an ebullient, claret-drinking voice which exuded English self-confidence and suggested stock-broking mammon with a foot in the door of the parish church. The pedestrians on the ferry, only partly a car ferry, were less affluent: families off to see the sea and the sights, just as in Carroll's day.

When Carroll came to the Isle of Wight for the first time in June 1859 he was accompanied, as was proper, by a clerical friend, the Reverend John Martyn Collins of Christ Church whose photograph was in the Christ Church album. Previously, the two bachelors had walked together in the Lake District. Carroll returned to the island in 1862 and 1864, and after that not again for a long time. These two long vacations were crucial to 'Alice', and then something seems to have gone wrong. Carroll, it appeared, had tried to ingratiate himself into the circle around Julia Margaret Cameron and Tennyson. This was characteristic of his attempts to move away from clerical and towards literary and artistic circles.

To our right the battery at Hurst Castle stuck out into the Solent, once important for the defence of England, now an anachronism. After twenty minutes in open water we were across and the ferry nudged the dock at Yarmouth.

We wanted to get to Freshwater where Carroll had stayed, although we had been told that there was no trace of Plumleys Hotel where he liked to put up. We bought an edition of Emily Tennyson's 'Island Journal', a booklet called *Three Freshwater Friends* about Tennyson, George Frederick Watts and Julia Margaret Cameron, and a book about Cameron's photography on the island, by a local historian, Brian Hinton. We also gathered up the Ordnance Survey guides to the island, stuffed these into our pack and managed to find a bridle walk enclosed in hawthorn and full-skirted willows that followed the little estuary of the river Yar.

Perhaps Carroll took a dray. Walking revealed a part of the Isle of Wight remote from tourism. There was almost no development at this western end. The path took us down what had the promise of being a secret tunnel to Carroll's island. It followed the river Yar which runs north and almost meets the Freshwater, which runs south. The watershed is only about twenty feet above sea-level. These two rivers make the western end of Wight an island off an island.

The square, stub-towered Freshwater Church was on the right. Emily Tennyson had been buried there, her husband in Westminster Abbey, a less democratic arrangement than the Kingsleys'. The footpath led on through the backs of gardens, a number with boats in them.

We were in search of Tennyson. Having seen the two Tennyson boys as possible models for Tweedledum and Tweedledee, we wondered whether Carroll might have mocked the Poet Laureate, their father, as well. There was certainly trouble between them. On Carroll's side relations had gone from good to bad, on Tennyson's from acceptance to refusal-to-see by the time that *Alice* was written. Yet Tennyson's verse, particularly his resuscitated Arthurian legends, echoed throughout the period. Before he rebuffed Carroll, the Poet Laureate was a major influence on Carroll's creative writing.

In the earliest diary entries concerning Tennyson, Carroll described himself walking out of a lecture on Tennyson's poetry because he thought the reading affected; then he read 'Maud' alone, with great concentration, at Croft in the autumn of 1855. At first he did not like it – it is too passionately purple for most modern readers as well. Then he decided he liked it after all. He thought Tennyson must have been inspired by the pangs of first love:

> Read 'Maud' again in the evening: I enjoyed it much more on second reading: the Canto beginning 'I have led her home' is true, passionate poetry, one can scarcely believe but that it must have been written under the inspiration of a first love.

Carroll was constantly in search of verse to parody and listed a handful of target poets on the left-hand page of his diary. A principal target was Tennyson's *Collected Works*. In October 1856, he sent to the magazine, *The Train*, a parody of Tennyson's 'The Two Voices'. Carroll's parody was called 'The Three Voices', he drew an accomplished sketch to go with it, and it was published in the following month's edition. Carroll liked what he had written and reprinted it in *Phantasmagoria*, the nonsense verse collection he published between the two 'Alice' stories in 1867.

All the same, an interview or a sitting with Tennyson was more important to Carroll than readings, recitations and the imitation of Tennyson's verse, and that was what Carroll set out to achieve.

Less than a year later, he managed to get one. This was the occasion we studied in Texas, when Carroll went by train from Croft to the Lake District with his younger brother, named after his inventor uncle, Skeffington Lutwidge, and his camera equipment.

> Sept:18. (F). I . . . walked with Skeffington to the head of Coniston Water, and from that point he went down the west side of the lake . . . while I went down the other side, intending at least to see Tent Lodge (where Tennyson is staying) if not to call. When I reached it I at last made up my mind to

take the liberty of calling. Only Mrs. Tennyson was at home, and I sent in my card, adding (underneath the name) in pencil 'artist of 'Agnes Grace' and 'Little Red Riding Hood'. On the strength of this I was most kindly received and spent almost an hour there. I also saw the two children, Hallam and Lionel, five and three years old, the most beautiful boys of their age I ever saw. I got leave to take their portraits . . .

I mark this day with a white stone.

These were the photographs of the bumptious Tennyson boys held in Texas. We had also seen the photograph that Carroll had used as a calling card on this first visit. That was of Agnes Grace Weld, a plain Tennyson niece dressed as Little Red Riding Hood, one of the only five photographs Carroll ever put on public display. All his other sittings and portraits were entirely private.

Familiarity followed. Four days later he had the photographs of the boys, but nothing of Tennyson himself:

At six I went . . . to dine at Tent Lodge, and spent a most delightful evening. I saw the little boys for a short time; I had met them in a donkey cart near Coniston during my walk. Mrs. Marshall sent over [Carroll's photograph books – she had been viewing them] . . . Mr. and Mrs. Tennyson admired them so much that I have strong hopes of ultimately getting a sitting from the poet, though I have not yet ventured to ask for it.

They talked about Carroll's photography and the relation of a monkey's skull to a human's, a subject which interested Carroll and which he had drawn and photographed for his own amusement before he published *Alice*. Then, as we had noted in our search for the Gryphon's identity, Tennyson moved on to another topic:

We talked a good deal of Ruskin, whom he seemed to have a profound contempt for as a critic, though he allowed him to be a most eloquent writer . . . He threw out several hints of his wish to learn photography, but seems to be deterred by a dread of the amount of patience required. I left at what I believed to be a little after nine, but which to my horror I found to be after eleven . . . The hotel was shut up for the night, and I had to wait and ring a long while at the door.

Dies mirabilis.

A year later, in 1859, Carroll met the Tennysons again, this time at Farringford on the Isle of Wight, where we were now destined. Tennyson had purchased this large house where he hoped to be able to live in isolation from the increasing number of people clamouring to catch a glimpse of him.

That year, Carroll was allowed to take a portrait of Tennyson, and we had seen that photograph in Texas. They spent a long evening together in Tennyson's private sanctum at the very top of the house where the poet gently ribbed the ordained Carroll for associating with his indulgence in tobacco and late nights. But no lasting friendship grew from it. Carroll wrote to his sister after his 1862 holiday to say 'I have seen hardly anything more of Mr Tennyson – and daytime does not seem propitious to getting much conversation out of him.' However, he taught the two Tennyson boys 'elephant hunters' and had some games with them.

In the afternoon I was on the beach again, when there came a troop of 5 small soldiers, with banners, and got up in a sort of uniform – the 2 Tennysons, the 2 Camerons, and Harry Taylor – all between 12 and 7 years old. I was just showing Hallam how they ought to represent the battle of Waterloo, when who should lounge down on to the beach but my old brother-tutor Joyce (some of you saw him at Christ Church), who has lately been made vicar of Harrow. I spent the evening with him at *his* hotel.

On Friday Joyce and I went to Freshwater Church, about which I have no remarks to make.

On the 1864 visit, Tennyson would not see Carroll, who had to put up with photographing his garden staff. A second cousin of Hallam and Lionel, Charles Tennyson, reported as a piece of family wisdom in 1949 that Tennyson would not let Carroll look at the proofs of his latest addition to *The Idylls of the King* because he had been stung by the parody of 'The Two Voices' which Carroll published in *The Train*. Charles Tennyson paid Carroll the compliment of agreeing with his criticism of Tennyson's original verse, which had been more perceptive than the objections of other critics. He had been right to parody it. There actually *were* three voices in Tennyson's original.

In the meantime, Carroll, supervising his sisters, had made a joint effort at writing a useful if sombre Index to Tennyson's *In Memoriam*, which he persuaded Moxon, Tennyson's own publishers, to put on the market. Carroll and his sisters benefitted, not Tennyson. Carroll recorded the sales of this early publishing venture in his diary from time to time. The Index had used up so many copies of the letter 'S', a favourite with Tennyson, that the typesetters ran out of font and had to cast more.

These two sides of Carroll, the over-zealous admirer and the secret punster, may have alerted Tennyson to watch the quiet Oxford don. And then he pounced. On Sunday, 3rd August 1862, a book agent called Mrs Hotten urgently requested that Carroll return a pirated American copy of Tennyson's early and fresher verse, which he had suppressed on the English market. Carroll, who was working on some more spoofs for 'College Rhymes', put his hand in the cage of the Cambridge bear. He wrote:

> The sale of the American reprint of Tennyson's early poems is objected to as an infringement of copyright. Wrote to Tennyson begging permission to keep the book.

Tennyson took umbrage and Carroll took umbrage at his umbrage. The quarrel centred on the fact that Tennyson told Carroll that by seeking to retain the suppressed material he showed himself to be no gentleman. The waspish Carroll was then on his mettle: he had slavishly read every line that Tennyson had ever written, pursued him from the Lake District to the Isle of Wight and invented endless games for his spoilt little boys, only to have Tennyson question strongly whether Carroll was even a gentleman.

Their letters of mutual repudiation survive. Carroll was quarrelling with Queen Victoria's beloved Poet Laureate and was by this time totally *non grata* at Freshwater Bay. Nevertheless he insisted on having the last word. On 31st March 1870, as he was devising the scenes of *Through the Looking-glass*, Carroll claimed he was taking Tennyson's advice – literally – that poets were 'dowered with the hate of hate . . . the love of love.'

Another layer of personal insult added to the dispute. Carroll offended Emily by giving a penknife to Lionel, to make up for a telescope he had given to Hallam. The Tennyson boys enjoyed war-games, and were encouraged in this by their jingoistic papa. This gift from Carroll caused a fierce quarrel between the two boys. By the time Carroll saw the boys at Farringford with their latest harassed tutor, they were older, more unruly and more like Tweedledum and Tweedledee than ever.

As if the quarrel with Tennyson over the pirated texts of his poems and the divisive and dangerous gift of a knife to the boys were not enough, Carroll photographed Emily with her sons. He did this at her request and against his better judgement. Her appearance in the finished photograph was so haggard that she dreaded her husband seeing it. Later, with Julia Margaret Cameron's connivance, she blamed Carroll for this final embarrassment. The Tennysons refused the prints.

Perhaps in 'Alice' Carroll had his revenge on her husband and sons with three comic children's characters. We had come to the Isle of Wight with the thought that Tennyson was the White Knight in the *Looking-glass*, alias the Wight Knight or the Knight of Wight.

In Kingsley's parsonage at Eversley, Graham Fuller had told us that Tennyson had thought of buying a house along the cul-de-sac lane by Eversley Parsonage, where we had seen the house's present and secular incumbent with a tumbler of ice-cubes and drink. Kingsley had warned Tennyson off, telling him that the valley was damp. Perhaps he did not wish to inflict on his parishioners the crowds of sight-seers that Tennyson tended to draw. Although the house at Farringford was secluded, Tennyson's presence made this western end of the island popular with an artistic and literary set he enjoyed for a while – and the tourists he abhorred.

The Queen and Prince Albert had built their own home,

Osborne, at the other end of the island. The Queen had
knighted Tennyson when she appointed him her Poet Laureate.
While Tennyson was living at Farringford, Prince Albert called
on him, and the visit was returned. After Albert died in 1861,
Tennyson was granted royal permission to dedicate *The Idylls* to
his memory, and everybody knew that the Queen knew that
King Arthur at his Round Table was Tennyson's tribute to her
late Consort. Tennyson really was a Wight Knight.

The chapter of 'Alice' dominated by the White Knight was
called 'It's My Own Invention'. At this time, Tennyson was
engaged in writing the official poem to be read out at the opening of one of the major Victorian Great Exhibitions, filled with
new patents and devices. The White Knight himself claimed to
Alice, who liked him, to be extraordinarily inventive. One of
his inventions was a Carroll standing-on-its-head or upside-
down-in-a-mirror joke. The White Knight's way of getting
over a gate was based on the observation that the '*head* is high
enough already'. He explained:

> 'I put my head on the top of the gate – then the head's high
> enough – then I stand on my head – then the feet are high
> enough, you see – then I'm over, you see.'
>
> 'Yes, I suppose you'd be over when that was done.'

Over and done with. The idea of the White Knight as an
inventor was interesting. Martin Gardner had suggested that the
shaggy hair (which surely was not Carroll's) and inventiveness
pointed to Carroll himself as the model. Carroll did invent a
flying-bat and a postage-stamp case and was interested in world
standard time zones and cipher systems and many other set-
piece games and ciphers, but it was his uncle, Skeffington
Lutwidge, the Commissioner for Lunacy, Carroll's first photography teacher, who was the member of the family most
fascinated by gadgets.

Carroll insisted, when he saw Tenniel's first sketch of the
White Knight, that he did not want him to look too aged and
asked Tenniel to make the Knight look younger. It has been
observed that the White Knight's long moustachios and
youngish face suggested those of Tenniel, an inveterate ham

JOHN TENNIEL, BY HIMSELF (LEFT), HIS WHITE KNIGHT (RIGHT)

actor who very likely did portray *himself* in the White Knight engravings. But these may have just been disguises. The character, setting, mood and circumstance of the White Knight scenes belong more meaningfully to Alfred Lord Tennyson, Carroll's erstwhile and closely-observed 'friend'.

The chapter title 'It's My Own Invention' contains the letters of Tennyson's surname. The Poet Laureate's reiterated themes of dream and reality, which intrigued Carroll, the possible Tweedledum and Tweedledee connection, which would make Tennyson father of two boys in *Through the Looking-glass*, and the 'over and done with' jokes, which may refer to poetic decline, all suggest Tennyson.

In *Through the Looking-glass*, Alice first encounters a Red Knight. She is a White Pawn, so the White Knight has to protect her. But for most of the scene the White Knight falls on to his head from his horse — never on to his feet — and when he is settled, starts off on endless talk about fresh inventions. In the end, the White Knight recites a poem about inventiveness, which Carroll had written. As an instance of how close to the bone Carroll worked, he based the verses the White Knight recites on a childish verse he had coaxed out of little Lionel Tennyson. Carroll's spoof emerges as the poem the White Knight recites 'A-sitting on a Gate':

I'll tell thee everything I can:
There's little to relate.
I saw an aged aged man,
A-sitting on a gate.

In a different way Carroll may owe Tennyson a debt. In trying to trace the origin of 'Alice' as a strong and independent female central character, Tennyson's Princess in *The Princess: A Medley* may well be important. Carroll undoubtedly had read this. Only the Princess goes on, as did the Unicorn's daughter, Helen Gladstone, to play a senior role in a newly founded women's college in Cambridge. Neither 'Alice' nor Alice Liddell were quite like that. Nor did Carroll ever fully declare himself on higher education for women. He did give logic lessons at the newly founded Cheltenham Ladies College. Conversely he reported the extent to which his friend Dr Liddon disapproved of the idea. Carroll's view of the aptitudes of young girls is expressed through his heroine in 'Alice'.

The heroic idea of a 'perfect, gentle knight' as set out in Tennyson's complex drama, the *Morte D'Arthur*, is heavily mimicked in the White Knight episode. A part of Carroll's scene parodies 'The Last Tournament' and other episodes in the *Idylls of the King*. The White Knight looks all ready to joust. Alas, he falls off his horse on to his head. In a gory death scene from this idyll, published in 1871, one incautious knight fell on his head in the twilight into a steaming swamp, never to be pulled out again.

We were still looking for the place where Carroll certainly saw Tennyson standing in the sun, even if not riding on a horse. The way to Farringford led past 'Bed & Breakfast' houses and small hotels close to a little thatched church crouching like a hedgehog in a green field. The church had been built in 1908 when the community had expanded because of the popularity of Tennyson and Julia Margaret Cameron. Someone had told us that Farringford had become a hotel and we thought we might stay there. We imagined spending an evening absorbing the atmosphere, watching the light fade over the Downs in a *Morte d'Arthur* haze.

·ALFRED·TENNYSON·POET·

CARROLL WAS NOT THE ONLY PERSON TO DEPICT
TENNYSON IN ARMOUR, AS THIS 1898 ENGRAVING
BY ROBERT BYRON SHOWS

We walked by the back way, overgrown with spindly
hawthorn, that was used daily by those passing between the
thatched church and the residential houses round Tennyson's
home. Then we saw the large, sprawling house on its rise,
placed just as in old photographs. Could Tennyson have
deserved what we found? If the black-bearded, dark-visaged
White Knight who was Queen Victoria's Poet Laureate left a
ghost anywhere, it was not here. In the 1980s municipality had
seeped into Farringford on its sluggish tide.

The tarmac driveway, the car-park, the rose-beds, the sheltered swimming pool and golf course flew in the face of Tennyson's wild-haired love of heroism and easy-going friendship. In his view these were the two most important treasures of ancient England. They were missing from the age in which he wrote.

Tennyson, a wrestler when he was a youth in Lincolnshire, used to scythe this garden himself; now it was maintained by machines on wheels. The gothic-windowed exterior of the house was in period; inside, the decorations seemed deliberately anti-Victorian. One room high up a winding staircase had a few pieces of Tennyson memorabilia in a glass case. There was his microscope with a slide of the wing of a tortoise-shell butterfly. There was the 'wide-awake' hat in which he walked over the Downs, his cloak and scarf and tobacco jar and pipes.

The poet's memory seemed truly far away and long ago, lost against the beige anaglypta walls, red plush chairs, the colour television in its cabinet and the heavy pea-green velvet curtains. The bar was linked to a patio, and on the great folding doors over the bar itself two huge, faded, identical photographs of Tennyson had been blown up to a gigantic size and placed behind laminated plastic panels, as if symmetry could be made of the old bard. They had not even made the two copies of his head face opposite ways. Carroll might have smiled inwardly. Tennyson would not have been amused.

We looked across the sun-dried and manicured garden. We recalled that Alice had found the sight of the White Knight making his recitation 'the one that she remembered the most clearly'.

Years afterwards she could bring the whole scene back again, as if it had been only yesterday – the mild blue eyes and kindly smile of the Knight – the setting sun gleaming through his hair . . . the horse quietly moving about . . . and the black shadows of the forest behind.

Carroll himself had been greatly moved by his first sight of Tennyson.

I was shown into the drawing room. After I had waited some little time the door opened, and a strange, shaggy-looking man entered: his hair, moustache and beard looked wild and neglected: these very much hid the character of the face . . . His hair is black: I think the eyes too; they are keen and restless – nose aquiline – forehead high and broad – both face and head are fine and manly. His manner was kind and friendly from the first: there is a dry lurking humour in his style of talking.

This may have been the 'young' look Carroll insisted on for Tenniel's White Knight character, part of the similarity between Carroll's impression of Tennyson in the diaries and the poetic description of the White Knight in *Alice*. When Alice bids farewell in *Through the Looking-glass* after listening to the Knight's poem, she (and probably Carroll) has an odd experience. No tears come into her eyes. It is the Knight's character, his sadness, that touches her, not his verse.

The sense of sadness which deeply affects Alice in the White Knight's presence also overwhelmed Carroll himself when he met Tennyson. Yet the young Tennyson, who wrote his greatest epitaph *In Memoriam* on the dead friend of his Cambridge days, Arthur Hallam, was to suffer all his life, as did Tennyson's brother Charles and other members of their family, from bouts of depressive illness.

At the time when Carroll was still acceptable to Tennyson and photographed him, his photograph showed Tennyson sitting bolt upright, like a horseman, in a draped chair at an angle to the camera. The poet was wearing a frock-coat. His hair was quite orderly and he held on his knee an open book and a bowler hat. His eyes were just off the lens and the portrait showed a dignified man with sadness in his eyes and considerable learning in his high brow.

In another photograph in Princeton, Tennyson's posture was more hunched. He wore his wide black hat and in profile looked more bohemian, more relaxed and 'poetic' than in the three-quarter length pose Carroll had attempted first. The chair on which Tennyson sat, with its carved back, was the same as that on which Carroll photographed the sulky and mischievous Hallam standing, wearing dancing shoes tied with satin ribbons, and holding a cane he looked just ready to use.

In building up our image of the two Tennyson boys as
Tweedledum and Tweedledee, the photographs by Oscar
Rejlander had been important. He had had more access to the
Tennysons than Carroll at this time. His photographs make
the boys look even more bumptious. It is Rejlander's outdoor
photograph of Tennyson, Emily and their young sons moving
towards the camera in the garden at Farringford, their coats
flowing, back-lit by the sun, that must be among the most dramatic family pictures ever taken.

As clear evidence that Carroll knew about Rejlander's
Tennyson photographs, he purchased prints of them on 20th
July 1863 at Rejlander's London studio. In the morning he had
been with a wood engraver, working on preliminary illustrations for *Alice*. In the evening he dined at a club with Liddon.
It was Rejlander's photographs more than any others that had
suggested Tennyson might be the White Knight. Like the
White Knight in 'Alice', they portrayed the Tennysons back-lit
against a low Isle of Wight sun.

Under Carroll's photograph in Princeton, the one of Tennyson
in his hat sitting in the upright chair, Tennyson had signed his
name. Carroll had written in his mauve ink, all in upper case:

THE POET IN A GOLDEN CLIME WAS BORN,
  WITH GOLDEN STARS ABOVE;
DOWER'D WITH THE HATE OF HATE, THE SCORN OF SCORN,
  THE LOVE OF LOVE.

Judging from the chair – the one on which he stood young
Hallam, whom even his mother, Emily Tennyson, called 'dae-
monian' from time to time – it seemed that Carroll took this
photograph when he first met Tennyson in the Lake District.
Perhaps 'love of love' and 'golden stars' hung above Carroll
when he stayed up late with Tennyson, who never invited
him to stay. If the White Knight was indeed a parody of the
Knight of Wight – a great, much-photographed and bearded
poet – it was audacious of Carroll to have published it.

We walked away and sat down to eat sandwiches beside the
thatched church. Inside was a photograph of St Agnes, taken by
Julia Margaret Cameron. One of Cameron's maids had modelled

for it. A quarter of a mile further down the road was Dimbola Lodge, now being restored as a Cameron museum. This was the house which Julia Margaret Cameron converted out of two cottages joined by a central tall high tower, now painted cream, but distinctly recognisable from old photographs.

Mrs Cameron settled here after her life on a plantation in Ceylon. Her first husband, a coffee planter, had died. The house had gothic details in its gables and windows but on a less majestic scale than at Farringford. For the home of an ex-colonial it was more bohemian than imperial; Farringford was more imperial.

Inside, the floors were bare. There was little furniture and the restoration was under way. The greenhouse where Cameron manipulated and judged light for long exposures had been taken down after she eventually returned to Ceylon. According to Virginia Woolf, whose mother she photographed, she took cows with her on the steamer. Mrs Cameron was eccentric and she was generous with hospitality. Dr Benjamin Jowett, lampooned by Carroll for his sceptical Christian views, was a favourite with her household as well as the nearby Tennysons, and he with them. She had built a garden house for him so that he could work on his *magnum opus* on Plato in peace. Part of that still exists and the book is a great classic. The scholars Carroll took on were right at the cutting edge of higher learning and culture.

Looking down to the beach from the upper floor, a single long room with bay windows, it was possible to imagine gaggles of Cameron's guests going to and fro with parasols and wicker picnic baskets and the paraphernalia of the fancy dress she provided for them when they modelled for her. Mrs Cameron was famous for her untidiness, shrillness and energy.

On the wall there were a number of Cameron photographic prints, all or almost all originally posed, photographed and developed there. Her camera came so close to the subjects who posed for her that it is possible to feel the kisses and hugs of the drawn, wispy-haired woman in her wind-blown open-work shawl. The pictures suggest gentleness and affection, and also the most wild and lonely yearning. There was the sad-faced and bearded Henry Taylor in a crown as 'King David', one of her

maids as a biblical Rachel with a pitcher on her head, a naked
child, a boy with girlish curls, holding a quiver and bow. There
is not a single humorous or light-hearted photograph among
them: humour was not her medium. Her models were dressed
up for scenes describing Tennyson's Arthurian legends or stories
from the Old Testament that no one but she could remember.
Alice Liddell was there, dressed as Cordelia in *King Lear*.

Cameron drew heavily, as Carroll did, on Tennyson for her
scenes and for the exploration of dream and reality she devised
in her photographs – though sometimes there was more dream
than reality to Cameron's poses. In some of her photographs,
the sets were tumbling down among the models. When she
photographed Tennyson she squeezed every ounce of wild
shagginess out of her model, producing a picture very unlike
the bolt upright Tennyson of Carroll. She dressed the poet in a
monk-like outfit and seems to have preferred him not to wash
when he came in from the garden to pose for her.

We also found, from the book written by Brian Hinton, that
Plumleys Hotel still stood. It was no longer trading as Plumleys
but it remained a solid, square resort building, cream-faced and
sedate on the cliff. As always with Carroll, he had chosen a
beautiful location. To the south Plumleys looked over the
English Channel; to the west it looked down the flow of white
cliffs.

The sun had burned through, the sea was dotted with yachts with white sails and young men and women army cadets were learning to abseil on the chalk-face visible just above the hotel. Plumleys was in direct line of sight with the upper floor of Dimbola less than a quarter of a mile away. As in the Library at Christ Church, we felt at Farringford and Dimbola that we had a glimpse of how closely Carroll stalked his subjects. When he came to the Isle of Wight he had no more than a passing acquaintance with Tennyson. He did not know Cameron, nor had he more than slight knowledge of the photographic skills she was beginning to reveal.

During his 1862 visit, Carroll fell in with the group of guests at Mrs Cameron's house. He got to know her and, while walking to the beach, had his first recorded meeting with Benjamin Jowett – just in time, for he was writing anti-Jowett spoofs and drawing anti-Jowett sketches and distributing them round Oxford. In 1864 Carroll recorded in his diary:

> July 28. (Th). Called on Mrs. Cameron, who begged I would bring over my pictures in the evening. She showed me her pictures, some very beautiful.

> Aug: 2. (Tu). Went to the Camerons in the evening and met Mr. Henry Taylor and Mrs. Colonel Franklin (her little girl was one I had observed at the school-feast, and had enquired her name, with a view to getting Mrs. Cameron to photograph her for me). Sent off to Mr. Combe Chap: III of *Alice's Adventures*.

The next day, Carroll wrote to his sister Louisa, the eighth in the family, who was then twenty-four and lived until 1930. The letter was sent from Plumleys Hotel.

> In the evening Mrs. Cameron and I had a mutual exhibition of photographs. Hers are all taken purposely out of focus – some are very picturesque – some merely hideous. However she talks of them all as if they were triumphs in art. *She* wished she could have had some of *my* subjects to take out of focus – and *I* expressed an analogous wish with regard to some of *her* subjects.

Lord Cranbrook (Gathorne Hardy),
the Tory candidate who defeated
the sitting M.P. for Oxford
University, W. E. Gladstone

Carroll's photograph of John Ruskin who danced
the Quadrille at Winnington Hall (*right*)

The Deanery garden, taken from
the Christ Church Library where
Carroll worked

Alice Liddell as a beggar child,
the Carroll photograph
Tennyson most admired

The boathouse at Nuneham, where Carroll sheltered
from the rain with Alice and her sisters

Alice Liddell as a beggar child photographed by
Carroll in the Deanery garden

The Dean of Christ Church and his family,
grown-up Alice Liddell by his right knee

Mrs Lorina Liddell,
Alice's mother

Professor H. W. Acland,
Alice's doctor . . . and friend

The Natural History Museum, Oxford, soon after it was built
in the 1860s, with Ruskin's photograph of O'Shea carving a portico

Dean Liddell, the portrait
in Christ Church

Pen Morfa, the Liddells'
summer house in North Wales

Bishop
Wilberforce
(*right*) and
Professor Owen
(*below*), who
briefed him on
evolution, with
his grand-
daughter

Thomas Henry
Huxley (*right*)
by Carroll,
from the album
he gave to Alice

The Rev. Henry Parry Liddon, Carroll's favourite preacher

Furies Allies and the Mice

The Rev. Thomas Vere Bayne, collector of Christ Church satire

The Rev. Osborne Gordon, who wrote Latin spoofs with Carrol, his pupil

The Rev. T. J. Prout, 'the man who slew the Canons'

Fury said to a mouse, That he met in the house, "Let us both go to law: *I* will prosecute *you*. Come, I'll take no denial; We must have a trial: For really this morning I've nothing to do." Said the mouse to the cur, "Such a trial, dear sir, With no jury or judge, would be wasting our breath." "I'll be judge, I'll be jury," Said cunning old Fury; "I'll try the whole cause, and condemn you to death."

H. P. Liddon

T. Vere Bayne

Osborne Gordon

T. J. Prout

HIGH CHURCH MEN: Cardinal Manning, the man in a hurry; Dr Pusey, photographed by Carroll who called him his 'dear old friend'; and Cardinal Newman, Manning's spiritual rival

BROAD CHURCH MEN: Canon Stanley, photographed by Carroll; Benjamin Jowett, photographed by Julia Margaret Cameron's son; and the Rev. F. D. Maurice, Carroll's photograph of one of his favourite preachers

Hallam

Above: The Tennyson boys, photographed with Julia Marshall by Carroll

Above: Ellen Terry in her wedding dress, the portrait Carroll saw in Watts' studio J. E. Millais (*left*), after his election as a Fellow of the Royal Academy

D. G. Rossetti with his sister Christina, his mother and brother in the garden at Cheyne Walk

Carroll did not have his camera with him, although he was about to send for it. The letter continued:

> The next two or three days were very enjoyable, though very uneventful. I called on Mrs. Cameron on Monday, and told her I felt rather tempted to have my camera sent down here – there are so many pretty children about – but that it was too much trouble, and instead, I asked if she would photograph for me (*in* focus) the prettiest two, one being a child of Mr. Bradley's . . . , and the other unknown, but constantly to be seen about: I described her as well as I could. 'Well then,' said Mrs. Cameron, 'next time you see her, just ask her name,' and this I half-resolved to do . . .
>
> On Monday afternoon I was lounging about on the beach, and came on the same little unknown child – such a little gipsy rich brown complexion and black eyes. I was afraid of frightening her if I asked her name, so I came up to the hotel and got the landlady to come out on the cliff, who made out for me who she was . . .

Carroll met this child with Mrs Cameron and, a few days later, photographed her with her mother at Farringford. At the same time he met the Camerons' great friend, Henry Taylor, the white-bearded civil servant and poet who sat frequently for Cameron as King Arthur or as King Lear when Alice Liddell posed as Cordelia. Many people staying locally would come to lunch in the course of a chaotic day's photography at Dimbola. Carroll, of course, would not dream of exchanging clerical black for fancy dress. The distance between Farringford, Plumleys and Dimbola was small and guests went to and fro all the time, but Carroll, on the fringe of these circles, would plod off down the road to Plumleys for lunch, hoping to make the acquaintance of some little girl or other.

The source that encouraged us to seek Cameron connections with Carroll were the memoirs of Henry Taylor's daughter, published at the turn of the twentieth century. Una Taylor, one of the pretty gipsy-like children on the beach who sat for Carroll that summer, recorded that Mrs Cameron wrote to her father:

Your photograph by Dodgson I heard described as looking like 'a sea monster fed upon milk' . . . The Tennysons *abhor* that photograph . . . I hope it will not be circulated, for it was printed so ill – come out so white *and* feeble *and* grotesque . . . I am going to order no copies of it.

Una Taylor neglected to mention in her book that she had been a child-friend of Carroll's and posed happily for him in London and on the Isle of Wight, and that her parents had initially taken to him. That, too, we found odd. Either she had genuinely forgotten the experience, or she had chosen to forget it as she took sides with Cameron and the Tennysons in condemning Carroll when he became, for several reasons, very much a *persona non grata*.

In seeking to photograph Henry Taylor, with his refined old face and long beard, Carroll was treading on Cameron territory. Later, when Carroll had very limited social connections with the Liddells, Cameron photographed the beautiful grown-up Alice Liddell as 'Flora', flanked by sprigs of white jasmine. Alice looks hard-eyed, ambitious and stares into the camera. The year was 1872, the year of Cameron's Lear photographs. That year Cameron photographed Bishop Wilberforce in an untidier pose than Carroll would have permitted. All these sittings took place soon after Carroll published his Isle of Wight skits in *Through the Looking-glass*.

Alice was also photographed by Cameron at Dimbola dressed in a Persephone costume. The Liddells had given up their summer villa at Pen Morfa on the North Wales coast because of the trippers and moved to the island for the summer. They had rented a house half-way between royal Osborne and poetic Freshwater. Mrs Cameron obliged Alice to sit at lunch between two housemaids who doubled as models and photographic laboratory assistants. Wedged between the two rustic maids, Alice said that she was completely lost for conversation. Confident with equals or social superiors by virtue of her mother's training at the Deanery, she was not at ease with the less educated.

Carroll could have predicted the occasion, and indeed had already done so in print. He knew Alice well. Carroll had

teased her in print for objecting to the fact that the White
Rabbit mistook her for Mary Ann, his maid.

Cameron could command circles, indeed be the centre of
them, in a way that Carroll could never have done or been.
Standing here in Freshwater and reading in Brian Hinton's book
the many contemporary descriptions of Cameron's gushing
manners and muddled dress, we realised that if Tennyson
inspired the White Knight, and quarrels between his two boys
suggested Tweedledum and Tweedledee, it was possible that
Cameron, too, was portrayed here. The tension between
Carroll and Cameron may have resolved itself in Carroll's imagination in the wild and flying shawl that the White Queen wore
when Alice helped her put the pins back into her dress and hair
before she turned into the Sheep in *Through the Looking-glass*.

THACKERAY
– from a self-portrait
in a letter

ALICE STRAIGHTENS
OUT THE WHITE QUEEN

The face of the White Queen in Tenniel's drawing looks
startlingly like the face of William Makepeace Thackeray,
whom Tenniel and Carroll had both met; Tenniel weekly at
Punch editorial board meetings and Carroll at breakfast in Christ

Church. After Thackeray's death in 1863, Mrs Cameron and the Tennysons befriended his orphaned daughters, Hester and Annie, the latter growing up to be a writer. So there *was* a Thackeray connection on the Isle of Wight, which appeared as the face of a character in *Through the Looking-glass*. And though the White Queen behaved like Mrs Cameron, she had the face of one of her most talented guests: author, satirist and graphic artist, William Makepeace Thackeray.

We left Dimbola and walked up the chalky path that led from Plumleys Hotel westward along the cliff-face of the Downs. The cliff to the west of Freshwater Bay has been designated Tennyson Down. We walked up there on the path Carroll would have taken to see the Needles, the line of rocks at the extreme western end of the island. The path led along the windswept grass interspersed with harebells and small wild scabious. The rolling Down, its chalk almost vertical to the sea, is 482 feet above the waves at its highest point. We passed a few leisurely walkers, then fewer. The trodden part of the grass narrowed. We felt we were walking Tennyson's song-line, sensing his energy and love of the wild high coastline of southern England.

As so often in this investigation, an incidental word or phrase or visage led to an important breakthrough. On this occasion, a fresh and provoking incident was Alice's encounter with the Talking Flowers.

Before meeting the White Knight, Alice enters the Garden of Live Flowers. Some of these flowers have faces, others speak. The idea for them owed a good deal to Grandville, artist to *Charivari*, the French satirical journal and precursor of *Punch*, much admired by Carroll and Tenniel. Several commentators had pointed out that there were references here to the garden in Tennyson's 'Come Into the Garden, Maud'.

Then, at Dimbola, we had seen one of Mrs Cameron's photographs which showed a group of five soulful girls in the garden, their heads inclined at awkward angles towards each other. It was entitled 'The Rose-Bud Garden of Girls'. The impression was developing that the Garden of Live Flowers was not only a spoof on 'Come into the Garden, Maud'. It also echoed the pushing and shoving and temperament that was displayed at Mrs Cameron's fancy dress photographic sessions where quarrelling between rose-buds in the garden was likely to break out.

We sat down on the high cliff and read through the scene. Alice has as much trouble getting into the Garden of Live Flowers as she does into the secret wonderland garden. The looking-glass path up which she is trying to climb keeps taking her back to the looking-glass house which she expects to leave behind her. Characteristically, she persists. Then she 'came upon a large flower-bed with a border of daisies and a willow tree growing in the middle'. Falling into conversation with the first flower, she says it was 'waving gracefully about in the wind'. This turns out to be a passionate Tiger-lily, and Alice's first words to it are: 'O Tiger-lily! I *wish* you could talk!' Immediately, she finds that the Tiger-lily and all the other flowers in the looking-glass flower-bed talk and complain and cast aspersions on each other in the most clear and lady-like voices, just as in photographic sessions at Dimbola.

The Tiger-lily which first catches Alice's eye is approachable, confiding and stagey. It did not, like one of Mrs Cameron's maids, have an Irish burr. Its voice, as Carroll portrayed it, was 'lady-like'. Instead, the Tiger-lily sounded like a leading lady with a wide dramatic range, used to playing to full houses as occasion demanded. It could not prevent itself from swaying from side to side and working itself into a passion as it spoke. Yet the Tiger-lily was a kindly-spoken flower and tried to protect Alice, the innocent newcomer.

We had seen in the Cameron photographs another model whom she and Carroll shared – the actress Ellen Terry.

Early in 1864, the painter George Frederick Watts had married Ellen Terry who had been in love with him since the age of fourteen. She was by then sixteen. Watts' home, 'The Briary', also in Freshwater, was to make up the third point of the artistic triangle of which Tennyson and Cameron were part.

When Ellen Terry came on her honeymoon to the Isle of Wight, Cameron photographed her. The young actress was wearing a summer shift, bare at the shoulders. Her eyes were closed, as if in a dream, her head on one side. She looked serene but not happy and Mrs Cameron entitled her picture 'Sadness'. It is one of the loveliest she ever took. For some private reason, ultimately connected with cruel interference in the relationship by one of Cameron's sisters, Watts snubbed Ellen after he had forced her to abandon what he unkindly called her 'services to the theatre'. Although Ellen had already made her name, she had promised him to give up the stage in return for a pension paid to her family. That was her part of their marriage contract. She kept it for the next few years. Watts did not keep his. He abandoned her.

Carroll knew about this. He had visited Watts' studio in Holland Park before coming to the Isle of Wight, and had seen Watts' canvas of Ellen in profile among the camellias, entitled *Choosing*. (Perhaps the title concerned her wedding promise.) He had seen Cameron's photograph of Ellen, the one that Watts used as a reference, near the canvas. More important than this, he himself hoped to meet Ellen, whose acting he had admired from afar for nearly a decade. There was only one person in Carroll's diary of this period who could double as a Tiger *and* a Lily and that was Ellen Terry.

If Ellen Terry was the Tiger-lily in the Garden of Live Flowers, her conversation with Alice made sense. The Tiger-lily spoke as a professional actress would to an amateur who had only ever played silent parts in drawing-room 'tableaux vivants'.

Alice was overwhelmed with shyness in the Tiger-lily's presence and asked timidly:

'And can *all* the flowers talk?'
'As well as *you* can,' said the Tiger-lily. 'And a great deal louder.'

This was certainly true. However well brought up the Dean's daughters were, the Terry sisters could project their voices and manage their passions better than any young Deanery daughter. The flowers criticised Alice's face and hair because they were not flower-parts. (The Looking-glass Insects did the same in the very next scene.) The Willow Tree in the middle of the looking-glass flower-bed gave the game away further. Alice asked the Rose: 'Aren't you sometimes frightened at being planted out here, with nobody to take care of you?'

Alice was well-protected compared with real child-actresses like the Terrys – Carroll had made friends with the whole family by the time the *Looking-glass* stories were ready for press. The Terry girls had been on the stage as tiny children, Ellen herself having acted before large audiences in London and the provinces from the age of eight.

The Rose explained to Alice: 'There's a tree in the middle. What else is it good for?'

'What' appears to be a name joke on Watts, who developed the image of being a sturdy, oak-like figure, rescuing the young Ellen from the theatre. In fact he abandoned her, a twist in this tale being that he did so partly under pressure from

Ellen Terry

Mrs Cameron's sister. So perhaps Carroll was right to put him in the garden as a bending willow.

What *was* Watts good for? The answer is, he was good for nothing in Carroll's eyes. He had let down the Tiger-lily and all under-age professional actresses, many of whom were leading ladies and still children. All his life Carroll lent them his active support, believing in their talents and longing to help them in any way he could. And it does not appear that he received any rebuffs. Yet Watts had wed and abandoned Ellen, with the encouragement of his patroness, Julia Margaret Cameron's sister.

'Look after the sounds, and the sense will look after itself', the Duchess said to Alice. The Tiger-lily sounded like Ellen:

'How is it you can all talk so nicely?' Alice asked.

'In most gardens they make the beds too soft – so that the flowers are always asleep,' explained the Tiger-lily.

Hard training, early discipline and no shirking for child-actresses was practised and preached by the Terry acting dynasty. Ellen, the most talented of them, loved exotic flowers, chinoiserie and Japanese kimonos. Her lover after the collapse of her marriage to Watts was a member of Whistler's bohemian circle in Chelsea, the architect and designer, Edwin Godwin, with whom she shared Whistler's passion for oriental art. The flower Carroll chose to match to Ellen's name was a tribute to her taste for the exotic and her passion on the stage. For a description of her, we re-read Kate Terry's grandson Sir John Gielgud's account of Ellen as an old lady in her seventies, still a great actress. The magic of her presence had not left her.

She moved with an extraordinary spontaneity and grace, holding her skirts gathered in two hands or bunched up over one arm, and crossed the stage with an unforgettable impression of swiftness . . . Shaw said that she had a genius for standing still when she was not making the most beautiful movements. She had known and talked with all the great men of her time – Tennyson, Browning, Ruskin, Wilde – and had learned a great deal from them. Yet she had a real humility. When you met her you felt that she was ready to learn from children.

Ellen's great-nephew, Gielgud, omitted Lewis Carroll from his list, but she knew him better than she knew the other great Victorians he mentioned. Carroll's first visit to the Terrys was in London. One of the 'white stone' moments of his life was the four days he spent on a photographic engagement with Ellen and her whole family in Kentish Town. His comments on her fit the thumbnail sketch he drew of her in the Garden of Live Flowers where she is the most exotic and commanding flower in the garden. This is how he depicted Ellen at the age of sixteen in a bevy of girls:

> The air seemed quite full of little shrill voices. 'Silence every one of you!' cried the Tiger-lily, waving itself passionately from side to side, and trembling with excitement. 'They know I can't get at them!' it panted, bending its quivering head towards Alice . . .

For eight years before he met her, Lewis Carroll had watched Ellen as a child-actress playing both male and female parts. He was devoted to her artistry and that of her younger sister Marion. Her willingness to encourage younger actresses and her Pre-Raphaelite affiliations increased his admiration.

Carroll's photographs of Ellen show her in her black and purple brocade wedding-gown, and Carroll catches a haunted, tragic gaze as she faces his camera. He commented on the humiliation of her ill-fated marriage. We had seen the haunting print in Texas, cut to an oval. Ellen had signed it for Carroll, 'Truly yours, Ellen Alice Watts' in a hand that is architectural in its authority and sloping slightly backwards.

For that pose, taken after the summer of 1864, Ellen wears a paisley pattern skirt. The body of her dress is made of what seems to be satin with velvet slashes. She has a windswept look, head sideways but with an expression the exact opposite of pert, the look of a wise and nurturing woman, particularly a wise one. She wears beads round her neck, of costume jewellery, and a wedding-ring on her finger. Her hands are slightly short: they look like working hands.

Though her marriage was over, she still loved her dress. The costume, with its paisley drapes, was the one she had worn

when she posed for Watts for 'Choosing'. We had found the live
flower Carroll called on after Alice had ceased to pose for him.

Carroll photographed Ellen's younger sisters alone and with
their family in the garden and in their house in London.

He ate with them when he was working with them, and was
not sent away for his lunch as at Dimbola. He had in common
with Ellen that both were spurned by the catty Pattle sisters. As
his biographer Anne Clarke was the first to realise, she was a
more mature, more adult Alice – an inspiration. He had recon-
ciled himself to her uneasy status as an abandoned child-bride
and then common law wife. She remained a confidante of his.

With the Terrys the rules which were set were to prove helpful to him: Carroll could eat at the Terry table but Mrs Terry, a
street-wise middle-class woman without Oxford pretension,
never let any of her four daughters, grown or tiny, go off into
London alone with Lewis Carroll. He asked her once about
Polly, whom he adored, but after Mrs Terry refused him he
never tried again.

CHAPTER TWELVE

The Pink Boathouse

O N TOP of the Down there was a Tennyson memorial, a
cross 'raised as a beacon by the people of Freshwater and
other friends in England and America'. After another undulat-
ing mile it was possible to see the chalk-coated Needles erect
against a glimmering sea. Portly German tourists came puffing
up from the car-park. Up here was the emplacement where
Britain's potential moon rocket was tested in the late 1950s.

We were in search of another place where Carroll had been
treated as an equal, the Needles Hotel, to which he had walked
and where he had visited Henry Kingsley on his honeymoon.
We found it, not so far out on the point of the island as the view
of the Needles themselves, but nestled from the prevailing wind
in a cup of land behind the cliff at Alum Bay, famous for its layered, high cliffs of different coloured sands.

The old white hotel building was a modest place, now mod-
ernised and built around with a glass-fronted patio, but with the
hunched look of an old inn. It stood in the middle of brightly-
coloured rides and stalls, a small amusement park on the edge
of pine woods. It was more modest than Plumleys and,
although only a couple of miles from Farringford and Dimbola,
much more modest than they were.

Like Carroll, Henry Kingsley had not been a member of the
inner circle on the Isle of Wight.

We walked eastward, just the two of us, like Carroll and his
parson friend, when no one had invited them to dinner. There
were scurrying rabbits on the warren, but no one else was in

sight. The globular sun was lowering itself to the horizon, like an old man lowering himself into bed. We could smell the mixed perfume of honeysuckle unusually growing among the purple bell-heather.

Guide books we had seen recorded Carroll among the island's famous visitors, giving him as much or more precedence than the others. But they, now rather forgotten, did not accord him that privilege at the time.

The light was failing fast. When we looked out towards the jutting rocks of the Needles, the Sealink car ferry came into view from Cherbourg or Le Havre, prickling with bright lights and moving imperceptibly through the water. From somewhere we thought we could hear dance music. Perhaps we were mistaken. Perhaps it was the clank of an encumbered White Knight falling into a gorse bush.

Next morning we took the bus to the royal palace at Osborne. Perhaps we had a sense that in this particularly royal love-nest we might find something of the pantomime view of royalty that Carroll himself displayed. We knew that the Liddells, Aclands and Tennysons were invited to this summer residence, and were flattered by the tokens of favour they felt they had received when they answered each royal summons.

Plumleys Hotel and Osborne were diagonally opposite each other, one south-west on the island, the other north-east, one a celibate kind of place, slightly elevated and looking over the bright sea, the other on lower ground. Osborne was not at all modest or celibate.

The driveway to Osborne had a parade-ground look to it, sandy-coloured gravel on tar and precision cut grass edges. It seemed to suggest to visitors that they were there on sufferance, like platoons at an inspection. The lawns were interspersed with large cedars and other trees from imperial lands or the lands of other empires. The turreted and balconied house came into view, built of a creamy-coloured brick. It looked awkward and asymmetrical, as if it ought to have palm trees around it. It was Prince Albert's design, built with the help of an English architect, and suggested mostly Italian idioms. The interior was 1840s German, and amazingly so.

We were in a world of royal fantasy. This place was pure Victoria and Albert vanity, their specifications untrammelled by any Georgian past.

'V' and 'A' were inscribed with regularity in plaster or iron or porcelain or stone. Portraits of richly-dressed royals and their family were everywhere, but the second striking theme of the decor was that of royal undress. Royal or allegorical, everywhere there were nude figures, in marble and porcelain and in gold leaf. There were nudes on the candelabra, on the candlesticks, on door handles and ceilings. There were female nudes and male nudes and on the main stairs a statue of Albert dressed as a Greek warrior with a mini-kilt barely covering his private parts (or where they would have been), emblems of nude ladies clinging to his breast. There was a pair of large porcelain pugs on porcelain velvet cushions, the male showing *his* privates and the female suckling a puppy. High fecundity was decisively royal at this time. Where there were not nudes and portraits of Albert and Victoria there were further statues and portraits of the royal children. Here and there were a few landscape paintings. The most striking non-portrait was a large canvas by Landseer, showing significant numbers of stags dead, writhing in near death or about to be killed.

A section of the house was done up in Durbar style, but the dominant impression was of a German royal love of self, dressed in a baroque idiom, a thundering chorus to the principle of sperm and egg.

The King and Queen of Hearts in *Alice* were not like this at all. They were a pack of cards, but perhaps that in itself was a snub. Carroll never managed to photograph a real queen, consort, or heir to the throne. He said that he found the real Queen disappointing and 'dumpy' when he cast eyes on her at Christ Church. In April 1868 Carroll wrote to Margaret Cunnynghame, a child-friend:

My dear Maggie,
 I am a very bad correspondent, I fear, but I hope you won't leave off writing to me on that account. I got the little book safe, and will do the best about putting my name in, if only

I can remember what day my birthday is – but one forgets those things so easily.

Somebody told me (a little bird, I suppose) that you have been having better photographs done of yourselves. If, so I hope you will let me buy copies. Fanny will pay you for them. But oh, Maggie, how *can* you ask for a better one of me than the one I sent! It is the best one ever done! Such grace, such dignity, such benevolence, such . . . as a great secret (please don't repeat it) the *Queen* sent to ask for a copy of it, but as it is against my rule to give in such a case, I was obliged to answer: 'Mr. Dodgson presents his compliments to Her Majesty, and regrets to say that his rule is never to give his photograph except to *young* ladies'. I am told she was annoyed about it, and said, 'I'm not so old as all that comes to,' and one doesn't like to annoy Queens, but really I couldn't help it, you know.

Your affectionate friend . . .

Carroll saw Queen Victoria at close quarters on two occasions. On each he disparaged her appearance

Then we noticed a few portraits of the Queen's servants at Osborne, grouped with those of her dogs. Also in the photograph collection was a portrait of the royal photographic tutor whose pictures lacked Carroll's flair and candour. There were two other portraits in the Queen's study. One was of Benjamin Disraeli. This was hardly surprising. The Queen doted on him and he on her – so unlike her feelings for the old Unicorn when in power.

The other portrait was of Dean Stanley, a small rather serious oil painting in rich colours. Despite its size, it had an important place near the Queen's bath-chamber and was framed in a heavy, box-shaped gilt frame. It caught Stanley's sharp features in the same way that the photograph by Carroll had done, the one in Alice's album. Dean Stanley, her father's friend, who had been Canon at Christ Church during the reform crisis, officiated at the marriage of Alice Liddell and Reggie Hargreaves at Westminster Abbey.

Could Stanley be the Cheshire Cat in *Wonderland*? The way

the picture had suddenly turned up, small but important, was just like Stanley, hovering in the most intimate of royal places.

Stanley was the first Canon at Christ Church to be appointed by Liddell. He was a reformer in the college and in the university. The main branch of the Stanley family came from Cheshire. So did the Cat. Stanley knew a good deal about the comings and goings of the Queen, for, to the Queen's momentary indignation, as both were well into their middle-age at the time of his suit, he married her most trusted of the ladies-in-waiting, Lady Bruce, who was also accustomed to walking in the corridors of power. He knew a great deal about the Kingsley circle, and he included them among the theological innovators with whom he wished the Abbey to associate.

The Stanleys were the family which had owned Winnington Hall. Arthur Penrhyn Stanley – Canon Stanley, then Dean Stanley of Westminster – was the son of the Bishop of Norwich, a bishop known for his liberal views, particularly towards the theatre: Dean Stanley's father had entertained Jenny Lind, known as the 'Swedish Nightingale', at his palace. Stanley, his son, even before his promotion from Canon at Christ Church to Dean of Westminster, had always been a royal favourite. He was less formal and stiff than Liddell in royal company.

In *Wonderland* the Cheshire Cat is found where the King and Queen are to be found. Its grins and wide mouth are not unlike the portrait the Queen kept on the wall with her little board painting of Disraeli in her personal sleeping quarters. The Cheshire Cat appeared on high. Carroll, who dined with Stanley at the Deanery, would not have missed his aloofness. Carroll barely mentioned Stanley in his diary, but he equated him with Liddell as the butt of Common Room satire. Liddon and Pusey were at loggerheads with him throughout the 1860s.

Carroll had an ideal source of gossip about Stanley in A.J.C. Hare, whose elder cousin we posed as a possible Hare at the mad Tea-party. The young Hare was Stanley's unpaid secretary and thereby enjoyed the privilege of using the Christ Church Senior Common Room. Later he became known as a country house gossip and teller of ghost stories. It was Hare who reported how Stanley wrote his sermons standing up at a lectern, writing with his right hand and eating buns with his left, rapidly covering yellow sheets of paper with his sermon and letting them fall to the floor for young Hare to pick up.

The Queen loved Stanley and appointed him Royal Chaplain. Like the Hares, Stanley was a Liberal. His German leanings appealed to the royal household.

At Oxford he had been associated with the defence of Benjamin Jowett. One of Carroll's longest and most approachable spoofs was called *The New Method of Evaluation as Applied to* π, pi being the algebraic symbol that was important in measuring Jowett's large girth and the pie being what Jowett and others in the Broad Church party, including Stanley, swallowed whole. Part of this long mock-mathematical explanation was a discussion of 'Penrhyn's Method', a mathematical approach – too obtuse to bring results – devised by Arthur Penrhyn Stanley.

A favourite of the Liddells, Stanley was above all a favourite courtier, on a par with Disraeli. Carroll wrote of the Cheshire Cat: 'The Cat only grinned when it saw Alice. It looked good-natured, she thought: still it had *very* long claws and a great many teeth, so she felt that it ought to be treated with respect.'

There he was, in this little oil-painting in Osborne House, looking obsequious, dreamy and shy, but also very intelligent.

We passed the royal bathroom which was an enclosed chamber and went through the royal bedroom. The bed was made as it was left, a sash across one pillow and an emblem of Albert on the sash.

It was time to wake up from this mad English dream, to leave behind what we had learned about Carroll and his standing on the Isle of Wight and get out of this summer palace, dedicated to royal fecundity.

Or were they only a pack of cards? We took the ferry and returned to Oxford.

★

'Little Canon Stanley' used to walk briskly in the Oxfordshire lanes, pondering a Broad Church sermon or plotting to save Jowett from High Church attackers. Dons like Stanley and Carroll on occasion walked thirty miles in a single day, alone or with a suitable companion, pondering the religious schisms of the moment.

We wanted to see the lower part of the river where Carroll rowed when he went downstream with the girls. So we walked from Abingdon, where the railway ran from London, across short golden stubble and past the Radley College boathouse. Determined fishermen with large square boxes and twenty-foot poles had placed themselves every fifty yards along the banks. One had arranged his box on a frame so that he sat firm as a rock in the slow water of the river. On the far bank was the Nuneham boathouse, a Victorian building painted sugar-almond pink. It was built in imitation of a little summertime Swiss chalet, like one that Ruskin might have drawn and coloured in Schaffhausen. The Harcourts' chalet boathouse had a prettily carved balcony above the entrance for boats and a black lattice pattern of woodwork on its high gables.

Later in the afternoon we went round to Nuneham itself which belonged to Carroll's friend, the chemist Harcourt, later a Fellow of the Royal Society, sometimes a boating companion with the girls and a substitute for Duckworth. The large Georgian house at Nuneham Courtney was originally Palladian before it was extended. It was built by the first Earl of Harcourt and in 1993 became the Global Retreat Centre for the Brahma Kumar's World Spiritual University. Two white-shrouded

German women showed us the way down to the boathouse, unlocking the wicket-gate which was hung with small orange flags. The sun was shining brightly and we could hear a combine harvester. No Red King was in sight.

Around the boathouse was a coppice. Entering the coppice through the iron railings which defined the borders of much nineteenth-century wealth was like entering a darkened church. The boathouse was deserted. This was where Carroll and the girls had tea and sheltered on more than one occasion. We tried climbing the staircase that ran half-way up the back of the chalet building, on the side away from the river where he had tied up their boat. It was all locked up, but it must have been a comfortable and roomy place in which to dry off.

In *Under Ground*, Carroll had described real people in a real place, but he cut out the section in *Wonderland*. They were soaked to the skin, either because they had been in the Pool of Tears, or because they had been in the Oxford riverside rain.

> The whole party moved along the river bank . . . in a slow procession, the Dodo leading the way. After a time, the Dodo became impatient, and, leaving the Duck to bring up the rest of the party, moved on at a quicker pace with Alice, the Lory, and the Eaglet, and soon brought them to a little cottage, and there they sat snugly by the fire, wrapped up in blankets, until the rest of the party had arrived, and they were all dry again.

After this they sat on the bank and the Mouse told his 'long and sad tale'. Stanley was high on the list of those the mice had to fear. Less exposed than the Dean, he could always be seen in the background, grinning slyly, rich enough not to bother about teaching income, yet holding views on what new priorities the real teachers, the mice, should espouse.

Christ Church and its controversies faded to insignificance, although only three miles upstream. The oak trees and plane trees allowed a dappled sunlight to come through and the river was green and alive. Earlier in the afternoon we had seen a boat from Salters go upstream, a pleasure boat with varnished wood and seats on the upper deck of what must originally have been a steamer. Now it came down again past the boathouse and

there were strains of music that might have come from Radio 1
and the beery talk of an un-Christian Sunday on the river. Its
wash sploshed against the bank. We could not see into the
boathouse over the river but we could hear a craft inside creaking on a chain.

Perhaps it was a rowing-boat trying to get out.

Why had Carroll removed from the published version of *Alice*
this seemingly innocent passage about the river party? And why
had he eliminated his description of the side of the Pool
of Tears lined with 'rushes and forget-me-nots'? It was as if he
had suppressed the place that inspired the story, with its soft
romantic focus, and edited out the innocent (or not so innocent) section about himself and the three wet little girls for the
meat of the Mouse's tale, the part closer to Christ Church and
its controversy with Dean and Canons. The 'Alice' books are
set out as a child's dream laced with hidden adult characters.
Here the literal part about the children's role in the expedition
on which the dream was based had been suppressed.

The suppression may have been self-imposed. Carroll's relationship with the girls he took on the river was tinged with the
adult language of procurement. When he wrote to Duckworth
about the occasion of a forthcoming trip on the river with the
Dean's little daughters, he suggested dinner in Christ Church
Hall and joked: 'should you be disposed any day soon for a row
on the river, for which I could procure some Liddells as companions?'

CHAPTER
THIRTEEN

Sue it And Suet

THE NEXT MORNING we set off along the High Street for Balliol College. We also wanted to see the circular Sheldonian Theatre surrounded by its Roman statues. It was here that Carroll and Ruskin later cast their votes and lent influential voices in protest in the press against the proposal by Acland, tacitly supported by Liddell and Jowett, that vivisection should be practised in the physiological laboratories of the University. It was here that the 'Jowett issue' had been debated over a number of years, ending in 1867 in victory for Jowett. Of all Carroll's targets, Benjamin Jowett expressed more strongly than any a world of changing theological values in which the innocence he claimed for Alices was gone for ever.

Because Jowett wanted (and deserved) a salary of more than the £40 a year he was paid for being Professor of Greek, because his theological views were held against him, because he was dogged in the communication of his views, loved by those who loved him and distrusted by the rest, he was the butt of satire, cartoons, lampoons, gossip and vitriol. These squibs were whispered in the Common Rooms, shouted along the streets and, in Carroll's case, posted on every college notice-board for all the world to see.

We passed Magdalen, All Souls, St Edmund Hall and New College. Carroll sent his squibs around to all of these, and more of them were about Jowett than anybody else in the period when *Wonderland* was published. The funniest was deemed to be the mathematical joke about Jowett's girth, which was combined with the joke about his appetite for pie – having it, eating it and being measured for it. This was the squib in which Stanley also featured.

The colleges were emptied of undergraduates on that damp August morning as we mingled with the tourists, who gazed intently at the stone edifices, and the shoppers. There were a few people out and about, on foot and on bicycles, with a distinctly donnish air. They wore old coats and seemed to stare fixedly at some distant abstraction, as if they wished to avoid the risk of engaging with a coterie of potential enemies.

In Jowett's case, until 1867, the coterie consisted of everyone from the University Vice-Chancellor to Dean Liddell, to most of his own college's High Table to Lewis Carroll and numerous other pin-prickers. These were backed by the country clergy who came with their Bibles and copies of Bradshaw's railway guide to vote on University matters in the Oxford parliament, Convocation.

Jowett looked cherubic in the pictures we had seen of him. His small amount of hair was brushed, but it was hard to think of him as not having flying hair and frayed cuffs, with ink stains on his handkerchiefs.

> They passed beneath the College gate;
> And on the High went slowly on;
> Then spoke the undergraduate
> To that benign and portly don . . .

This was how Carroll had started *The Majesty of Justice: an Oxford Idyll* which accused a 'portly don' of twisting the law in high places. The don in question was identified by name in this squib, the only time this occurred in any Carroll squib, so important did the issue seem to Carroll: 'You're talking nonsense, sir! You know it!/ Such arguments were never used' (viz. arguments for High Court justice rather than religious court justice)/ 'By any friend of Jowett'.

Jowett, we realised, almost rhymed with 'suet' in the 'Old Father William' verses. Carroll set both squibs in the form of a conversation, written as a dialogue between an old and a young man, just as Plato (Jowett's favourite author) set out his Socratic dialogues. The dialogue took place between a young man, who looked like Carroll in his own drawings, and an old country-man who looked like a fatter, more self-satisfied Jowett.

We walked on past the circular library, the Radcliffe Camera, and into Broad Street, crossing diagonally from the Bodleian Library and the Sheldonian Theatre where the High Church clergy gathered to stem the tide of unbelief. Here Carroll gave his maiden speech against Jowett. Opposite was Blackwell's Bookshop, and beyond this Balliol College. Like Carroll at Christ Church, Balliol was home for Jowett from the time he arrived as a scholar, the son of a bankrupt father, until he died in 1893, gradually accumulating power and prestige – and, in Carroll's view, girth.

'Little Jack Horner/ Sat in a Corner/ Eating his Christmas Pie', the mathematical Pie spoof began and went on: 'Let U= the University, G= Greek, and P= Professor. Then GP= Greek Professor; let this be reduced to its lowest terms, and call the result J.' It went on to call for the elimination of J from the equation. Carroll thought of the Pie Squib on Wednesday, 1st March 1865, in the press of other matters, including *Alice*, and within a fortnight he had had it printed and distributed to every Common Room in Oxford.

It had long been perceived that the chief obstacle to the evaluation of 'π' was the presence of J, and in an earlier age of mathematics J would probably have referred to rectangu-lar axes, and divided into two unequal parts – a process of arbitrary elimination . . .

'Talking of Axes', the Red Queen had said, 'Cut off his head!' It had all been so much simpler in Tudor Oxford.

The entrance quadrangle to Balliol was small, enclosed, medieval in spirit, Victorian in that it was rebuilt during Carroll's and Jowett's time. Balliol was the oldest Oxford foun-dation. The Library was in the Old Hall. We knew that Jowett had, in the period in which his tenure was under threat, so dis-approved of the High Church regime at Balliol High Table that he preferred to sit down among the undergraduates. It was on the site of the Library that he had sat.

His former pupils, who became senior civil servants and distinguished colonial administrators, left many accounts of the fact that Jowett was not in the traditional sense the best of company. Undergraduates invited to breakfast in his rooms would sometimes endure the meal in silence. Jowett is said to have considered very little worth saying, and if he thought nothing worth saying, he said nothing. Yet Father William, the fat man of Carroll's new ballad, boasted to his young – student – companion:

'In my youth,' said the old man, 'I took to the law,
  And argued each case with my wife,
And the muscular strength, which it gave to my jaw,
  Has lasted the rest of my life.'

'Took to the law' suggested the intensely tough defence Jowett put up to keep himself in Balliol when accused of heresy by his High Church enemies. Turned down for the Mastership in 1854, denied by Convocation the salary he deserved in 1864 when Carroll voted against him and wrote many squibs, Jowett triumphed in 1870 when he finally became Master of Balliol, publishing his own translation of Plato, now an English classic, which he worked on in Freshwater in 1871. The rebuilt, revitalised Balliol owed its pre-eminence to his vigorous tutorial style, his fundraising and his powers of organisation and mobilisation.

The Balliol Library was small. While Christ Church was full of space, there was a serious, enclosed feeling to Balliol. It was

BALLIOL OLD HALL AND NEW LIBRARY

hard to imagine Liddell at Christ Church tolerating Jowett's intensity of thought and serious concern to broaden the undergraduate basis of the University. Liddell's view was that he could improve Christ Church's academic performance and do it with the 'existing material'. By the existing material he meant the 'country house set' of undergraduates.

We found the Jowett papers described in a printed catalogue. Two books, it appeared, led Jowett to be prosecuted for no less than heresy. They were innocently entitled *Epistles of Saint Paul* and *Essays and Reviews*. Of the first he was the author, of the second the editor, and author of the final essay. There were seven essays and he wrote the longest of them. The authors became known in High Church circles as *Septem Contra Christe*, the 'Seven against Christ'.

The Jowett issue was, as Carroll entitled one of his poems, 'A Tangled Tale'. From Martin Gardner's annotations to *Alice* we knew that the 'Old Father William' verses were a parody of a similar poem by Robert Southey, Poet Laureate before Tennyson and Wordsworth; in its Oxford setting poor little Alice recited Southey's ballad all wrong. She was growing taller and shorter, being barked at and charged by a giant puppy with rolling eyes, smiled at by a disappearing Cheshire Cat and quizzed about her identity by a blue Caterpillar.

> 'You are old, Father William,' the young man said,
>   'And your hair has become very white;
> And yet you incessantly stand on your head –
>   Do you think, at your age, it is right?'

> 'In my youth,' Father William replied to his son,
>   'I feared it might injure the brain;
> But, now that I'm perfectly sure I have none,
>   Why, I do it again and again.'

Right and wrong had become all mixed up in Carroll's Oxford. Jowett stood mostly for wrong. So, in Carroll's eyes, did Dean Liddell, but Liddell did not back Jowett. He, like Jowett, had Broad Church leanings, but he was much less openly sceptical

FATHER WILLIAM STANDING ON HIS HEAD, by Carroll

than Jowett, more of a theological fence-sitter, a less impassioned man.

The problem of the Greek Professorship was none the less partly of Liddell's making. The reforms which Jowett, Liddell, Stanley and others had instituted in the University after 1854 had put a greater teaching-load on to the Professors. In any case, £40 a year was anachronistic as a salary. It was even more degrading when Jowett's increasingly heavy teaching burden was taken into account. The trouble was that the salary was in the gift of the Dean and Canons of Christ Church and the C and D did not want to give any more of it to J. Jowett's salary and his own raised a number of conflicting objections in Carroll's logical mind.

He decided to take the opportunity to voice his position in a maiden speech in the Sheldonian Theatre, facing the high throne and standing up erect in posture, trying to control his stammer. He was prepared to take a chance on an issue about which he felt as strongly as this, the strength of his feeling revealed in his many Jowett verses. On 20th November 1861, he wrote:

Promulgation, in Congregation, of the new statute to endow Jowett. The speaking took up the whole afternoon, and the two points at issue, the endowing of a *Regius* Professorship, and the countenancing of Jowett's theological opinions, got so inextricably mixed up that I rose to beg that they might be kept separate. Once on my feet, I said more than at first I meant, and defied them ever to tire out the opposition by perpetually bringing the question on . . . This was my first speech in Congregation.

It may also have been his last. There is no other record of Carroll speaking in the University bodies. Instead he used other, odder weapons for attack, of which 'Alice' achieved greatness.

One reason Liddell may have had for being lukewarm about supporting Jowett was that Robert Scott, who edited the Greek Lexicon with him, was the same High Church Scott who had been elected Master of Balliol when Jowett was turned down for the post. There happened to be a 1925 edition of *Liddell & Scott* on the Balliol Library reference shelf and its preface listed the previous editions, in 1843, 1845, 1849, 1855, 1861, 1866, 1882 and 1897, some editions selling nearly 15,000 copies at almost £2 per copy. It was a valuable commodity. Liddell and Scott had been Christ Church undergraduates together. They were at variance in theological dogma but they were financial partners. Did this explain why Liddell gave only lukewarm support to Jowett? The Lexicon had paid for extensive internal renewal at the Deanery in Christ Church, including the Lexicon Staircase, up which the Liddells' guests would troop to meet Mrs Liddell..

Listed in the well-organised Balliol Manuscript Catalogue are letters from Dean Liddell (who left little trace of his power-broking in any archives) to Benjamin Jowett. There are also letters from the Cheshire Cat, Canon Arthur Penrhyn Stanley to Jowett, as well as other documents under the heading 'Greek Professorship'. The first document we looked at was a pamphlet entitled, 'The Case whether Professor Jowett in his essay and commentary has so distinctly contravened the doctrines of the Church of England that a Court of Law would pronounce him guilty; with the opinion of the Queen's advocate thereon'. It was published in London and had cost sixpence. (Carroll's squibs expressing similar views were distributed free.) It discussed the writers whom Jowett persuaded, without revealing the identity of any one to the other, to create the innocuous-sounding *Essays and Reviews*. It said, coyly, of the first of these essayists that 'Professor Powell, who wrote against miracles, was removed before a higher Tribunal, at no advanced age . . . ' Supporters of Jowett claimed that the furore about the book had killed a benign old scholar.

The next, Mr Goodwin, who questioned the 'Mosaic account of Creation', had been obliged to resign from Christ's College, Cambridge. One of the next two essayists was Mark Pattison of Pembroke College, a future Master and later a free-thinker with whom Carroll dined at the Liddells'; the pamphlet denied that anything 'could make *his* arguments answerable to a court of law'.

Two others, Dr Rowland Williams and Henry B. Wilson, were ruined as a result of condemnation by the revived Court of Arches, which had stripped them of their livings, pupils, parish duties and incomes. Most significant of all was the Headmaster of Rugby himself, William Temple, who was said to have written his essay secretly at night by candlelight. This was Carroll's own school and his younger brothers were still enrolled there as the furore over *Essays and Reviews* broke out. It penetrated to the heart of the public school system. The document continued, 'Professor Jowett is the seventh', and questioned whether the University could indeed take Jowett to court for his heretical views:

> The question involves the whole present and future of the University as a place of religious education. The subjects, upon which Professor Jowett has, in the opinion of Counsel so contradicted . . . the Church of England . . . comprise both the source and the substance of faith. In denying the super-natural inspiration of Holy Scripture he takes away from those who trust him the groundwork of all faith . . . These points are provable by law . . . as the talented young men influenced by him become tutors in other colleges, the extent to which Oxford may become a destroyer of souls is incalculable.

The bitterness of the debate is encapsulated in this argument. A memorandum from Dean Liddell wonderfully caught his character as a nebulous but all-powerful Red King. First it said: 'The Dean and Chapter of Christ Church have under their consideration the question of augmenting the salary of the Regius Professor of Greek . . . The Dean and Chapter are unanimous' (many crossings out) 'in thinking that they are under no legal obligation to increase the annual payment of £40.' In support, the letter cited the opinion of the Attorney-General and other highly-paid counsel: 'Nor can the Dean and Chapter recognise any moral obligation in the matter . . . '

In spite of this lofty string of negatives, the letter eventually got round to saying that the Dean and Chapter had decided at long last to grant the increase 'on the ground of general expediency.'

We were getting close to Jowett. We were getting closer to Liddell. Normally Stanley and Liddell were hand in glove, and in one letter of her father's found in Alice's papers, we noticed that Liddell wrote to Stanley of Bishop Wilberforce and his High Church allies that, 'I fear the Philistines will be too strong for us'.

In this case the association with Robert Scott (otherwise a 'Philistine') was too close for comfort. Stanley, meanwhile, came off as a model of tolerance in the correspondence about Jowett. He did not come and go at all, like Carroll's Cheshire Cat. He argued his principles in the matter of the Jowett case and held his ground throughout, warning, in a balanced way, of the fate of a university that espoused such extreme views as those of the High Church party of Pusey and his supporters. No wonder Carroll made the Cheshire Cat smile through very sharp teeth.

Stanley supported the Portly Don, lambasting the 'intricacies of argument' of the opposition. Where Carroll was perceptive was in his recognition of the fact that the Portly Don, more than any other figure, symbolised the changes ahead for Oxford. It was to cease to be a place of religious education and emerge as a university in the modern sense, multi-disciplinary and multi-sectarian. To Carroll's chagrin, a decade later, Oxford was on the way to becoming the seat of secular belief. John Ruskin moved away from his evangelical past towards a worldly belief in beauty for its own sake. In parallel with his public recantation of his Christian art criticism, the 'Art for Art's Sake' movement grew up in the form that was mainly associated with Walter Pater at Oxford. Other Oxford intellectuals, such as Mark Pattison, the Jowett supporter who wrote for *Essays and Reviews*, moved from High Anglicanism into plain unbelief. How threatening to the religious and artistic views of the Archdeacon's son from Croft! How threatening, too, to the climate of opinion surrounding the innocent child of the nursery.

We were looking at the small Balliol quadrangle, its flagstones shiny with rain. A monastic silence, an air of intense calculation hung over the quad. This had been Jowett's home and power base for five decades. We looked again at the lines of 'Father William', or rather between them. The Old Man's white hair and his fatness fitted the Professor of Greek's personal appearance well enough.

So possibly did the suppleness of the old quack in Alice's verse. Jowett, while portly, was fit, a sturdy urban-living fell-walker who believed, as Kingsley did, that fresh air would dissipate desire among the chosen young men he took on reading parties. Carroll's satire against the transformation of part of the Oxford Parks into University cricket fields had alerted us to Jowett's athleticism.

Jowett trained his students for First Class degrees. In the view of his opponents, echoing the charges brought by the Elders of Athens against Socrates, he 'infected' them with his sceptical doctrines.

As to Jowett's facial identity, Carroll's own illustrations were more striking and more savage than those by Tenniel. Carroll's smiling, balding Father William in his silly striped socks caught Jowett as we had seen him photographed, wispily out of focus, by Julia Margaret Cameron, and drawn reverentially by George Richmond. Carroll's Father William stood on his head, somersaulted – an upside-down and backwards joke about Jowett's ideas. And he held forth at his own meagrely spread table (he was not paid enough to entertain well) and balanced an eel on his nose.

The jokes suggested a man who was constantly turning the world upside-down, going round in circles, laying down the law, balancing slippery ideas and getting away with it. Tenniel's illustrations slightly dissipated the face Carroll had captured. His Father William had more of a benign John Bull-ish face and figure.

There also seemed to be some hidden word jokes.

> 'You are old,' said the youth, 'and your jaws are too weak
>   For anything tougher than suet;
> Yet you finished the goose, with the bones and the beak –
>   Pray, how did you manage to do it?'

First we spotted a rhyming joke about school mastering. Jowett prided himself on his punctilious didactic technique. (The same could not be said of Carroll. His maths tuition was dreaded and sometimes accompanied by heavy punishment – mediated when necessary by the Dean himself.)

'Weak' and 'Beak' (slang for a public schoolmaster at some schools) rhymes with 'Greek' (Jowett's Professorship).

The Goose the Old Man ate up in front of his two astonished guests (a young man and an unnamed person of indefinable sex shown in Carroll's illustration) supplies the initial 'G'.

So 'Weak' and 'Beak' carry the sound '-Eak', or '-Eek', to describe Jowett's Chair of Greek, the one Pusey and Carroll hoped the University would deny him.

In the fifth verse 'Jaws' and 'Suet' are associated with 'Do it!' and 'Sue it!'

'Do it!' rhymes with the hidden 'Jew – it', a scarcely disguised surname joke on Jowett. The echo of 'Jew – it' has an undertone referring to Jowett and Stanley's 'heretical' interpretation of the Old Testament in its original Hebrew. Their interpretations from the Hebrew were a source for the sceptical remarks in Jowett's remarkable essay, 'On the Interpretation of the Scriptures'. The Hebrew exegeses, together with his Greek and Hegelian studies, exemplified Jowett's tolerance as a religious thinker. Carroll sought to mock what he regarded as his unstoppable audacity in the 'Father William' skit.

Jokes about 'Jaws' also target Jowett – 'Jaw – it'. Asking in Oxford, we could find no consensus on how to pronounce

Jowett's surname. We also learned that Liddell can either be pronounced 'Liddle' (to rhyme with 'fiddle') or Lidd-ell (to rhyme with 'hare bell'). The most famous Oxford rhyme about Jowett – not a Carroll rhyme – was about his self-importance. (There were plenty of other punsters and squib writers at work beside Carroll.) It ended 'I don't know it', rhyming with 'Joe-it'. The point is that everyone knew who the squib was mocking, in whatever form his surname turned up in its rhyming pattern.

As a curious footnote to the way Carroll worked, we discovered in one of the few pieces of the 'lost' diaries retained by his nephew that he lifted the idea that runs through verses five and six of 'Father William' from Dr Oliver Wendell Holmes, the New England physician and essayist. In May 1861, Carroll picked out a piece of Holmes hearsay at dinner with Canon A. P. Stanley. A visiting American guest described how Dr Wendell Holmes had observed the head of a real turtle 'freshly killed . . . whose eyes and jaws still showed muscular action'.

Carroll was not only a Dodo; he integrated ideas from all kinds of sources. He, as well as his friend Osborne Gordon, was a magpie.

There is an abundance of tortoise and turtle jokes in 'Alice'. In this ballad, which we knew was fishy, Father William's human jaws show an identical action to Holmes' dying New England turtle:

'the muscular strength' which it gave to my jaw
   Has lasted the rest of my life.'

Jowett, like Father William, 'took to the law' frequently, using 'muscle' to fend off the battery of heresy cases brought against him, above all by Bishop Wilberforce, whose photograph by Carroll we had seen in Alice's album. Nevertheless Jowett triumphed. The answer to the young man's question in the Jowett case – 'How did you manage to do it?' – was unspoken in the 'Father William' ballad. Jowett had been tenacious in arguing cases through the secular courts, presided over by judges who shared his scepticism of Anglican doctrine. Carroll must have been sure, even though matters were *sub judice* at the time he published his ballad, that Jowett would eventually prevail.

Another idea struck us. There is a difference in the price of the ointment between the two versions of the ballad. In Alice's 1864 *Under Ground* poem the Old Man's ointment cost five shillings and in the 1865 published version in *Wonderland* it had gone down to one shilling. From Carroll's point of view, Jowett was peddling tawdry spiritual doctrines in his book *Essays and Reviews*, which had become a bestseller, going into cheaper and cheaper editions. The reduced price of the ointment reflected the lowering price of the banned book. Besides, the Old Man offered to sell a couple of boxes, and Jowett no doubt hoped that the success of one book would lead readers to his earlier offering, *Epistles of Saint Paul*.

> 'You are old,' said the youth, 'as I mentioned before,
> And have grown most uncommonly fat;
> Yet you turned a back-somersault in at the door –
> Pray, what is the reason of that?'
>
> 'In my youth,' said the sage, as he shook his grey locks,
> 'I kept all my limbs very supple
> By the use of this ointment – one shilling the box –
> Allow me to sell you a couple?'

Like the travelling patent medicine salesmen who were commonplace before the drug industry became regulated, Jowett can be seen selling a cheap remedy, indeed trying to get rid of 'a couple'. Cheap salve makes a nice parody for cheap theology, and the fat old salesman says he used it successfully in his youth to help him limber up, his limbs being a metaphor for his mind, loosening away from the rigours of High Church discipline.

The country clergy were in uproar about the damage the book could do. Among others condemning Jowett was Gladstone, who said on one occasion he was glad not to hear Jowett preach because 'his Gospel is dry and poor and thin and barren'. Another who attacked Jowett (far more tenaciously and less condescendingly) was Wilberforce, the Bishop of Oxford. He lost the case he brought in person against Jowett in the House of Lords, and this lost cause gave the clue to the joke about the Eel – a truly fishy joke – that Dr Jowett balanced on his nose.

'You are old,' said the youth, 'one would hardly suppose
　That your eye was as steady as ever;
Yet you balanced an eel on the end of your nose –
　What made you so awfully clever?'

The battle of wits in the House of Lords was between Samuel Wilberforce and the Lord Chancellor, Lord Westbury. Westbury failed to show a vestige of judicial impartiality. He was a grammar school boy who had suffered as an undergraduate at Oxford from the snobbery of those who were public school boys, and there became a free-thinker. He had been a member of the Jowett camp long before he gave judgement in his favour against Carroll's Bishop.

The 'eel' on Jowett's nose wriggled into the ballad out of the speech with which Westbury dismissed Wilberforce's religious argument for the removal of Jowett from the Chair of Greek at Oxford, in accordance with an earlier ruling by the revived Church Court of Arches. The Lord Chancellor described the High Church party's argument as: 'simply a series of well-lubricated terms – a sentence so oily and saponaceous that no one could grasp it – like an eel it slips through your fingers and is simply nothing'.

Samuel Wilberforce, first Bishop of Oxford, and at the end of his not altogether successful career Bishop of Winchester, was landed for life from that day onwards with the cognomen, 'Soapy Sam', which had nothing to do with his duel with Huxley over evolution. He acquired the name in the House of Lords while trying to take Jowett's Chair of Greek away from him.

To be thorough about what Carroll depicted in the 'Father William' *Under Ground* version, the line 'Allow me to sell you a couple' may identify not just one heretic, Jowett, but two. The colonial Bishop Colenso of Natal, a most interesting figure, whose daughter was at Winnington School, was in trouble for his heretical religious views about the legality of Zulu marriage customs, including the 'bride-price', which were being passed off to the general public at the same time as *Essays and Reviews*.

Carroll's ballad, surely one of his best university squibs, ends with a number joke. Father William digs in his heels: 'I've answered three questions, and that is enough . . .'

Three times Jowett had been put to the test. Three times he had survived attempts on his tenure. By 1865, he was safe, preserved by the highest court in the land. Westbury was not. He ceased to be Lord Chancellor not long after he had had the temerity to twit the High Church faction in the Lords. In Carroll's skit, Jowett had the last word:

'Do you think I can listen all day to such stuff?
Be off or I'll kick you downstairs!'

Alice recites the ballad, her hands clasped in front of her, but the Caterpillar grumbles that it is 'wrong from beginning to end'. It was wrong when heretics like Jowett, Colenso and Westbury got away with it. Yet more and more of them did. Carroll, as in his evolutionary skits, was nothing if not a realist. He did not duck the issues. He merely pointed out any inherent illogicality he could spot in newly received opinions.

Near the Balliol Library was the chapel, rebuilt in gothic much to Jowett's displeasure, the gothic being a visible and permanent symbol of the High Church values against which he fought. As in the Dining-Hall, this relentless man, capable of inspiring great hate and great love, chose to sit in the undergraduate pews and, on occasion, even answer back. Jowett was a force to be reckoned with, and Carroll knew it.

From Balliol we went across Broad Street to the spacious tiered Sheldonian Theatre, where Carroll had spoken against Jowett in public for the first and last time, in an amphitheatre facing a big throne. We also wanted to see where the University Convocation met, and where most of these debates were argued. The larger University parliament, Congregation, was a body which all M.A.s could attend. Convocation was similar, but attendance there was limited to those living within a mile and a half of Oxford. This was the usual debating forum for University issues, an upper house that could veto but not amend University statutes.

Behind the Sheldonian was the courtyard of old university buildings. Over each door was a gilded inscription showing the schools of learning that had preceded the reforms of the Liddell, Stanley and Jowett era – Music, Logic, Metaphysics, History and Grammar lumped together, Natural Philosophy encompassing science.

Architecturally the world that Carroll wanted to preserve was still there, out of sight of the concrete and brick blocks of the science buildings. High up, on one side of the courtyard stood King James, almost as regal as Liddell on the wall at Christ Church. The King who sponsored the translation of the English Bible was protected by an angel and a trumpet and was described as *Doctissimo Magnificantissimo*. He sat up there in a building decorated with harps and gargoyles and pillars of different designs that did not appear to be holding up the structure. Opposite was the delicately embellished stone facade of the Bodleian Library. The courtyard was deserted except for the statue of the smiling scholar and benefactor, the Earl of Pembroke, and an electrician who was smoking a cigarette and wearing a baseball cap. He seemed to be in charge of chucking out old neon light fittings that did not quite meet the architectural standards around them. We knew that we would have to get permission to look at Convocation Hall and so asked the Keeper at the entrance to the Library. He was a silver-haired man, having a conversation on the phone in a patrician accent about a visit to Dorset.

He told us to tell the man on guard in the Divinity School to give us the key, and that this authority would be sufficient. The man on guard in the Divinity School looked as if many generations of people with patrician accents had tried to squash him and told us we had not got the right authority. We really needed to see a secretary in the University offices across the way underneath King James and his royal arms if we were to have any chance at all of getting to look at the Convocation Chamber. We went in search of this functionary and, with the deliberation of a professional woman in a university where men still dominate, she guided us straight back to the man who had refused us entrance, took the key with her and let us in.

Convocation Hall was dominated by a fantastic wooden throne, a single throne like the one in the trial scene at the end of *Wonderland* as drawn by Tenniel and placed in the frontispiece of the story. In Carroll's *Under Ground* there was room for two on the throne and two were seated in it, The King and the Queen. His was just like this one. As with Father William, Tenniel's illustration seemed more competent, but less true than Carroll's.

Behind the throne was a window of thick ancient panes of glass. It was a room entirely panelled with dark, fine-grained wood which had been cut into benches and seats and a speaker's dais many generations before. The wood from which it was made must have been growing in the English ground for many years before that. It was without clutter, a beautiful small parliament. The only view from the high windows was of trees and stone buildings of similar age. It was one of those rooms that has the effect of creating a whole world within its walls.

This was where Convocation was held and where Carroll heard debates on University issues, a room small enough for everyone to know everyone else, their views and their cabals. The empty chamber we saw as an expression of Carroll's view that the world was best left unchanged, its understanding of God left unchallenged, the view we had felt at Croft.

The building was still and authoritative, and explained the well of bitterness that Jowett's resistance to persecution had brought into the open. It expressed the gentler idea of a school, a university as a school of thought, a centre of orthodoxy, not a melting-pot of ideas.

For better or worse, those days were now long gone. The Oxford Movement and the spread of High Church ideals had emerged from the desultory and secular-tending Oxford of the eighteenth-century. The Jowett movement had emerged in violent intellectual reaction to all this religious turmoil. Carroll and young Alice were somewhere in the middle, trying to be good.

CHAPTER FOURTEEN

Left-hand Side of the Notebook

WE LOCKED UP the hall and returned the key to the desk. By now the guard had gone and been replaced by a silver-haired woman. The patrician keeper on the Library entrance had gone too. He was a very Oxford figure and his accent had reminded us of the historian, Hugh Trevor-Roper, now Lord Dacre. Clues were like corpuscles in a blood vessel, recognisable as one shape for one moment in the capillary, then squeezed on among the crush.

We bought a few postcards in the Bodleian shop and stood behind a woman who was buying a book of Oxford and Cambridge Latin graces and a tea-towel. Perhaps the patrician guard had gone to lunch or perhaps he had just vanished like the Cheshire Cat. We bought a sandwich on Broad Street opposite Balliol's Victorian facade, part of which is the Master's House. No large Deanery garden there. This side of Broad Street opposite Balliol was also where Dr Acland lived.

We ate our lunch with this view in sight.

We had recently seen a copy of the annual Christ Church Report for 1994. That, too, had reminded us of Lord Dacre, previously a member of the Common Room. In the Report he had written a memorial piece about Sir Dick White. The article was about how Dick Goldsmith White was recruited into MI6 by the tutor of Modern History at Christ Church, J. C. Masterman, before being joined by Trevor-Roper in the Second World War secret service. Trevor-Roper remarked that there was a 'sub-audible grumble about a Christ Church *mafia* in the secret world'. He remembered that Gilbert Ryle, the philosopher, and Denys Page, the classicist, were also members of the Christ Church group and it was 'regarded with some suspicion by our superiors – unlike the Cambridge *mafia* (Philby, Blunt, etc.) who won golden opinions'. He went on to describe Philby's part in slating White and White's part in tracking down Philby.

Without taking sides in the issue of Philby and White, how important, we wondered, had Carroll been in the birth of the British cryptographic tradition? Certainly the Liddell era Common Room was a breeding ground for conspiracy, secrecy, squibs, and certainly Carroll was its most able code-maker and code-breaker in his odd child-like way.

In 1976 Trevor-Roper had written, with what we could only take to be a Christ Church sensibility for these cryptographic matters, *The Hermit of Peking: the Hidden Life of Sir Edmund Backhouse*. This mysterious unveiling of a forger and British envoy extraordinary was particularly useful to us in our quest because it suggested that the psychology of Carroll was not unique. Trevor-Roper had written:

> Little by little as I pressed the evidence, I was able to satisfy myself that the memoirs were . . . fantasy which was spun with extraordinary ingenuity around and between true facts accurately remembered and cunningly bent . . .
>
> His contrivances were not random hallucinations . . . Shot through though they were with grotesque sexual obsession, they were highly rational constructions, artfully designed to be coherent in themselves, indestructible by obvious fact, but able to corroborate other figments of the same mind.

'Grotesque sexual obsession' was not quite Carroll. Or was it? The unexpurgated version of his diaries (of which we had the microfilm from the British Library) listed beside more prayers to God than we knew he had composed at this troubled time in his life almost a round hundred girls who might take over as models as he was losing Alice. There was something of an obsession here and it persisted from the 1860s right through the 1880s. Figments of Carroll's imagination, 'indestructible by obvious fact' in Trevor-Roper's words, were exactly what we

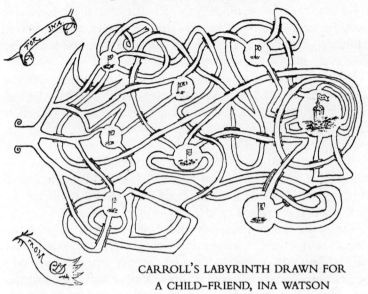

CARROLL'S LABYRINTH DRAWN FOR
A CHILD-FRIEND, INA WATSON

were dealing with in our journey through Carroll's reality, both of places and people.

We knew by now, or strongly suspected, the identities of more than twenty real people in 'Alice' – Carroll and Alice's sisters, Duckworth, Gladstone and Gathorne Hardy, Disraeli, John Ruskin, several Christ Church dons and their adversaries among the Canons, strong hints about Dean Liddell and Lorina Liddell, his wife, Charles Kingsley and possibly his brother or Augustus Hare, Tennyson and strong hints about his sons, Cameron, Watts and Ellen Terry in the Garden of Live Flowers, Benjamin Jowett and a strong hint of his and Liddell's ally, Canon Stanley.

In 'Alice' we could locate original and linked models for the Dodo and Alice, the Lion and Unicorn, the Gryphon, the Mouse, the Magpie, the Red King and Queen, the Hatter, the Hare, the White Knight, Tweedledum and Tweedledee, the Tiger Lily and the Willow, Father William and the Cheshire Cat.

We were convinced that Carroll was using these people as models in one way or another. Sometimes the real individual helped Carroll to build up a character, a part of a composite.

Sometimes he used an aspect of a real character in a minor way; or sometimes in set-pieces, as with the Hatter or the White Knight or Father William. We felt we had moved closer to the sources used by the hermit of Christ Church.

Why had Carroll done this? We knew a certain amount about what he had done – hidden real people – and how he had done it, sometimes in a word joke, sometimes by look, most brilliantly by replicating character and voice, but that did not explain why he had done it.

We went back on to Broad Street, left Balliol behind and edged through the shopping crowds in the Cornmarket until we came to St Aldate's and Christ Church. In the Library we looked again at Carroll's pictures of Alice Liddell.

Earlier in the summer we had been to Paris to look up French sources for 'Alice' in the Bibliothèque Nationale. Here we had learned how to use the computer system that enabled a book to be directed to a reader's desk number without filling out a call slip. This happened so rapidly that there was hardly time to sit down between ordering the book and its arriving at the desk on the floor above. It was something that would surely have intrigued Carroll who made his own elaborate letter-numbering system for correspondence, lost with the missing diaries.

One substantial French authority on 'Alice' was a study by Jean Gattegno. What came across from this and other French work about Carroll was an uncomplicated and unabashed sense of how piquant it was that the black-suited Carroll should have loved Alice and other small child-friends.

In England, and in some circles in America when we mentioned our interest in Carroll, we were frequently asked about his relations with little girls in a way that implied the real interest would be the discovery that he had abused them in some way or another. 'Oh, yes, Carroll went with little girls, didn't he?' 'I wonder what he got up to?' That was the tone of many, though by no means all enquiries.

The French view was refreshing, because it accepted the evident possibility that Carroll's desire to amuse these little girls was the driving force in his life. Because human beings are not one dimensional in the way they direct their energies, he expressed his fascination for them in the stories he wrote for them and the photographs he took of them.

The pictures of Alice Liddell in front of us showed her in Chinese costume, seated with a small fern in the corner of the frame, and with a wreath of wild flowers on her perfectly balanced head. This must be one of the most beautiful child photographs ever taken. These pictures were the result of hours and hours of patient work. There was no financial reward, only friendship and the pleasure the images gave to Carroll and those who saw them.

On 29th April 1863, Carroll wrote in his diary in a section we discovered was cut from the edited version:

> There is no variety in my life to record just now *except* meetings with the Liddells, the record of which has become almost continuous – I walked with them in the meadows this morning. Coles of Pembroke came to see my photographs in the evening.

Three days later he went to the Deanery at eleven o'clock, played croquet until lunch, went on the river with Duckworth and the girls from half past two until five, and then stayed at the Deanery in their company for another hour. On the river he sang them a new song he had written, (though it is hard to imagine a Dodo singing like a bird) – 'Miss Jones'.

Nobody took to 'Miss Jones', but the 'Alice' stories were different. He was deeply involved with Alice Liddell that spring. These entries covered the few days before her birthday on 4th May when he sent her as a birthday present *Scenes and Characters* by Charlotte Yonge. (Carroll had photographed the author with her old mother, as he had Christina Rossetti by then.)

Alice was nearly eleven and he was infatuated with her. He drove the energy released by his infatuation into his portrait of her in his book. During that spring he was also preoccupied with the beliefs, ambiguities, doings, and public successes and failures of Gladstone, Ruskin, Tennyson, Kingsley, Jowett, Dean Liddell and Lorina, Alice's mother. These were the people around her, whose views were discussed, whose poems she recited, whose orders she obeyed – or occasionally evaded.

The grown-up characters in 'Alice' he was to describe later in his life as 'grotesques'. The 'why' – why did he portray these people? – was Alice Liddell. She was the driving force, the source of so much emotion he may not even have known he had inside him. The other source was real people. Between the age of twenty-four, when he first saw Alice and started photography, and the age of thirty-nine when the *Looking-glass* story was published, Carroll matured as a tireless finder and loser of child-friends. In these years, he developed his opinions, made a certain mark in British amateur photography and developed a wide and lively range of contacts, to his credit for he was an extremely shy man, in the University, the church and the artistic world. In addition, a particular set of his stories for children started to be read all over the world.

These fifteen years, 1856 to 1871, were the years when the debate over the future of Oxford was won by the school of Jowett, when the debate over the constitution of Christ Church was partly won by the Students, when the debates over evolution and vivisection received far too few set-backs for the likes of Carroll and Ruskin, when the Pre-Raphaelites lost their ideals and the Church of England world of Carroll's father lost its dominance. All of this troubled Carroll. So he dressed up the players on his stage in animal or part-animal costume. He secretly based them on what he felt, sometimes consciously, sometimes less so. So the real secret of his literary success was that, even if we did not know who they were, their real presence was, and is, felt by the reader of 'Alice'.

The reason why he hid real people in 'Alice' was inseparable from Alice herself. Almost everything else Carroll wrote lacks the fire of 'Alice', which succeeds because of his drive to place the little girl he loved in a controlling position in the pantheon of grown-up people and ideas that made the world seem uglier.

Five years after the *Looking-glass* was written, Carroll tried to vouch for the innocence of the 'Alice' books in a mysterious statement.

If I have written anything to add to those stores of innocent and healthy amusement that are laid up in books for the

children I love so well, it is surely something I may hope to
look back on without shame or sorrow (as how much of life
must then be recalled!) when *my* turn comes to walk
through the valley of shadows.

This solemn afterword was written to accompany editions of
Alice published after the Easter of 1876.

One way of looking at this would be that it was Carroll's
statement of regret that he would never again write anything as
vivid as the 'Alice' stories, since he had lost the girl who
inspired them.

Another more suspicious view might be that he was imply-
ing there was indeed more to these 'innocent and healthy' stories
for children' than met the eye. With the idea of 'who dreamed
it', Carroll hinted at a second dream.

In his book *The Raven and the Writing-Desk*, Francis Huxley
pointed out that there were three dreams involved in 'Alice' –
Alice's, the Red King's and Carroll's. Carroll's statement in
An Easter Greeting to Every Child Who Loves Alice was the nearest
he came to admitting in public that there is a riddle about his
motives and sources for the worlds of *Wonderland* and *Looking-glass*.

We put away the photographs of Alice. One is in a little oval.
Another shows her as the beggar-child, the lesser-known and
less formal one where Alice has broken out into the most imp-
ish of smiles being the liveliest of all. There is her sister Ina, very
young and with a hat on her lap. There is Edith holding a little
bag and sitting on a table beside a white china jug to the right
of the sitter, a jug full of fading wild foxgloves. The foxgloves
reappear on the left of the image when Alice is holding the pig
that evolved from the Ugly Duchess's baby. We put the photographs of the three little sisters away with their companions,
Bishop Wilberforce, Thomas Henry Huxley, the Christ Church
dons, Vere Bayne, Quentin Twiss, Osborne Gordon, Southey,
and Prout, the Crown Prince of Denmark and Canon A.P.
Stanley. We closed this album full of real people whose fingerprints we were beginning to have in our files. More of them
Carroll had portrayed in his 'Alice' stories than not. We took a
final look out on to the Deanery garden, empty now, the lawn

parched yellow and the shrubs exhausted from flowering.

This was a garden that Carroll had been denied. We realised that there might have been another crisis in his life when his father died, a religious crisis. The crisis was always near the surface, but it came more to the fore in 1868 between the publication of the two 'Alice' books.

We knew of his decision not to become a full Priest, one he worked out in the panelled rooms we were now leaving. Below was the garden with its soft lawn and promise of a child's inno-cent world from which the children's voices drifted up to the Library. On the other side was Peckwater Quadrangle with its gravel under foot and the noise of rowdy undergraduates.

We stepped out from the room lined with leather-bound books, from the wisdom and secrecy of scholars, to the follies of a breezy Oxford summer's day, with dust blowing across the college from a new building where the yellow crane was sway-ing slowly and deliberately. We walked under the statue of Dean Liddell, looking out on high and holding up the fold of his clerical robe so as to show the world a glimpse of his left ankle. We wondered what kind of gesture Carroll would have made if he had had to walk underneath it, knowing that he was far too secretive to show anyone what he thought – as Mark Twain had noticed when he met him. Mark Twain called him the 'stillest' man he ever met.

His secretiveness hid the pain of his enforced celibacy and his failure to penetrate circles where he might have belonged as a man and as an artist as well as a don. The pain showed itself in his seeing the world differently from those about him – with the exception of his favoured child-friends. It showed in the hidden dimension of his work, in the follies of his characters on the stage of 'Alice'.

In the soft light of a side chapel in the Cathedral there was a strikingly-coloured window showing Saint Catherine holding a quill pen and standing among meadow flowers. The window is dedicated to Edith Liddell, the Eaglet, youngest of the three sis-ters whom Carroll took on the river. She died in 1876 when she was twenty-two. She was engaged to be married to Aubrey Harcourt, one of the family who owned the old house where

Carroll and the girls sheltered in the pink boathouse. The memorial was designed by Edward Burne-Jones, friend of the Liddells and the Gladstones, who had taught with his wife at Winnington Hall where Ruskin danced the Quadrille.

Dean Liddell tried to open up the Cathedral to better the view of the congregation, but its huge pillars made it rather a squashed space in which to worship, as if its medieval architects aimed its tower to heaven at the expense of space on earth. There was a lot of room for the C's and D in their carved, numbered stalls, but the rest of the congregation, the poor Mice, had by the standards of many cathedrals obscured views round the edges.

Yet there was something human in the scale of the building. Two or three precisely-dressed middle-aged lay members of the diocese of Oxford stood around ready to give information to tourists and to emphasise that this was a church. This was a very old Christian space on a piece of raised ground above the marshy Thames where the original monastery of St Friedeswide had been erected.

On the Cathedral walls were memorials to Canon Pusey, to Dean Liddell, to Henry Wentworth Acland and his wife. Together Liddell and Acland had gone underground to inspect the junctions of the Oxford sewers in their efforts to prevent repeated outbreaks of cholera. When it did break out, Sarah Acland, a pioneer of convalescent nursing like Mrs Gladstone, had persuaded Canon Pusey to open up the Christ Church kitchen in the long vacation to provide soup and succour to survivors.

Then we saw a bas-relief of Bishop Wilberforce's head, high up. He had died from a fall on his head in 1873 when his horse bolted out riding with Lord Granville. He had tried to insult Thomas Henry Huxley in the debate in Oxford about evolution, and removed Carroll's closest friend, and indeed confessor, Dr Henry Parry Liddon from the Vice-Principal's post at Cuddesdon Theological College because he suspected him of being closer to Rome than he was, thereby putting the Mock Turtle in the soup.

Could Wilberforce, Jowett's and Huxley's prosecutor, be hidden in 'Alice'? Or would that have been too daring? After all, the Bishop was Carroll's spiritual superior; he had ordained him Deacon, and nothing that concerned Carroll's spiritual well-being could be hidden from him. Or could it?

In Christ Church Cathedral, Carroll was reported sometimes to be so deep in prayer that he would remain kneeling, head in hands, after the service was finished and the congregation had drifted away. He wept copious tears in Cologne Cathedral in 1867 in Liddon's presence. In that third of Carroll's diaries which Lancelyn Green did not publish in 1954 were short sections which show his turmoil about Alice.

In these sequences of what is generally a clipped and formal account of his social engagements, Carroll reprimands himself, notably using the word 'vile', employed by other Victorians in their private diaries in this period to describe their revulsion at their physical urges. On a surprising number of occasions in the diary Carroll bumps into the Liddell girls as though by chance.

He took himself to task for self-indulgent behaviour of this kind in simple, deeply-felt Christian prayers. It was less the message and brevity of each prayerful entry in the diary than the frequency of the prayers written in the summer of 1863 that surprised us. Carroll was in turmoil that summer, a hypocrite when he preached, and guilty about his escape routes via his 'child-friends,' via art and photography. He resolved these in the composition of 'Alice'. The notes from the microfilm summarise the prayers:

> May 19 (Tu) A guilty prayer.
> June 12 (F) Wants to start a new life.
> June 23 (Tu) Watches the Liddells go. Prays
> for a new life.
> July 2 (Th) Trial page proof of *Alice's
> Adventures* arrives from Combe. Carroll prays
> for 'more regular and better habits'.
> July 3 (F) Adds 'Amen! Amen!.
> Aug 21 (F) Adds 'Help me, oh God, to amend . . .'
> Aug 22 (Sat) Adds 'Yea – Amen'.
> Sept 12 (Sun) Prays 'Help me!'

Sept 21 (Mon) Begs to 'leave my old life and sins
forever behind!'
Nov 7 (Sat) Prays 'Oh that I could rouse
myself from my life of dead works!'

A note of disengagement from Alice follows:

> 'Dec 5 (Sat) Christ Church Theatricals: 'I held
> aloof from Mrs Liddell and the children as I
> have done all the term.'
> Dec 7 (M) Prays 'my old life may die out in me'.
> Dec 16 (W) Seeks 'a holier and better life'.
> Dec 28 (M) Prays to 'die in me the old evil life'.
> Dec 30 (W) Repeats 'Amen! Amen!'
> Dec 31 (Th) Urges himself to: 'Consecrate to Thee
> my life and powers, my days and nights, myself'.

We examined these unpublished jottings from Volume 8. He
called these diaries the volumes of his 'Private Journal'.

During two summer weeks at the end of April 1863, a
revealing period in Carroll's friendship with Alice, there was a
sense that the published diaries were a genteel version of the
original. An important vote in the University Convocation over
the issue of the curriculum for scientists was left out. The fact
that Carroll reconnoitred by train a downstream river journey
on which he planned to take the Liddell girls was also omitted.
He did this alone and then persuaded his friend Francis Vere
Bayne to go over the same route on foot and by train.
Everything had to be right for these river expeditions. Edited
out was Carroll's cryptic comment that 'the record of my meetings with the Liddells has become almost continuous'. The
sense of these meetings being continuous and Carroll joining
the Liddell girls uninvited was missing. The actions of Lancelyn
Green's Carroll appear less premeditated and less emotionally-
charged than Carroll's own account indicated. His name lists
reveal the extent to which Carroll worked on his bookings of
photographic subjects at this time. He preferred runs of sisters.
Sometimes their fathers' work interested him, as we had noticed
from the start in his albums.

All the names of little girls he listed had been or were regarded by him as potential sitters for his camera. Carroll's list carried on over five pages and had been left out of the printed diary by Roger Lancelyn Green. By the time he published *Alice*, Carroll was engaged as Maths Examiner for Cheltenham Ladies College, newly-opened. His ambition as a photographer was on a scale that can only be wondered at. So was the statistical sample of girls and young women whose reactions to his children's writing and word games he could test at first hand.

Carroll had listed in Volume 8 of his manuscript diaries 102 girls by their Christian names in alphabetical order. The names were written on several consecutive left-hand pages opposite the daily entries. The list was compiled in 1863 when he was writing 'Alice'. The entries opposite these lists are filled with prayers.

We recognised a few of his entries from the research we had done on his Isle of Wight and Oxford contacts. The list served as a summary of these. They also served to remind us of the many trails we had no doubt missed in searching for the real people who inspired his grown-up characters. If his diary was anything to go by he worked on the basis of a densely-peopled canvas.

There are two sitters named Agnes. One is Agnes Weld, Emily Tennyson's little niece, his pass-ticket to the Tennysons, whom Carroll finally snubbed as a middle-aged lady for failing to hide his identity. The other Agnes is little Agnes Hughes, daughter of the Pre-Raphaelite painter, Arthur Hughes. There is one Aileen and there are five Alices. Alice Liddell's birthday is listed, 4th May 1852. (*Alice's Adventures* is set on her seventh birthday. *Through the Looking-glass* is set six months later.) There are two Amys, two Annies, one Antoinette, one Augusta and one Ada. There are four Beatrices, and one Bertha, Bessie, Blanche, Cecilia and Caroline respectively. There are six Constances, a Camelia, a Dymphna, a Diana and seven Ediths.

The birthdays of two of the Ediths are noted. They include Edith Liddell – 23rd January 1854. 'Tillie' in *Alice* was five at the time of the story. All the children whose birthdays are given received first editions of the 'Alice' stories, the most favoured bound in vellum.

There are three Emilys and one Effie, named after her

mother Euphemia, wife of Millais. Her portrait for the painting, 'Her First Sermon' inspired Alice's pose in the railway carriage in *Through the Looking-glass*. There is one Elizabeth and
two Ellas, one Evelyn and five Florences, including 'Flo', Ellen
Terry's little sister, a tiny child actress. Her birthday is noted as
16th August 1856. She was two years younger than Edith
Liddell, and Carroll photographed her and took her to see her
elder sisters in their dressing-rooms.

The list continues with three Franceses, two Georgias, two
Graces, three Helens, one Hilda, and one Irene. Grace and Lily
were the resourceful, unspoilt, well-read children of the author
George MacDonald, his favourite child-friends in London.
None of them were pretty but all were good at acting.

One Jane, a Joanna, a Kathleen, two Katies, one Laura and a
Lizzie follow. Lorina Liddell is the oldest on Carroll's 1863 list
of subjects to photograph. Her birthday is given as 11th May
1849. She was only ten in the year the *Wonderland* story is set,
1859, when Alice Liddell was seven. So Lorina was actually
rather young to have served in her governess's absence as the
older sister chaperone in Carroll's 'Alice'.

On 20th March 1863, Carroll 'fell in with the Liddells with
whom (after a race with Ina on the bridge over the reservoir),
I walked back to Oxford'. He had, besides, walked with the
Liddell girls on the Broad Walk all morning, a fact which is
noted in the original diary only. Ina was fourteen at the time.
His and her behaviour was certainly dashing. This entry comes
in a matter of fact way opposite the unpublished lists of Carroll's
child models.

Continuing down the list of sitters there are three Louisas,
one Madeleine, three Margarets, all together nine Marys, of
whom most is known of Mary Donkin, older sister of the Alice
who was to become his sister-in-law and spied on Ruskin at
Winnington Hall. Mary MacDonald and Mary Millais are two
other Carroll sitters. So is Mary Terry, ('Polly'), two years older
than Flo. There are two Mabels, two Mays and an Olive, a
Rose, a Rosamund and Una – Una Taylor who forgot she had
sat for Carroll – followed by a Winifred.

Little Rhoda Liddell, older than Violet, but younger than

Edith, is listed with her birthday – 1st July 1859. She was born too late to appear in *Wonderland* but not too late to catch Ruskin's eye in her young teens at a Deanery banquet which Disraeli attended. She may be the model for a Rose in the *Looking-glass* Garden of Live Flowers.

When Mrs Liddell finally denied Carroll access to her daughters in 1864, he noted drily of her ban on his presence, which she had often encouraged: 'A rather superfluous caution'.

Carroll made two corrections in Volume 8 of his diary, deeply-incised ink erasures rolling over the offending notations. One concerns an undergraduate whom he had had to rusticate. Carroll scribbled out his name. The other concerns his agitation about Alice, who had been petulant when he went to see her. His erased comment of 21st April (Tu) 1863 runs: 'Alice was in an unusually imperious, ungentle mood, by no means improved by her being an invalid'.

Shortly afterwards, Carroll and she patched things up and they were back on the best of terms. He sent her a letter in French (burned with all the other letters he wrote to her by her mother) to which Alice replied in French. This interchange took place on 6th March 1863 and is omitted from the published diary, along with all but a few of the longer prayers. The prayers and the long lists of little girls' names suggest Carroll's agitation in the period in which he wrote 'Alice'. He prayed he might cease to feel the need to write exculpatory prayers, a sentiment matched by his ambiguous statement about the innocent basis of his story in *To Every Child Who Loves Alice*. The guilt never left him but his ingenuity as a puzzler buoyed up his spirits in moments of self-reproach. Above Carroll's list of sitters of 1863 is written his latest rhyming scheme.

An idea has occurred to me of trying rhymes at the *beginnings* of lines (like 'Earth' – 'Early'). Why should not the ear learn to appreciate them as well as final rhymes?

First letters and syllables interested him as a poet and as a cipher-maker. While photographing the daughters of dons and artists, such as Dean Liddell and George MacDonald, he wrote stories and invented rhyming games with which to divert them.

These strands he elaborated over a lifetime. They mingle in the construction of the text and pictures of 'Alice'.

The concept of his rhyming scheme of 1863 matches the lists of alphabetised sitters by Christian names, the Agneses, Aileens and Alices. Their Christian names were the names that those of them learning to write could and did sign under their portraits for him. It was in early childhood he found the fullest inspiration, in beginnings, not in fulfilment or ends.

" she will be happy!
and with a — 😊 — I went
on my way.
Your aff.te friend
CLD

CHAPTER FIFTEEN

The Cardinal
and her Shawl

IT WAS A GREY September afternoon with a low sky when we drove through small lanes just beyond Oxford's southern industrial fringe. In the hope that a place connected with Bishop Wilberforce might help us discern something more about his character, we had organised a visit to Cuddesdon Theological College which had been built by the Bishop to train young men for the parishes in his diocese. Setting the college outside Oxford, he hoped to discourage defections to Roman Catholicism by young men influenced by the Anglicans of ability who had gone over to Rome, John Henry Newman and Henry George Manning. We were still unsure whether we were caught up in our own prejudice or whether we really did touch some old ghosts of bitterness from Carroll's time – and the bitterest bitterness of that time was of the religious kind.

With some of the figures in 'Alice', the identity was clear. Some, like the Frog Footman, we had not come close to. With others, such as Alice's own parents, the King and Queen of Hearts and later, Alice's father lurking in the personality of the Red King, it was possible to take an educated guess. With the Ugly Duchess two identities seemed to be mixed up in one and the identities were antagonists, as if a single, violent character reflected a conflict between two individuals. The two individuals were the Bishop of Oxford, Samuel Wilberforce, and the man he tried to mock in the debate over evolution, Thomas Henry Huxley. It was the Duchess who handed to Alice the baby that evolved into a pig. This, and the kitchen set like a laboratory gone mad, argued for Huxley. Yet many of the Duchess's remarks to Alice on the croquet ground sounded like the conversational gambits of 'Soapy Sam' rather than the trenchant Huxley. The Ugly Duchess keeps on telling Alice about morals: 'Tut, tut, child! . . . Everything's got a moral, if only you can find it.' Huxley would not have agreed. Life, biological life, was governed by different rules.

Cuddesdon was five miles from Oxford, up on a ridge with commanding views over the northern part of the Thames valley where Wilberforce hacked and hunted. It was a heavy gothic building, with crosses on the tops of the drain-pipes. Wilberforce had constructed it on the doorstep of what had been his palace. At the time, the word 'infected' was used to describe the allegedly 'poisonous' influence of other religious disciplines. With a monastic regime of six services a day, and no time to walk to Oxford between them, Cuddesdon was designed to be isolated from the spiritual infections that young men might pick up in Oxford. Ripon College, as Cuddesdon is now called, is no longer confined to training students for the Oxford diocese alone.

We had made an appointment to see the archivist, and we thought the moral of that was to see the archive. We were shown the buildings, and we found an old print of Carroll's friend, Henry Parry Liddon. The photograph had been taken by Carroll and Liddon looked handsome and buoyant, a celibate man fired by conviction; too much as it turned out for Bishop Wilberforce, alias Soapy Sam, who removed him from the position of Vice Principal of Cuddesdon. Members of Wilberforce's own family had defected to Roman Catholicism and he feared that Liddon was about to do the same. That was how Liddon became a Mock Turtle, rather than a proper Turtle, and was so tearful on the beach.

Now it was our turn to be tearful. We managed to meet the archivist at a communal tea, but as we had not given notice we were told that we could not see the archive. We had given notice, we said. It had not been in writing. We had not been asked for it in writing. They were short-staffed. The archivist had to leave to teach. These decisions could not be reached immediately. They were sorry we had come such a long way.

'I quite agree with you,' said the Duchess; 'and the moral of that is – 'Be what you would seem to be' – or, if you'd like it put more simply – 'Never imagine yourself not to be otherwise than what it might appear to others that what you were or might have been was not otherwise than what you had been would have appeared to them to be otherwise.'

Alice says that she would have understood it better if she had it written down. Which sounded exactly like the kind of firm politeness that Alice Liddell might have shown faced with an obtuse grown-up such as Wilberforce, Soapy Sam. At the tea where the atmosphere was of babies and beards and big shaggy sweaters and Christian *bonhomie*, we tried to show the same politeness, although for the first time on these researches we had been firmly rebuffed. Making conversation, we said to a young woman priest that we were interested in nineteenth-century disputes of High and Low Church and Roman Catholicism as they affected Cuddesdon and its foundation.

'We're interested in the issues of today's society,' she said, ending the conversation by looking down at her shoes. Even the old chapel from Liddon's day was closed to us, 'because it was full of books'.

Possibly we did interpret this visit with some prejudice. It was difficult not to blame what was just a muddle about our visit on a prejudiced view of the sanctimonious nature of High Anglicanism in Carroll's day. Perhaps something of that nature still resides in the Church of England. We certainly left the college more convinced than ever that Carroll had come as close to the wind as he dared in spoofing Wilberforce's prejudices in the ugly moralising of the Duchess. However much the facial ugliness might be Huxley's, the obtuseness had to be Wilberforce's. As we drove out of the car-park, we nearly went straight into a tractor. It was a Russian tractor, from the land where Carroll and Liddon had gone on their Church mission.

At the croquet party the Duchess's moral this and moral that sounded like Wilberforce. Alice, saying that when she was a Duchess she would not have pepper in the kitchen, sounded like a not unreasonable joke for Carroll to put to Alice Liddell whose mother would have liked her to be a Duchess, preferably a royal one. Whether Wilberforce oiled up to Alice Liddell in the way that the Duchess does to Alice is not clear.

Among Alice Liddell's correspondence in Christ Church we found a letter that expressed Dean Liddell's total frustration with the ability of 'Sam Oxon' to twist arguments in his own particular High Church way. It related to Wilberforce using influence with Mr Gladstone's son Stephen when Stephen Gladstone was a student at Cuddesdon. It was the only time, in looking at letters from the Dean, that we thought he admitted he had met his match. Only the Queen's threat to behead the Duchess stops her from talking about morals. Alice says she has a right to think, perhaps a reflection of the right to free thought that people in the Oxford world might claim.

'Just about as much right', said the Duchess, 'as pigs have to fly; and the m . . .'
But here, to Alice's great surprise, the Duchess's voice died away, even in the middle of her favourite word 'moral' . . .

So poignant were the issues of conscience and the nature of a young man's Christian thinking that undergraduates from Oxford who were interested in the Roman Catholic faith had to creep under shadow of darkness to the small retreat that John Henry Newman, later Cardinal Newman, established in Littlemore, by geographical coincidence − or was it? − in a straight line between Cuddesdon's lofty position on the ridge and the spire-spiked horizon that is the centre of Oxford. The retreat had been made from a row of working cottages, their doors blocked off on the street side and a single entrance created so that they turned inwards. Looking in at this entrance, not quite sure what we had come upon, we saw a delicate garden with red geraniums and little box hedges around a fountain and a statue of Newman. It was a place as still as Cuddesdon had seemed turbulent. The cottages had been made into rooms that were occupied by a small community of five nuns. Notices in the entrance advertised sister communities in Rome, Jerusalem and Austria. We peeped in at the bronze head and shoulders of Newman who looked unpriestly or rather unsolemn, hair brushed forward boyishly on his forehead, the bow of his tie arranged rakishly.

'Please come in!'

A young woman with a trace of a German-speaking accent surprised us and welcomed us where we might have been intruding. She was dressed simply in a grey skirt and a white blouse. She was amused at our idea that Newman and Manning might be parodied as the White and Red Queens. She knew 'Alice'. She told us a little about the institution and took us into the library, a plain white room with beams exposed, making the foot of 'L' around the small garden.

'Here's Shane Leslie,' she said, 'and Lytton Strachey.' She looked for books. 'They are at one another.'

'You mean Manning and Newman?'

'And the Queens.' she said. 'We have these disputes now.' She took down Newman's *Dream of Gerontius*. 'That was the one Elgar set to music,' she said, 'and here . . . this is what he had to say about Dr Pusey . . .' She brought out Newman's *Apologia*. 'Have you read what Lytton Strachey said about Newman at Oxford?' She found the passage.

> Newman was a creature of emotion and memory, a dreamer whose secret spirit dwelt apart in delectable mountains, an artist whose subtle senses caught, like a shower in the sunshine, the impalpable rainbow of the immaterial world . . . At Oxford he was doomed. He could not withstand the last enchantment of the Middle Age. The air was thick with clerical sanctity. His curious and vaulting imagination began to construct vast philosophical fabrics out of the writings of ancient monks and to dally with visions of angelic visitations.

Strachey was an atheist. And he went to Cambridge.

'He could still understand the power that ritual has to move us,' she said, smiling.

The White Queen, we ventured, was in a terrible muddle in *Alice*, anxious, illogical, highly-strung and introspective. The young woman smiled again, a particular kind of smile that some people with deep faith have, in no way smug. We showed her the passage at the beginning of the chapter called 'Wool and Water', where the White Queen is upset about her shawl being crooked. She blames the shawl, not herself for her disarray. 'It's out of temper, I think. I've pinned it here, and I've pinned it there, but there's no pleasing it!'

'It's a cruel portrait,' she said, 'High Anglicans used to post guards outside this building. Carroll's colleagues would wait here for undergraduates. If they were caught, they could lose their place in the University.'

We said we felt that Carroll, in his portrait of the White Queen, caught Newman's idiom as he wrote of his Catholicism in *Apologia*, emotional, breast-beating and suggesting that others were to blame for his spiritual anguish. 'The strange thing about Carroll is that he seems to catch the pomposity in everyone.'

'Manning was very different to Newman,' the young woman sought to assure us.

In the Looking-glass world, the two Queens are locked in dispute and competing for Alice's attention. Most of England saw Newman and Manning as co-defectors to Rome. As we understood it, Carroll had inside information from Dr Pusey or from Liddon about the doctrinaire Manning having serious differences with Newman. They had, for example, very different goals for the spread of Catholicism in England. The practical, strict and able Manning looked down on Newman's introspection, in particular his public self-doubt. They snatched at converts from Wilberforce's flock at Cuddesdon separately, not together. So what, we wanted to know, was Manning like?

'Very precise and systematic – a realist, a political person . . . ', explained our guide. 'This is what Manning said when an interlocutor asked why he never mentioned the Holy Ghost in his sermons –

> I found it to be true. I at once resolved I would make a reparation every day of my life. This I have never failed to do. I bought all the books I could about the Holy Ghost. I worked out the truths about His presence and His office. This made me a Catholic Christian.

She excused herself and left us in the library to browse for a few minutes. She said we could come back whenever we liked. The other sisters would be interested to meet us. Towards the end of *Looking-glass*, Alice is 'queened' in what Shane Leslie had thought to be her triumphant conversion to Roman Catholicism. The Red Queen in *Alice* did not look unlike Manning, who was frequently parodied in *Punch*. The emotional White Queen complains that 'It was *such* a thunderstorm. you can't think!' The Red Queen puts her down immediately. She never could think, anyway.

The Red Queen explains, 'She never was really well brought up . . . but it's amazing how good tempered she is!' and advises Alice: 'Pat her on the head, and see how pleased she'll be!'

In this power game, the Red Queen seems very much in charge. 'All the ways about here belong to me,' she explains to Alice. It echoed the idea of 'Papal Aggression' (much satirised in *Punch* at this time) from Carroll's Anglican perspective.

That perspective was sharpened by practical experience. This brought to mind the journey taken in 1867 when Carroll represented the Anglican Church as Dr Liddon's fellow-traveller on their journey to Russia, an official attempt by the Anglican leadership in England to make overtures to the leaders of the Russian Orthodox Church, who were being courted by emissaries of the Vatican. Carroll knew from firsthand experience what was at stake in the sectarian struggle for the minds of English and Russian Christians, when he described the traps set for Alice by the Red and White Queens she met in *Through the Looking-glass*.

Alice hears about the Queens in the Garden of Live Flowers which she enters in a looking-glass way by walking away from it. A Red Rose, rooted to the spot, warns Alice that she may expect to meet 'another flower in the garden that can move about like you'. This two-legged red flower has 'nine spikes' round its head. Then the Larkspur hears a thud. 'Thump, thump along the gravel walk!' It is the Red Queen, who takes charge of Alice, trains her in how to behave and what to believe, offering her a dry biscuit when she is thirsty, and rushes her off, covering no ground at all. The Red Queen wants to know, 'Where do you come from? And where are you going?'

The 'm's and the '-ing' in that question suggest the name of Dr Henry George Manning. (As we know, the Duchess said at the Croquet Party: 'the moral of *that* is – 'Take care of the sense and the sounds will take care of themselves.') The Red Queen continues to Alice, 'Look up, speak nicely, and don't twiddle your fingers all the time . . . Curtsey while you're thinking what to say. It saves time.' This joke could be against the spiritual exercises of the strict Roman orders to which Manning subscribed, and we hoped our companion would not feel insulted when she came back to the library. She did not.

'Most of Manning's converts were wealthy women,' she explained. 'Newman's successes were with the students – Gerard Manley Hopkins was chief of his prizes – a poet *and* a scholar. Manning's attempt to convert people would have been too impatient and too dry!'

The Red Queen certainly takes a broad view of the world, we said. Alice reaches the top of the hill and senses the struggle: 'I declare, it's marked out just like a large chess-board! . . . It's a great huge game of chess that's being played – all over the world – if this *is* the world at all . . .'

This had contemporary echoes, though we felt it not tactful to say so to the nun. And if the contemporary Papacy was not unhappy to see the contemporary world as a chess-board, perhaps the reverberations of nineteenth-century Anglican turmoil really had been felt in our visit to Cuddesdon. We

We closed the books, made a few notes and said 'thank you'. As we were leaving, a possible solution to a puzzle in *Alice* came to mind.

Manning had been only the second Catholic Cardinal appointed by the Pope in England since the days when Wolsey, founder of the modern Christ Church, lost his head. Manning was appointed in 1870. Newman followed Manning into the office of Cardinal, in spite of Manning's attempts to prevent this. Newman, old and frail by this time, was never a candidate for Supreme Pontiff. Manning was.

The puzzle was to do with the way in which Alice helped the White Queen, who, like Newman, is very untidy, to pin up her hair and her shawl. 'Living backwards the White Queen explained to Alice, '... always makes one a little giddy at first ...'

'What sort of things do *you* remember best?' Alice ventured to ask.

'Oh, things that happened the week after next . . . for instance . . . there's the King's Messenger. He's in prison now, being punished: and the trial doesn't even begin till next Wednesday: and of course the crime comes last of all.'

The King's messenger was none other than the Hatter, reappearing in the second 'Alice' book in the form of the Anglo-Saxon Hatta in Tenniel's vignette. He sits pathetically in jail, his leg manacled to the wall and his hat hung above him in his cell. At the Tea-Party in *Wonderland* we thought the Hatter was, for several reasons, very like Charles Kingsley in his most imperious mood. In 1865, in the most famous controversy of the decade, Kingsley had accused Newman of being a liar. Kingsley maintained that Catholic doctrines were based on untruths.

In the ugly dispute which followed, Newman raised a banner that rallied much popular support. Regardless of people's sectarian affiliation, they saw Newman as a wrongly affronted gentleman. Newman's appeal in the monthly journals against Kingsley's lack of courtesy in debate worked in his favour. Kingsley had come out badly indeed, most of all in High Church circles at Oxford. Newman had entered the public eye again. He had been in seclusion for a decade, beyond the pale of public attention. We left his small shrine. We wanted to go back once more to the river, not to the calmer waters where Carroll rowed with Alice and her sisters, but somewhere that expressed the turbulence of conscience.

In the scene between Alice and the White Queen, the White Queen pricks herself on a shawl pin, feeling the prick before it happens. Alice says that she hopes the finger is better. 'Oh, much better!' cried the Queen, her voice rising into a squeak as she went on. 'Much be-etter! Be-etter! Be-e-eetter! Be-e-ehh!' The last bleat is the first bleat of a Sheep. The Queen's voice and body change in appearance. She 'seemed to have suddenly wrapped herself up in wool'.

When Carroll was a boy, Canon E. B. Pusey's closest ally in the Oxford Movement was John Henry Newman. In 1845, Newman broke with Pusey and converted to Roman Catholicism. Could the White Queen have turned from Newman to Pusey as a looking-glass way of saying that they had drifted apart?

Alice meets the Sheep, which has human hands and spectacles, as she knits behind the shop counter. (The Sheep is a 'she' although in the text Carroll's animals were usually described as 'it' even when they had human hands.) One moment the Sheep is in her shop, the next Alice is rowing her in a small dinghy.

We decided to revisit the pink boathouse at Nuneham, where Carroll had rowed with Alice below the weir at Stamford. Approaching across stubble fields form Radley, we came to the place where the river divides. There was one channel for traffic coming through the lock and a wider, wilder channel which took the main stream from the weir. It had been raining hard the night before and it was difficult to hear above the thunder of Thames water sheeting over the lip of the weir. There was an ominous quality to the thunder of water around us. In the nineteenth century, before the sluice-gates were erected, floods on the Thames were dreaded. Alice's dinghy is small and the bulk of the Sheep, sitting upright in the stern and wearing her nightcap, leaves only a few inches of boat above the water-line.

'Feather! Feather!' the Sheep cried again, taking more needles. 'You'll be catching a crab directly.'

'A dear little crab!' thought Alice . . .

Alice does catch a crab, is caught by the oar under the chin and is 'swept . . . straight off her seat and down among the heap of rushes'. The real Alice testified in 1932 that Carroll allowed the girls to take the oars and learn to feather, so as not to catch crabs. The *Looking-glass* Alice does not know the meaning of the term to 'catch a crab', nor does she yet know how to feather her oars. The White Queen has become the Sheep, mutated backwards into lamb in sheep's clothing like the old Canon. She and Alice are now nearly engulfed in the deep waters of religious controversy. Sir Keith Feiling described Pusey as 'Untidy, ill-shaven with downcast eyes. This small figure hardly moved outside a beat between the Cathedral, St Mary's and the Hebdomadal Council.'

This sounds like the Sheep at the Mill. Pusey was photographed by Carroll and his picture was there in Alice's album. He looks distinctly woolly, his wisps of white hair coming adrift. This was Pusey not as the scourge of Roman Catholics and Broad Church Anglicans but as an old sheep, a chubby and cunningly-confiding old gentleman. He has removed his mortar-board for the sitting, perhaps at the photographer's request. He looks more jolly and relaxed than his reputation for heretic-baiting suggests.

To his friends, Pusey was the embodiment of Christian humility and insight. In the wave of agnosticism, aestheticism and atheism that rolled through Oxford after his heyday there, few authors had good words for Pusey. To his followers, Liddon and Carroll, he was a Lamb of God. When he died, Carroll with unique tenderness referred to him in his diary as 'my dear old friend'. Ellen Terry and Liddon were also close friends of Carroll's and also hidden in *Alice*.

Returning to the beginning of the scene, the Sheep is knitting in its shop with fourteen pairs of needles when Alice meets it. By magic, it hands her oars. 'How *can* she knit with so many?' the puzzled child thought to herself. 'She gets more and more like a porcupine every minute!'

The Cardinal and her Shawl

PUNCH, OR THE LONDON CHARIVARI.—August 29, 1868.

CANON PUSEY TRYING TO CONVERT A NON-CONFORMIST TO
HIGH CHURCH WAYS, in *PUNCH*

'Can you row?' the Sheep asked, handing her a pair of knitting needles as she spoke.

'Yes, a little – but not on land – and not with needles –' Alice was beginning to say, when suddenly the needles turned into oars in her hands, and she found they were in a little boat, gliding along between banks: so there was nothing for it but to do her best.

In the main stream of the river below us, the water rushed and eddied. The banks were too high for a little girl rowing to see over them. Away from the centre of the channel, the green river water was still and stroked at the hair-like weed and the torn yellow water-lilies. The shallowest places were crowded with bulrushes. An old heron, disturbed, flapped away. A few iridescent blue dragonflies shimmered above the surface like *Looking-glass* insects. There were no sheep on the bank, but there might have been in Carroll's day.

ROWING IN DEEP WATERS, WITH WORLDLY TOYS
IN THE LOOKING-GLASS WINDOW

The Cardinal and her Shawl

Wild and secret river-banks were favourite subjects for Victorian painters and Victorian novelists built them into their plots. Crumbling river-banks where terrible things happened to defenceless girls were a stock-in-trade. Millais' 'Ophelia', modelled by Lizzie Siddal, was shown dragged under water by weeds and flowers. In this *Looking-glass* scene – and it is the more mature and complex book – the tranquillity of the 'Golden Afternoon' Alice spent in *Wonderland* is gone. The boat glides on, but it is now with its Sheep, the symbol of Godliness, stubbornly afloat on the waters of death.

> The boat glided gently on, sometimes among beds of weeds (which made the oars stick fast in the water, worse than ever), and sometimes under trees, but always with the same tall river-banks frowning over their heads.

Alice was impulsive:

> 'Oh, please! There are some scented rushes!' Alice cried in a sudden transport of delight.'

She fell backwards. The Sheep laughed scornfully and went on with her knitting.

Pusey was not one for the easy answer: Christian belief was a subject to wrestle with, for long hours in contemplation and agony. When Alice is rowing her little coracle in that turbulent mill-stream, Carroll's High Church agenda is just visible through the mirror of the water. He is seeking to persuade himself that the quest must be for salvation for himself and for his beloved, but *not* in this world. Shane Leslie thought that, at the end of her life, Alice is converted to Rome. If she really is in the Red King's dream and it is not her dream, then she has to face the agony of an adult conscience.

The Thames water kept on thundering, and the dragonfly did not notice. But then it, as Huxley would have argued, was a creature of nature.

CHAPTER SIXTEEN

More Than Half-baked

L EWIS CARROLL was always on the side of the Mice against the 'C' and the 'D'. In fact he was one of them. He was also sympathetic to the Dormouse at the mad Tea-party. A word joke had given a clue as to who might be the persecuted and sleepy Dormouse. We were looking for Vere Street which ran for only a hundred yards north of Oxford Street in London's West End. The heavy shoulder of Debenhams Department Store occupied the left-hand side and an unlet office building called Marietta House dominated the end of the street facing us. St Peter's Chapel, eighteenth-century and classical, seemed to be hiding under the shadow of these bland and confident facades. It was a stately, lovely Georgian city chapel which we had never noticed or heard of before, with a handsome stone portico.

The Reverend Frederick Denison Maurice had preached here. Now a largely forgotten figure, he was a leader among the group of reformers that included Charles Kingsley, Julius Hare (whose sister Maurice married), Stanley and Jowett. Could he be the Dormouse? The sounds of 'Maurice' and 'mouse' played into each other, and into the German 'maus'. All this group were involved in German theology. There was also an M joke at the mad Tea-party.

'They were learning to draw, and they drew all manner of things – everything that begins with an M –'.
'Why with an M?' said Alice.
'Why not?' said the March Hare.

Alice was silent. The Dormouse had closed its eyes by this time and was going off into a doze; but on being pinched by the Hatter, it woke up again with a little shriek and went on:

'– that begins with an M, such as mouse-traps, and the moon, and memory, and muchness – you know you say things are "much of a muchness" – did you ever see such a thing as a drawing of a muchness!'

'Really, now you ask me,' said Alice, very much confused, 'I don't think – '

'Then you shouldn't talk,' said the Hatter.

The Dormouse was a guest at the Tea-party. The Hatter always over-ruled it.

First there was the M joke, then there was the clue about the rude, overbearing behaviour of the Hatter to the Dormouse. The Dormouse tried to help Alice understand, particularly its complicated running gags about treacle. Much of the later part of the mad Tea-party was taken up with the Dormouse's story about living in a treacle well. There were jokes about drawing treacle from the treacle well and three little sisters being well in.

Alice asked: 'What did they live on?' – to which the Dormouse replied, 'They lived on treacle.'

Who ate treacle in the mid-nineteenth century? Certainly not little girls brought up in a Deanery. Treacle was given in poor relief, along with rice. Hence the nursery rhyme: 'Half a pound of tuppenny rice/ Half a pound of treacle'. Alice was incredulous that people could live on it.

Perhaps this was a reference to Maurice's concern for the poor. Perhaps it was a 'sticky' joke. The teapot the Dormouse was put into was a 'hot water' joke. Maurice was certainly in hot water – and Carroll knew as much about it as anyone in Oxford, Cambridge or London, for Dr Pusey had got himself into hot water at the same time, and Carroll was involved with both of them.

We went into the church. It was bright, neon-lit, which was not quite in keeping with its wide but delicately proportioned balcony and plastered ceiling. Christian life was going on inside it, and that was in keeping with Maurice. It was a church designed by James Gibbs, and of great beauty. That was in keeping with Carroll.

Even in Maurice's time, this part of London was running out of congregation as the environs became less residential, which was no doubt why he had been assigned it. It was active now, not as a parish church but as the Institute for Contemporary Christianity. Volunteers were bustling about, sending out a mailing, organising Christian books for sale, being cheerful. Two men came in off the street, one for information, another the worse for alcohol and needing to sit down. On Sunday the Chinese community in inner London held services here. After poking around for a time, and being told there was no memorial to Maurice, we found a plaque, tarnished with old grime and hidden behind the piano.

We had seen Carroll's photograph of Maurice, a short man with a large head, almost no neck, a broad mouth and kindly eyes, sitting in a chair with a large incongruous white lace doily behind his head. Carroll had taken it in London on 27th July 1863, the day after he took Sunday service in Vere Street Chapel as Maurice's officiating minister. Maurice *did* look like a dormouse. Rejlander's charming photograph of him, taken when he went to shelter from religious persecution with Tennyson on the Isle of Wight, showed him holding the arm of a much taller Cambridge companion, as a sensitive and friendly little boy would hold on tightly to a stolid, bossy aunt. Poor Maurice: dunked in life, he was dunked in death, forgotten now. He was a major nineteenth-century figure, persecuted as was Socrates, whom he studied closely.

We found Maurice through the M joke and by searching among the Cambridge Apostles who had London connections with Charles Kingsley. Maurice held two professorships at London University. He founded and taught at Queen's College for Girls, an offshoot of the Governess' Benevolent Institution. Maurice's approach to girls' education was rather more straightforward than Ruskin's. At Winnington Hall, Miss Bell hung his portrait above Ruskin's.

Then all this had come to a halt. In 1853, Dr Jelf, a relentless High Church Canon of Christ Church whose name we had already located on a bend in the Mouse's Tail, had Maurice removed from both his professorships, which were in Christ Church's gift. Maurice questioned the doctrine of Eternal Damnation which held that everyone but a member of the Church of England would suffer in hell for eternity. Jelf was one of the Cats who, with the Dog, attacked the Christ Church Mice. He had also attacked the Dormouse.

Maurice could not be rescued, either by Gladstone operating in high places, or by Tennyson who wrote a moving and very well-received poem about the incident, which cursed the Establishment and suggested Maurice make his base at Farringford for ever. Even when two of the Christ Church Canons who had helped Jelf question Maurice's right to teach felt the matter had gone too far, and said so publicly, Jelf could not be stopped from violating Maurice's academic rights. Maurice lost all his academic positions and salary. He took on St Peter's, where we were seeking him out, as a consolation prize.

Apparently he had no staff, or not enough, and Carroll helped him at services. During the time he wrote the 'Alice' books there were several entries in his diaries which referred to 'helping at Maurice's church'. Maurice lacked a curate or an assistant. Other entries refer to helping on a Sunday 'as usual' or just simply attending the service. Carroll worshipped there whenever he could, when he was in London. He corresponded at great length over the Jowett affair with Maurice who, despite Carroll's antipathy, supported Jowett. In Maurice, Carroll evidently found a gentle, assured and bent-over father figure with whose views he in part disagreed, but whose humanity and Christian spirit he admired. Once again here was a character in 'Alice' like Alice Liddell, Ellen Terry and Edward Pusey, with whom Carroll was closely involved by ties of friendship and admiration.

Maurice was dunked by Carroll's High Church party, but, if we were right about the identity of the Dormouse, Carroll chose to return the fire of those who should have been Maurice's allies.

What Carroll saw in the Maurice camp to satirise in 'Alice' was the intolerance and changeability of Charles Kingsley who, wild as ever, was to move away from Christian Socialism and Maurice's gentle doctrines into more conservative political pastures.

Along with Julius Hare, Maurice had been a founder member of the Cambridge-based branch of the Christian Socialist Movement, a powerhouse of educational doctrine supported by Carroll's publisher, Alexander Macmillan. This influential group drew attention to poverty and committed their time as teachers to the education of working men. Other teachers at the Working Men's College known to Carroll were Ruskin, Thomas Woolner, Thomas Hughes of Rugby, and Dante Gabriel Rossetti. Burne-Jones also taught there. Maurice's popular Christian writings had helped establish Macmillan as a publisher at the time Charles Kingsley came into his orbit.

We were standing by the altar of the church where Carroll had helped the Dormouse give Holy Communion when Betty Baker found us. She was writing a history of the church and was surprised by the connection with Carroll. We discussed Carroll's associations with Rossetti and the Pre-Raphaelites and she told us that the centre still followed the Maurice tradition. In the passage leading to the vestry, now an office, is a memorial window designed by Edward Burne-Jones and executed by William Morris on the theme of 'The Souls of the Blessed

being received into Paradise'. It was dedicated to the Snelgrove family of 'Marshall & Snelgrove', the founders of what is now Debenhams Department Store.

As he did for Edith Liddell's memorial at Christ Church, Burne-Jones designed a beautiful window of clear colours and flowing lines. There was St Martha in her rich ruby robe, supplicating before her ascent.

The lines of communication with Burne-Jones' commercial patrons were less flowing. The price they paid him for this little masterwork he called contemptible. The only revenge he could find was to refer to the job ever afterwards as one he had executed for Saints Marshall and Snelgrove, but the presence of works by Burne-Jones and William Morris and the Pre-Raphaelite design of the grubby Maurice plaque increased our sense of being close to certain real people in 'Alice'. We had penetrated another close-knit circle.

We walked out into the scurrying rough and tumble of Oxford Street. We had been struck by the extent to which Carroll, while based in Oxford, relished his liberation as a London person, not a Christ Church parson.

London permitted Carroll liberty in matters of faith and ritual. Here too he absorbed everything he could on his packed visits to the London theatre. His line of contact with Tenniel came from London through the playwright and *Punch* writer Tom Taylor and other mutual friends. His closest friends here, the George MacDonalds, were the only family other than his own he photographed with himself in the picture. At the MacDonalds' he could not have felt more at home.

People were coming out of what had been Marshall & Snelgrove carrying large plastic bags. As we walked along the street, we were more aware than usual of scores of reproductions of Pre-Raphaelite works on shopping bags, in poster shops, on address books. It was not in Oxford Street, however, that we thought the Pre-Raphaelite painters – including Burne-Jones – had been parodied, but back in Oxford. It was there that Carroll had had his first contact with this exotic group and there that a piece of their work had given us a clue to the way in which he parodied them in 'Alice'.

During the winter of 1857 to 1858, when Carroll was twenty-five and Alice five, Dante Gabriel Rossetti was persuaded by Ruskin to assemble a group to paint Arthurian scenes of the kind that Tennyson had made so popular on the walls of the new Oxford Union debating chamber, a gothic building designed by Benjamin Woodward, who had also produced the new Natural History Museum and Meadow Buildings at Christ Church. In a street off the Cornmarket, we entered the Union building and went down a passageway full of students. It had that used feeling of a Victorian school or university hallway, scuffed paint and woodwork coated in grime-encrusted varnish, neon paper notices flapping in the draught of constantly opened doors . . . until we reached the Library. This was hushed and empty, a dome-shaped room built as the debating chamber, a big space with a vaulted wooden roof, rather like an upside-down ship. The beams were decorated with what was clearly William Morris's work and the surfaces of the roof were covered in brightly-coloured murals. There was a forgotten feeling to the room; only one old man sat there in a grimy raincoat, reading *The Spectator*. It is no longer the debating chamber.

Rossetti's group worked on the scenes without pay, Ruskin insisting that this medieval practice be observed, although they were provided with bottles of soda-water from the Randolph Hotel. Burne-Jones had been among them, just learning to paint, so had William Morris and Carroll's favourite of the Pre-Raphaelites, Arthur Hughes. The small leaflet explained that we were looking at 'Merlin being lured into the pit by the Lady of the Lake', 'Arthur Conveyed by Weeping Queens to Avalon after his Death' and others of the kind the White Knight invented. They were intended to bring tears to the eyes. Among the models was Jane Burden, later Mrs William Morris, one of the loves of Rossetti's life. The poet A. C. Swinburne, a pupil of Jowett's and a friend of Burne-Jones, also posed. Among those of the Pre-Raphaelite group who shied away from this unpaid commission were Ford Madox Brown, W. Holman Hunt and John Millais.

A ten pence piece in a machine turned on the spotlights which pointed at the murals. The bright paint was not always

so. Rossetti knew nothing about the preparation of plaster surfaces. Even before the work was finished all had turned to a
muddy and brown mess. Rossetti left the job, and, medieval
ideals cast aside, even Ruskin's money would not lure him back.
In one of her poems, which 'comes out all wrong', Alice recites
to the Gryphon:

> "Tis the voice of the Lobster; I heard him declare
> 'You have baked me too brown, I must sugar my hair.'

'Baked me too brown' was the first clue to Pre-Raphaelites
lurking in this poem. The murals had indeed gone very brown
until a recent grant enabled them to be restored. Many Oxford
people, including Carroll, would drop in to see progress while
the painting was under way. Rossetti and the other painters
were full of hilarity and their joking irreverence must have been
an eye-opener to Carroll. They no doubt helped to liberate
Carroll's wit and allowed him to explore more difficult satirical
territory.

> June 13. (F). Saw Millais' 'Carpenter's Shop' at Ryman's. It is
> certainly full of power, but hideously ugly: the faces of the
> Virgin and Child being about the ugliest. The figure of John
> the Baptist, bringing water to wash the wounded hand is one
> of the best – wonderful flesh colouring.

Two years later, in 1864, he secured an introduction to Millais:

> April 7. (Th). Took Mr. Holman Hunt's letter to Mr. Millais,
> at 7 Cromwell Place: I went to 7A by mistake, and while
> waiting at the door noticed a gentleman who was walking up
> and down in front of the next house, and whom I thought
> like the pictures of Millais: we interchanged some remarks
> about getting the door answered: then came some children
> with a governess, and I said to myself, there comes 'My First
> Sermon', but they passed the door I was at, made a rush at
> the gentleman (evidently their father), and went into the next
> house. At last I found out my mistake, and that the gentle-
> man was Millais himself: he was very kind and took me into
> his studio . . .

Later he photographed John Everett Millais with his wife, Effie, who had divorced Ruskin for failing to consummate the marriage. Between them is their daughter, and the family is shown sitting on a window-sill. Taken from the outside, this must be one of the most touching pictures of a family ever taken.

Carroll liked a few of Millais' canvases, and included his pictures of a little girl, 'Her First' and 'Her Second Sermon', in the *Looking-glass* vignette where Alice sits opposite Disraeli in the railway carriage. It is possible he used in *Wonderland* the banter outside Millais' door that no one would open in the scene with the Frog- and the Fish-Footman. However, Arthur Hughes was the painter he collected, rather than Millais, who charged much more for his work. Besides, Carroll did not altogether approve of Millais' attitude to Christian subject matter and could smell a rat.

It seemed to us that Millais' voice was in fact 'the voice of the Lobster', and that Alice's 'Lobster' poem parodies Millais' nervous prostrations at the Royal Academy Exhibition. Millais was elected an Academy Associate in 1855 and so became the only one of the original Pre-Raphaelite brotherhood to accept membership. Having agreed to becoming an Academician, he paraded in front of the dressing-mirror for the Academy opening night in the customary evening dress. Other Pre-Raphaelites, such as Morris and Rossetti, refused to conform. Black coat, white tie and tails was not a medieval way to dress, and they chose to remain Pre-Raphaelite in appearance. After 1860 Millais' paintings became more sentimental and less religious, for he sought only one thing – commercial success. He stood his ground in stiff shirt and tails, and Carroll lampooned him.

'Tis the voice of the Lobster, I heard him declare . . .

The lines contain the letters that make up the name 'Everett Millais, R.A.' The R.A. marks his affiliation as an official, bankable painter attached to the Royal Academy Schools. Carroll, the gifted amateur, wrote a savage attack on academic professionalization in his book of verse, *Phantasmagoria*, which he published between the two 'Alice' books. In 'Alice' he wrote:

'Tis the voice of the Lobster I heard him declare
'You have baked me too brown, I must sugar my hair.'
As a duck with his eyelids, so he with his nose
Trims his belt and his buttons, and turns out his toes.
When the sands are all dry, he is gay as a lark,
And will talk in contemptuous tones of the Shark:
But, when the tide rises and sharks are around,
His voice has a timid and tremulous sound.

Baked too brown on varnishing day? Gone brown in the
Union? Brown was also Ford Madox Brown, and the burning
of the browning either Swin*burne* or *Burne*-Jones. Why the
Shark with a capital 'S'? Sharks were critics, and the biggest of
them was Ruskin, the Gryphon, to whom Alice was saying this
poem. Frederick Sandys was a lodger and friend of Rossetti
and it was he who sharked the biggest Shark. He spoofed
Millais' Arthurian 'Sir Isumbras at the Ford' in an etching that
was widely distributed. Instead of riding a steed, the Knightly
Sir Isumbras rides a wretched donkey on whose flank Ruskin's

ROSSETTI, MILLAIS AND BURNE-JONES RIDING ON THE ASS
BRANDED AS J.R. – JOHN RUSKIN by Sandys

initials, J. R., were branded. Ruskin had attacked Millais for submitting the painting to the Academy. Sandys, like Carroll, attacked them both.

In the second part of this poem, Alice recites her verse about an Owl and a Panther and a dish and a spoon, Alice feeling 'sure it would come out all wrong', but obeying the Gryphon in a 'trembling voice'.

> I passed by his garden, and marked, with one eye,
> How the Owl and the Panther were sharing a pie:
> The Panther took pie-crust, and gravy and meat,
> While the Owl had the dish as its share of the treat.
> When the pie was all finished, the Owl, as a boon,
> Was kindly permitted to pocket the spoon:
> While the Panther received knife and fork with a growl,
> And concluded the banquet by —

Concluded the banquet by . . . ? 'Eating the Owl' – words that even Alice might be afraid to say – would certainly fit.

If words lurk here, so perhaps do hidden letters. 'I passed by his garden and marked with one eye' has most of the letters of D. G. Rossetti and P.R.B. for Pre-Raphaelite brotherhood. There is, however, one 't' too few. Suppose 'I' was Carroll – he certainly did pass Rossetti's paved garden in Cheyne Walk in London's Chelsea, took a series of photographs of the painter and his family there and, presumably, looked through his lens, the 'one eye' necessary to Rossetti's lunch-time guest, Lewis Carroll. It is not hard to identify Rossetti with the Panther for he had a dark feline quality to him. William Morris, who taught design in the company of Rossetti at the Working Men's College, is a likely candidate for the Owl. Here is another joke levelled against political radicals, in this case Rossetti and Morris.

The verse hinges on Rossetti's business dealings with William Morris. The black humour of the ending – about eating the Owl – implies that Rossetti ate all of Morris's company funds, and no doubt part of the implication was true. Millais spearheaded the movement towards client satisfaction to the point of advertisement. Bohemians, such as Rossetti, did not pay their debts, especially with Morris, a man of means, always there to foot the bill. At the Union, Morris was left to rescue Rossetti's project — which he did. His repetitive leaf patterns create a ceiling that is as enticing a monument to this period as the spoof written on it.

Carroll did not approve of overspending. He thought artists and writers, however talented, must make their way without borrowing, pay their debts and keep a stiff upper lip. Rossetti did none of these things. Carroll had a row with him when Rossetti tried to snarl at Carroll over the issue of payment for photographs Carroll had taken of master-drawings owned by Rossetti at Rossetti's own request.

The Fork was a member of the company Morris founded near Fleet Street in which Faulkner was his reliable financial partner. The dish was the beautiful and dishy Jane Burden, with whom Morris spooned. And indeed, Morris does look like an owl. Rossetti, on the other hand, was dark and moody. Georgiana Burne-Jones said he could be as black in his moods as a panther. The whole tragic story of the death of Rossetti's wife, Lizzie Siddal, from an overdose of laudanum, is told in her *Memorials*.

Rossetti's house and garden, now as over-cleaned and corporate in appearance as the Oxford Union murals, were 'marked' by Carroll and so were his limericks and spoofs. Carroll admired the poetry written by Rossetti's sister, Christina, some of it for children. She was on the list with Alice Liddell and Alfred Lord Tennyson to whom Carroll sent vellum-bound copies of *Alice* when it was published. Rossetti, to whom he sent no copy, read Christina's and wrote to Carroll saying how much he admired 'the wonderful ballad' of Father William and Alice's perverted snatches of schoolgirl poetry'. He mentioned no other part of the book and made no further comment. If Rossetti was hidden in the poem, it was not surprising that he realised why Alice's recitation had 'come out all wrong'.

He was also good at code-breaking. Georgiana Burne-Jones, who had first given us the clue about the Lobster Quadrille, reported that Rossetti's nonsense rhymes were among the funniest she had ever heard. Rossetti's eye had been drawn to 'The

Rubáiyát of Omar Khayyám' which he came across in a London bookshop when it was still totally unknown. Rossetti himself started the process by which the name of the poet who wrote this anonymous and later world-famous translation was traced to Edward Fitzgerald, friend of Tennyson and Maurice.

Fitzgerald, we believed, was a possible model for the blue Caterpillar to whom Alice recited 'Father William'. As a Pythagorean, Fitzgerald believed that the soul migrates and therefore that it is best not to eat meat in case of destroying other living souls. Carroll could have seized on this when he depicted him as the Caterpillar who lived on vegetables and, being an orientalist, smoked a hookah.

Rossetti's translations of Italian sonnets and his brooding allegorical portraits of tragic female muses were admired; but in private, there was another side to him. He wrote limericks about his friends, disguising them as pet animals. His praise for Alice's poems suggests that Rossetti had spotted the hidden identities of the Lobster and the Panther and possibly the Shark and the Owl, all of whom were, at various times, his closest friends. Is it not likely he would have wanted – without making too much fuss about it – to let Carroll know he had blown his cover?

How did Carroll dare to stir up friction between Millais and Ruskin, which centred on Millais taking Effie Ruskin to be his bride, by writing a child's verse about their antagonism? It was all too close to the bone. The only answer to these questions is clear. The jokes are only near the bone if anyone spotted them, but nobody did, except Rossetti, who was fair game.

We left the Union. Less than a quarter of a mile away on Broad Street was the site of the house of Dr Henry Wentworth Acland.

CHAPTER SEVENTEEN

Dissecting a Dodo

WE HAD FOUND Ruskin and Stanley hidden in 'Alice'. Of those who were in a close coterie around Dean Liddell at Christ Church and whose names kept appearing, the one we could not find was Acland, the Professor of Medicine. We had a strong hunch that he should be there but neither a word joke nor a facial likeness seemed to fit.

It was the Aclands who had introduced Carroll to the Pre-Raphaelites. They in turn were not so nice to their hosts, and there were malicious whisperings against the Aclands. The painters called Acland 'The Rose of Brazil'. There were reports of Rossetti and William Morris avoiding social engagements at the Aclands' house. When invited to dine at Christ Church by Acland, Rossetti did not put on a dinner-suit but came in the plum-coloured frock-coat he wore while painting, and when photographed by Carroll. On another occasion the Aclands' maid would not admit Morris to a reception because he looked so disreputable in his old painter's smock. Swinburne had been asked to one of Acland's talks on 'Sewage' – Acland's favourite topic – and protested vociferously all through the lecture.

The first recorded encounter between Acland and Carroll was when Carroll, in his first summer of photography, met Acland in Christ Church and got leave for his children to be photographed in the Deanery garden. There were seven Acland sons and one daughter born in the span of eleven years. No record of whether this was successful survives, but Carroll commented at this time having to work outdoors, wasting 'many pounds this summer, by trying on bad days, etc.'

The next mention of Acland in the diaries was in December of the same year, 1856, the Christmas when Carroll gave Harry Liddell a mechanical tortoise and then left to show his new magic lantern to the children at Croft. Dr Acland was about to take the Dean to Madeira for a cure.

Acland had already saved Mrs Liddell's life in 1848 when her husband was still Head Master of Westminster School. He had nursed her round the clock when she had typhoid fever. Now he was concerned about the Dean's serious bronchial complaint. As a sign of how grand they were, the Dean was able to re-organise the passage of a naval ship to take the party to the island of Madeira. His detractors attacked him for being absent. His friends, including Gladstone, acknowledged that Acland saved Dean Liddell's life by persuading him to go.

J. B. Atlay's *Life of Acland*, which came to light in a second-hand bookshop, helped to bring Acland to the front of our minds. His had been a rumbling presence throughout our research, cutting across many topics, Oxford and the reform of science and medicine, Christ Church, Ruskin and Liddell. We had heard of Atlay but not seen the book.

Acland emerged from it as someone who brought a respect to medical practice in Oxford which it had never previously commanded. As Alice Liddell's doctor, he had set her broken arm, and had also attended Jowett and Pusey, two sworn enemies. He occupied a large family house in Broad Street, almost opposite Balliol, close to the Sheldonian Theatre and Convocation Hall, really in the heart of Oxford. He had patients throughout Oxfordshire and was known to travel up to seventy miles a day, either in a carriage drawn by two grey horses or by taking the train on one of the branch lines from Oxford station.

Here was an energetic, compassionate and rather wonderful man. He became an early patron of Rossetti and the sculptor Alexander Munro and collected Renaissance drawings and other works of art. The little notes about actual meetings in Carroll's diary suggests that he was interested in Carroll and treated him with tolerance and geniality.

The picture of his study in Atlay's biography showed it to be a professor's den, large enough for well-attended lectures on sewage, the walls covered in high bookshelves, a room full of carpets, tables, books on chairs, pictures on chairs, portraits of angels, statuettes and heavy curtains.

There were no specimens to be seen, however. These were kept elsewhere, and Carroll's next mention of him, apart from one where he sent the Liddell children to the seaside because of scarlet fever in Oxford, was on 26th May 1857 when 'Dr. Acland called, and took me to see the skeleton of his tunny-fish in the Anatomy Schools which he wants me to photograph'.

A sepia copy of this photograph is in the Vere Bayne album in Christ Church Library. We also knew that Carroll had helped to write a satire about Acland and Liddell's Madeira tunny-fish. At least that was what William Tuckwell reported in his *Reminiscences of Oxford*, a gossipy and not always reliable account he published in 1900 of life at Oxford in Carroll's heyday as a squib writer. Tuckwell, a Socialist, planted his own allotments and did not like Carroll, who in his view sniped at people too much and spoiled the amusing atmosphere of a Common Room.

The Tuna had a curious history, a twisted tale of the Oxford variety. Carroll photographed it, bones perfectly preserved, set out incongruously in the open air. It and Acland had had an adventurous trip back from Madeira. The ship in which they returned home had been washed up on the Dorset coast, although everyone had managed to clamber free. Acland made the passengers and crew all eat breakfast before they went ashore. When finally they were all safe on dry land it turned out that he knew the local gentry and everyone was warmed up in the rooms of a country house.

So the fish had come to Oxford where it was given a long and pompous inscription in Latin. A sepulchral notice dated 'Nov. 3, 1860', and claiming to come from the 'University Catacombs', probably originated with Carroll and Osborne Gordon of Christ Church – the Dodo and the Magpie in *Alice*. It announced the text of a University Statute which it was intended should be voted on in Congregation. This text was to replace the existing caption Dr Acland and Dean Liddell had written for the large brass label they had had engraved beside the Tuna Fish skeleton from Madeira deposited in the University Museum.

The vote in favour of the substitution was spoofingly dated as follows: 'Placuit Universitati, 2009' (i.e. the University was pleased to agree to the substitute label in the year two thousand and nine. Forward dating of this kind is one of the fingerprints by which Carroll's Oxford squibs can be identified. Carroll had a habit of attaching future dates to such documents).

The spoof was based closely on the original label, with certain shifts of meaning. It began: 'Thunnus quem rides' – altered from 'Thunnus quem vides' on the original label, and continued:

The Tuna which you laugh at [as opposed to the Tuna which you see] was moved from the Anatomical Museum by Henry W. Acland, Regius Professor of Medicine in the University of Oxford, in June 1860 in Henry G. Liddell's XII year as Dean. It was washed up in Oxford to raise high the hopes of the inhabitants of Oxford on account of its extraordinarily placid and mild disposition.

The substitute label confused the Dean's indisposition with the Tuna's ineffable mildness: thus the visitor no longer knew which was the Dean and which the fish. It also muddled the shipwreck of a puffing steamboat bearing Acland and the Tuna (from which he and his specimen had to be rescued in January 1857) with a puffing speech he made in Congregation where he was defending profligacy in the matter of the museum building for which he was directly responsible.

This speech was delivered by Acland to Congregation at the most controversial period during the construction of the University Museum: the hand and targeting of Carroll were everywhere apparent.

Historically, this was the first of Carroll's known Christ Church fishy jokes, and he was not its sole author. These were nonsense jokes but, in their culinary aspect and in their political undertow, all were triggered off by real people. This one set him on the path he was to tread until the finishing of *Looking-glass*.

Apart from this spoof, there was no sign of antagonism between Carroll and Dr Acland. On one occasion, Carroll reported asking Mrs Acland to introduce him to the Duchess of Marlborough with a view to photographing her children and Mrs Acland brushed him aside.

On the other hand, to Carroll's great benefit, it was Sarah Acland who introduced him to Alexander Munro at the time that Munro was carving a bas-relief to be set over the entrance of the new Union building. The Aclands also commissioned a head of Dante. The connection to Munro had proved invaluable as Carroll made his way into London and towards Tenniel and Macmillan.

The first sign of some antagonism between Carroll and Acland came a year after Mrs Acland's snub in 1863. On 25th January Carroll finally met John Tenniel, taking with him a letter of introduction from Tom Taylor. On that trip to London he saw four plays and bought a musical box for Edith Liddell. A week later he wrote:

> Feb: 1. (M). Invented and wrote out (with a suggestion or two from Bayne) a squib on the division of tomorrow . . . consisting of an alphabetical list of the names of voters and others, with the names left blank.

He dated the squib, 'February 2, 4681', a date that was futuristic and looking-glass; and this is part of it:

> A is for [Acland], who physic'd the Masses,
> B is for [Brodie], who swears by the gases.
> C is for [Connington], constant to Horace,
> D is for [Donkin], who integrates for us.

Donkin was the uncle of the lovely Alice B. Donkin who knew Ruskin and father of the other Alice Donkin. They were two of Carroll's favourite models. The squib continued:

> I am the Author, a rhymer erratic –
> J is for [Jowett], who lectures in Attic:
> K is for [Kitchin], than attic much warmer.
> L is for [Liddell], relentless reformer!
> S is for [Stanley], sworn foe to formality.

T's [Travers Twiss], full of civil legality.
U's University, factiously splitting –
V's the Vice-Chancellor, ceaselessly sitting.
W's [Wall], by museum made frantic,
X the Xpenditure, grown quite gigantic.
Y are the Young men, whom nobody thought about.

In 1850 Oxford had introduced honour degrees for science, law and history. In 1854 and 1856 Acts of Parliament were passed preventing the exclusion of non-conformists from the University as undergraduates. The rules committing dons to sign the Thirty Nine Articles of Faith in the Church of England and to remain celibate stayed in place in spite of frequent attempts to introduce Acts of Parliament to change this.

The internal statute which Carroll's alphabetical squib was designed to influence sought to allow undergraduates to give up compulsory study of classics after their first examination, Moderations. This particularly affected those studying science and the modern subjects of history and law. Most of the names on the list are scientists, doctors and mathematicians – for example Acland, Brodie, Donkin; or their Liberal supporters Jowett, Liddell and Stanley. Wall – 'by Museum made frantic' – was University Treasurer and a distinguished Professor of Logic. The main supporters of the Museum project were Acland, Professor of Medicine, and Ruskin who provided the impetus to design the building in the gothic style. Both had been pupils of Liddell in his early days as a Christ Church tutor. Both were now his friends and his allies on the massive budgetary overspend.

Three weeks after the vote in favour of the lowering of the requirements for classics was passed, Carroll wrote:

Feb:25. (Th) The new Examination Statute giving a degree for third class in any school, passed in Convocation by 281 to 243. I fear this is the beginning of very grievous changes in the University: this evening I have been seriously thinking about resigning my Examinership in consequence, and I have written a sketch of a letter to the Vice-Chancellor on the subject. March:2. (W). Left the letter [of resignation – which still allowed him to keep his Christ Church studentship] at the

Vice-Chancellor's. I am also having it printed . . . to be circulated tomorrow.

Here was a sign of Carroll's serious antagonism. It was not so
much aimed at Acland personally as at the reforms for which
he stood. On a personal level, 'physic'd the masses' was not a
pleasant comment about someone whose hospitality Carroll
had frequently taken. Acland and his wife Sarah risked their lives
when they nursed cholera victims.

Unlike Swinburne, Acland preferred a post-medieval septic
system for Oxford. With Liddell he had gone down to inspect
the Oxford drains, to find out where raw sewage and fresh
water were intermixing, and to remedy the situation.

It was during this period that Sarah Acland, who was a loved
Oxford figure like her husband, had nursed cholera victims. So
had Mrs Gladstone, another pioneer of convalescent nursing.
Dr Pusey had encouraged the opening of the Christ Church
kitchen to provide hot liquids for the victims and had taken
note of Acland at the time. Indeed Acland's promotion to
Professor of Medicine in 1857 when he was aged forty-two was
based on his public health work rather than on any advance in
research. Carroll was among those Christ Church M.A.s packing his election. It was on this occasion that Carroll observed
Ruskin at close hand and made a derogatory comment on him
in his diary. By 1864 Carroll had changed his mind about
Acland and brought his view of him into line with that of the
'rather dull' Ruskin.

On a misty evening, as we were driving out of Oxford to stay
with a friend, we noticed the Sarah Acland Memorial Hospital
at the Science School's end of the Banbury Road, and called in
search of something from the time of its foundation.

The matron on duty said there were indeed old photographs
of the Aclands that had been found in an Oxford library.
Among them we saw what had to be a picture of the White
Rabbit.

We had already begun to like Acland from his photographs,
particularly one of him smiling in a sou'wester hat on the
Madeira trip. The Latin inscription on the Tuna Fish specimen

might have been pompous, but we could not see Acland in that light. He seemed to have a lively and inquisitive air.

Here he was on the hospital staircase. In one picture he was sitting bolt upright with a little monkey next to him. They looked delighted with one another, sitting on a park bench face to face. The monkey was wearing a suit and a small chain and had its left paw on Acland's ear.

Just a little higher on the angle of the stairs there hung another old photograph of Acland with his eldest son, a Royal Navy captain who later became an admiral. Again Acland was looking just like the White Rabbit, standing to attention and beaming up at his tall son. There was no facial likeness to help identify the White Rabbit, but its disposition set our minds working on the connection.

Acland and the White Rabbit displayed a similar combination of alertness, an air of being in a hurry – Dr Acland was notorious for booking in more than he could do in a day – and a sense of the importance of officialdom (which reflected the White Rabbit's pomposity at the Trial).

There was a third photograph of the entrance of the hospital which was built in memory of Sarah Acland. Here the now aged Acland was the only person seated in the front of a large group. He had no whiskers, but big sideburns, just like the White Rabbit's whiskers, although in this case he looked overwhelmed by the memory of his wife's death. The Prince of Wales was standing next to him. Acland had been the Prince's doctor and had accompanied him on his American trip. In the photograph the Prince was wearing a top-hat and check trousers, looking as if he had just had a large lunch and not paid much attention to Acland's advice on diet.

Significantly, royalty was standing and Acland was sitting, a considerable measure of respect.

The White Rabbit dominates the first part of the *Wonderland* story and then comes back at the Croquet Match and at The Trial. Like the Cheshire Cat, the White Rabbit was part of a royal entourage and there, next to the Prince and standing behind Acland's left shoulder, was Mrs Liddell, wearing a hat with magnificent plumage, like a Mrs Beeton table-decoration.

Below the hat she wore the most wonderfully sour expression on her jowly face.

She had become more than ever like the Queen of Hearts in *Alice*. Next to her was the young Lorina Liddell. To give the additional courtly stamp, the picture was taken by Hill and Saunders, recorders of grandees and grand occasions with their photographic studios in Oxford and Eton College.

Finally there was a photograph which we had seen before of two friends: Ruskin hunched in a wicker chair as if the world had forced itself inwards on his mind, as if he saw his face in alpine boulders, and Acland next to him, looking concerned and tolerant. That reminded us of their connection over the building of the Natural History Museum in Oxford and their eventual rupture over the practice of dissection, which Acland supported and Ruskin, along with Carroll, abhorred.

Acland had to be heavily implicated in the portrait of the White Rabbit. Much of the early part of the book, the tunnels and jars and breaking glass, could be seen to evoke the building of the Natural History Museum. Carroll took Alice Liddell there on several occasions, even during the construction.

Alice saw the White Rabbit and followed him. She went down the Rabbit Hole, got bigger and smaller, ate the cake which said *EAT ME*, remarked 'Curiouser and curiouser!'

Alice was not able to address the White Rabbit until she had been through the Pool of Tears and witnessed the Caucus Race. Then the White Rabbit sent her off, thinking that she was its maid. It called her Mary Ann and wanted its gloves and fan.

Alice found its house with a brass plate on it, '*W. RABBIT*'. Inside she found the bottle labelled *DRINK ME*. She worried about doing so. Alice Liddell had had experience of the chemicals in Carroll's studio. But curiosity won.

She drank the liquid and grew so big she could not get out of W. Rabbit's house.

Did this nudge us any closer to the circumstances whereby the character of the White Rabbit overlapped with Acland? Certainly the dress and the big pocket-watch were right for Acland, so was the hurrying to appointments. So were the potions, the cake that has an effect, and the medicine jokes that set up others on this theme like Father William's ointment and the Dormouse's treacle. So was the brass plate and the bottles and shelves Alice saw on her descent underground. The fluid that made Alice grow and shrink could also be a joke about the development of photographic plates.

Forgetting the gloves seemed more difficult to tie to Acland except that we saw him carrying them when wearing Court dress and being photographed with his son. The nosegay and the fan were curious *in a man*. Nosegays certainly had been carried by doctors as an antidote to bad smells. The Mary Ann joke, confusing Alice with a servant, was quite possibly a joke that Carroll and Alice Liddell shared about an upstairs and downstairs confusion of identities in the Acland and Cameron households.

All these were clues. Stronger was the association with 'Pat', for whom the White Rabbit calls out. 'Pat' was slang for Irish 'navvies'. Navvies worked on the building of the Natural History Museum. There is talk here about potatoes eaten by the Irish and the glass-covered frame through which the White Rabbit falls.

The second chapter in which the White Rabbit appeared, Chapter IV, was called 'The Rabbit Sends in a Little Bill'. Our speculation was that the Rabbit sent in a big bill.

Ever since Acland, with the backing of Ruskin and the natural scientists at Oxford, proposed the building of a new museum, library and laboratory the opposition had been creating an atmosphere of panic.

These new buildings, like the tuna exhibit, were to prove sitting targets for parody. The bill *was* very large, Irish workmen were indeed employed, glass frames were used for botanical experiments and the glass-paned cast-iron roof did give serious problems – indeed it was an important cause of the little bill not being little at all.

Opposition to the Museum from the High Church and anti-science party grew. Even before the bill had become large, mockery hovered over the project. The architectural magazine, *The Builder*, reported on the designs submitted by competition as follows:

Gothic of all kinds	12
Greek, more or less German in treatment	3
Roman, more or less after Wren, with pedimented porticos, columns, &c.	4
Italian, more or less Barryan or Palatial	6
Elizabethan	1
The Order of Confusion	2
Original, Crystal Palace work tacked on to various regular book details	3
Abominations, about	2

Confusion continued to reign about money and about the designs. A prize of £150, a pittance, was offered to the winning design but was not given. A firm of consultant architects had decided that none of the designs could be turned into a build-ing for the maximum approved sum of £30,000. Eventually a 'Gothic of all kinds' design was chosen, described by the dele-gates selected by the University as having 'the air of a Belgian *Hôtel de Ville* with points resembling the Tuileries Palace'.

Alice went on site there with Carroll. We followed a hundred and thirty-two years later.

On South Park Street, we had passed the Natural History Museum on our Oxford wanderings but had not looked at its high gabled structure closely. It really did look like just a Belgian Town Hall! As if to hide it, the University had surrounded it with modern concrete structures, monuments to the 'science is brutal, material, unromantic and square-edged' movement that has imposed itself so universally in the very recent past.

Ruskin's view was that the Gothic expressed craftsmanship and that the Museum should be an architectural celebration of Creation – as Ruskin saw it.

DISRAELI AT THE TOP OF THE GREASY POLE,
AS PORTRAYED IN *PUNCH*

Our first excitement was seeing carved animals around the windows and central front door: only the ones over the front door were defaced. That really did confirm something we had read in Atlay's biography of Acland, but we wanted to see more.

To the right-hand side stood what originally was to have been the boiler house, a room for effluent laboratory gases. We had read that it was modelled on the Monks' Kitchen at Glastonbury Abbey.

There were shades of the Ugly Duchess's kitchen range here. Now through the grimy window of this monkish kitchen we could see the yellow and black signs that warn of radiation hazard.

Was this the chimney up which Bill the Lizard was kicked? We had realised at Osborne on the Isle of Wight that Lizard was an almost perfect name anagram for Disraeli, lacking only the 'e' and substituting the actual 'z' for a phonetic 'z', Dizraeli. By the association with both bills (money and lizard-like characters) Carroll's joke was in keeping with unattractive and anti-semitic *Punch* satires on Disraeli, Dizzy by nickname, at this date.

We knew that Carroll had in his rooms a scrapbook full of *Punch* cartoons which he shared with Alice Liddell.

We went back to the front door where Alice and Carroll had come into the Museum. Its workmanship was of the most beautiful and elaborate design. So was the tiling. The panelled door was embellished with filigree brasswork around its lock. Everything about the entrance displayed Ruskin's ideas of the honourable nature of craft, the sense of fulfilment it brings to the individual. One of the oddest books to cross our path was Ruskin's *Ethics of the Dust*, conducted as a dialogue between Winnington girls (including the bewitching Lily Armstrong). It was thought to express through their voices Ruskin's holistic ideas of creation.

Inside the sensation grew that the onlooker was entering a sky-lit architectural forest. There were clusters of iron pillars supporting high gothic arches, constructed of ironwork. That in turn supported the roof. Every surface was decorated in a way similar to William Morris's decorations on the roof of the Union. The flat surfaces of the ironwork were painted in cream stencils with flowers and *fleurs de lys* on an ochre background.

Gracefully placed, where each pillar sprouted its arch, was an arrangement of cut-out iron flowers and leaves, flat surfaces of painted iron. Around the edge of the main space was a cloister with another above it. Each pillar supporting this cloister was made of a different marble and each arch had at the top of it carvings of plants, corals, ferns and animals, of horned owls on ivy, rabbits among grapes, squirrels among oak leaves, parrots garlanded with foxgloves.

One impression was of something quite archaic, an Aristotelian trophy hunter's monument to science. The undergrowth of the forest of pillars was filled with a crowded array of skeletons, statues and animal cases, of the prehistoric and the historic, of buffalo, birds and butterflies. We stood and gazed.

No wonder the White Rabbit sent in 'A Little Bill'. The cost overruns were legendary. Ruskin and none other than Liddell had pushed hard for the gothic design by the Irish architects, Woodward and Deane. It had been executed in part by an expert in cast iron, Skidmore.

Acland had liked this design. We had discovered that Canon Pusey who should (with the rest of the High Church party) have opposed the building and the teaching of science, agreed to vote in its favour. He had been impressed with Acland's work during the cholera epidemic and a ray of liberalism shone through the otherwise dark cloud of his conservatism. It glimmered again, according to Jowett, in the last twist of the Jowett heresy tale. The Gothic of the building appeased him, but it was the Gothic that cost so much to create and irritated Carroll so intensely. He minded the extravagance, but even more he minded the fact that it was invested in a future he viewed as hazardous.

So the building went up, including the glass roof. Or rather the glass roof had a tendency to fall down. This made the White Rabbit even more directly responsible for the Bill. Ruskin supported the project, but not the iron and glass roof which, for all the problems its high pitch and novel construction might have given, is what brings the airy character to the whole. Ruskin fell out over this and went off in a sulk, believing he could replace the intellectual basis of science with his own ideas. The estimate

for completion of the building was £29,041. By 1867 the cost
had risen to £87,000, making the University Treasurer, Mr Wall,
in Carroll's word, 'frantic'. By 1865, when *Wonderland* was going
to press, the cost was already a long way above the estimate.

'We must burn the house down!' said the Rabbit's voice.
And Alice called out as loud as she could, 'If you do, I'll set
Dinah on you!'

There was a dead silence instantly, and Alice thought to
herself, 'I wonder what they *will* do next! If they had any
sense they'd take the roof off.'

We wandered around the glass cases and pillars, each of a
different English marble. A party of French schoolchildren

squealed with delight. The
rather sullen attendant at the
souvenir counter in the darker
part of the building looked on.
The main hall was bathed in top
light. Then we saw Acland's
Tuna, just as it had been photographed by Carroll. Dissected
and majestic, it was sitting in its
case on the museum floor, just
as it had been in 1862, museum
item number 17423, next to the
leatherneck turtle, item number
8655, and a huge killer whale,
Orcinus Orca.

We had found Acland's Tuna,
which Carroll had spoofed,
but where was Acland? Right
next to the case where the
skeleton of the Tuna was displayed was a gothic door with
a large keyhole, reminiscent
of the one that Alice found
down the Rabbit Hole. This was
the Professor of Medicine's

office, or rather it had been, but there was still no sign of the Professor.

Round the main hall of the museum, we found statues of Euclid, Carroll's source for several textbooks written during the time he wrote 'Alice' – even though leading mathematicians of the day had gone over to Boolean algebra, which Carroll preferred to ignore.

There stood the statues of Galileo, Darwin, Newton and Linnaeus in his Lapland costume, looking bemused and down on the ground for a plant specimen that seemed to have eluded him. These and many other scientists were named on their pedestals. One statue in particular was not named. It was a head, cast in a shiny black material so that the expression was hard to recognise from the ground because of the top lighting from the glass roof. We managed to stretch up behind it, lean round, and there was Acland's name neatly engraved below the base of the head.

The anonymity and position not very far from his Tuna skeleton was in keeping with Acland's persistent modesty as the leading benefactor, bar none, of Oxford science.

Or *was* he so modest?

Near the panelled door into what had been the Professor of Medicine's office there was a glass case containing a small specimen of the Dodo. This was a sad story. As we read it on its Museum labels we, like Alice and Carroll, felt we were slipping into our own biological pool of tears.

Oxford had acquired one of the last specimens of the poor flightless, exterminated Dodo, brought back from Mauritius in the seventeenth century. In the eighteenth century this specimen had mouldered in the old Ashmolean. In the nineteenth, while the new Ashmolean (previously the only Oxford Museum) was being replaced as a museum of art and archaeology, the specimens went to Dr Pusey's carriage house outside Christ Church. Rumour had it that they caused a stink. Perhaps that, besides his being impressed by Acland's humanitarian work, helped the wily Canon, Carroll's ally, to vote for the Museum as a place for their preservation.

It was well known among Carroll fans that a specimen of

the Dodo was in this museum, and that Carroll portrayed himself as the Dodo in *Alice*.

We looked at the small, sad, bony and extinct head, brought all the way from Mauritius on a sailing boat a third of a millennium before. On completion of its last journey from the old Ashmolean to the new Natural History Museum, the skin of its cheek had been dissected away to the bone. The dried extinct flesh had been jettisoned, and this was done by none other than Henry Wentworth Acland.

This great Victorian doctor, who 'physic'd the masses', and served as patron and physician to the Pre-Raphaelites, saw himself as an improver of nature. Acland, the real Acland in 'Alice', as Carroll portrayed him, did have a more arrogant streak than we had imagined.

We went back to the entrance. Around the gothic arch that was the doorway were the disfigured heads we had seen on entering. At first glance they looked as if they were eroded, but those carved around the window arches, especially the carved animals, were complete and in relatively good order. Many of the windows had no carving. The doorway's carvings were damaged.

In his biography of Acland, Atlay told the following story. The University had become dismayed over the excessive cost of the – very beautiful – carvings done by the O'Shea family. After a vote in Convocation, at which Carroll might have been present, funding had been stopped but, one afternoon, Acland found one of the O'Sheas continuing his work in spite of Convocation's ban. He ordered him to stop. The next day he found O'Shea again: 'on a single ladder in the porch wielding heavy blows'. He asked what he was doing. 'Parrots and Owls! Members of Convocation', was the reply.

On the bodies of the parrots and owls, which can still be discerned, O'Shea had carved, in the manner of the medieval gargoyles of which Ruskin so strongly approved, the heads of those members of Convocation that were halting work on this soaring hymn to science.

Acland ordered the heads to be destroyed.

There is a parrot and an owl at the Pool of Tears. In the White Rabbit's second scene in *Wonderland*, when the White

Rabbit asked Pat what he saw in the window of his little house where Alice has *evolved* into a very large person entirely blocking him out, Pat replied: 'It's an arm, yer honour!' But Carroll transcribed the stonemason's answer with the stage Irish pronunciation 'arrum'.

The Pool of Tears scene became the little Bill scene. The sending away of Bill became the scene of Alice's meeting with the Great Puppy, after Alice became small enough again to get her 'arrum', indeed the rest of her, out of the house.

Charles Darwin claimed in later life that what had most hurt him at this time was an unnamed caricature of him – not as a monkey or an ape, as he was often shown – but as a Dog. If Carroll chose to put a puppy in this part of *Alice*, to make fun of Darwin's accounts of the *Beagle* voyage, that would be a joke in the *Punch* tradition. That the young Puppy should be huge in relation to Alice suggested that Carroll had the theme of evolution in mind in this part of the book, as William Empson had maintained. If so, then it is a more gentle and friendly lampoon

than most that Carroll devised, but it seems nevertheless to have
upset the victim. More than anything, Carroll detested posturing and abuse of power, and whatever his views of Darwin's
theories, it is inconceivable that he wished to spite such a careful
and modest man as Charles Darwin.

In Tenniel's illustration the furry Puppy is turned into something more fearsome than in Carroll's drawing. However,
the animal bears a closer resemblance to the younger Darwin
as drawn by George Richmond and whose photograph from the
1850s is in the National Portrait Gallery. In the Tenniel vignette,
Alice protects herself from the Puppy's charge 'behind a great
thistle'. Thistleton Dyer, with Christ Church connections,
was an emerging figure in British biology at this time.

'Alice' provides no evidence that Carroll was opposed to the
logic of Darwin's theories. Yet through the Dodo's pronouncement
at the finish of the Caucus-race – '*Everybody* has won, and *all* must
have prizes' – Carroll is clearly disapproving of the denial of God
and Christian ethics which he sees in Darwin's and Huxley's doctrines. In upholding a reverence for life, Carroll would have been
a formidable opponent to Huxley, had he challenged him at the
British Association debate – but Carroll's genius worked along
more subversive channels. Not content with rejecting Darwin,
the Dodo takes a well-aimed shot at Lamarck's belief in the
supremacy of the environment over the organism.

Alice's elongated neck suggests an adaptation of her body
form which allows her to stretch up and look into the Pigeon's
nest, and, in the Pigeon's opinion, threaten to harvest its eggs.
This was how Lamarck (at the time of the French Revolution)
explained the origin of species. Contrary to Darwin, he held
that the neck and legs of the giraffe had 'stretched' so long
because this savannah creature needed them long to help it
browse in the tree tops. To Lamarck the environment directly
shaped the organism. To Darwin, the great variety of species
was what nature opportunistically filtered.

In the first version of the scene by the Pool of Tears in *Alice's
Adventures Under Ground*, Alice leads the other animals through
the Pool to the safety of the shore. She is followed by a Mr and
Mrs Monkey, while the Dodo keeps the crowd in order from

behind her right shoulder. In Tenniel's drawings a monkey is present, full face and in profile, but the sense of Alice evolving from anthropoid forebears is not so clearly made as in Carroll's drawing of this same scene. Carroll portrays Alice as the thinking, breathing pinnacle of creation, a human nymphet, the monkey pair swimming along in calm waters behind her.

Although invited, Darwin would not go to Oxford to debate evolution and thus never gave Carroll the chance to photograph him. Huxley went in his stead, as we know from Carroll's three-quarter length photograph of him in Alice's album: Carroll must have been proud of this coup. Huxley's biological acumen was appreciated by Acland. Indeed in the part of the Museum above the disfigured carvings, Huxley – with Dr Acland's willing permission – debated evolution with Bishop Wilberforce.

We went back into the building and up on to the landing. What once was the library above the entrance way had been subdivided. So, with all the skeletons below us and in the cloister where each pillar was made of a different marble, we had to imagine the packed and tense crowd in the locked room above Acland's office. Carroll was probably present. (His diary for this period is among those that are missing.) He attended other British Association meetings that were not held in Oxford so it is not unlikely he attended this one on his doorstep, with his own, not entirely well-loved Bishop as chief antagonist to the formidable young Huxley.

After Alice met the Puppy, she came across a mushroom higher than herself on which the Caterpillar sat smoking a hookah. We associated the Caterpillar with Tennyson's friend, Edward Fitzgerald, translator from the Persian of Omar Khayyám. There was even a name joke in his 'hookah'. The botanist, J. D. Hooker, who followed his father as Director of Kew Gardens, reported the meeting as frankly as other evolutionists:

Hearing that Soapy Sam [Bishop Wilberforce] was to [speak] . . . all the world was there. Well, Sam Oxon got up and spouted for half an hour with inimitable spite, ugliness and unfairness. I saw he was coached by Owen and knew nothing [but] he ridiculed . . . Huxley savagely . . .

The Bishop had been briefed by Huxley's chief in the community of biologists, Sir Richard Owen, but Wilberforce was out of his depth in the complexities of Owen's anatomical theories. Carroll must have known it. Owen was a pioneer in the study of flightless birds, including the Dodo. He was a bitter opponent of Darwin's, a favourite of the Queen, a friend of Gladstone and of the fox-hunting Wilberforce. The most ill-advised snub to Huxley was the question Wilberforce put to him asking whether the ape in his family was on his grandfather's or his grandmother's side.

Huxley, in the language of an Old Testament warrior, smote his side and cried out that God had delivered the Bishop into his hands. Huxley won the day on points. His logic was better, his sense was more appealing, and he knew a great deal more about the brain anatomy of monkeys than the Bishop, for all the advice he received from Huxley's chief rival.

Although in his behaviour Huxley was less like the Ugly Duchess than Wilberforce was, the facial likeness was compelling. The other figure in the Duchess's kitchen bears an uncanny resemblance to Sir Richard Owen, most expert among the scientists who sided with Wilberforce.

The costume of the Duchess as drawn by Tenniel is copied directly from a medieval painting by Quentin Metsys at the

National Gallery in London. There was, however, something about T. H. Huxley's determined face and angular jaw which was reflected in the face of the Duchess, as we knew from Alice's album, and the likeness is evident if Carroll's photograph is placed beside Tenniel's drawing.

In the story, Alice goes into the Duchess's kitchen where the atmosphere is full of smoke – a cooking joke. There is pepper in the air, and everyone is sneezing except for the Duchess's Cat, the Cheshire Cat, which keeps on grinning. The Duchess is rough in her handling of her baby and of Alice.

There was also a hint of Huxley's uncompromising manner in 'you don't know much . . . and that's a fact' – the Duchess's frequent comment to Alice. This was Huxley's debating technique against the Bishop – and it worked.

At this point the Cook starts throwing the implements at the Duchess and her baby. 'The Duchess took no notice of them even when they hit her.' Then the Duchess throws the baby to Alice, and it starts another test of survival. Alice catches the baby, holds it, but it evolves backwards, turns into a Pig and trots off into the wood. Alice appreciates this event with equanimity and gives voice to Carroll's traditionalist view:

> 'If it had grown up' she said to herself, 'it would have made a dreadfully ugly child . . .'

Huxley's scientific rival, Professor Owen, was a notoriously quarrelsome experimental biologist. He was personally disliked by Carroll and other anti-Darwinian intellectuals. His face in photographs is unmistakable, staring, with goggly eyes, a long chin, and a long, stooping body, and his appearance had a great deal in common with the stooping figure stirring the pot of bones of old flightless birds and monkeys in the Duchess's kitchen – the Duchess's Cook.

Who cooked up Wilberforce's argument?

Owen did.

It was felt by anti-Darwinians that Owen's weak briefing of Bishop Wilberforce on the anatomical arguments Huxley raised had caused the collapse of the anti-evolutionist side. The joke Carroll made was that Owen cooked the facts and the Duchess ignored him. Huxley and Owen were at the time rivals to be Principal of the School of Mines in London – an institution under siege. Did the Duchess, meeting Alice, refer to their dispute? She states, her chin wedged into Alice's shoulder: 'The more there is of mine, the less there is of yours.'

Still, the Duchess was not all Huxley. Perhaps Carroll sympathised a little with a scientist who had resisted the bullying and innuendo to which Wilberforce had subjected Huxley. We argued earlier that the language about morals was all Wilberforce. Now we found another name joke lurking in the notion of 'Will-by-force', a jibe against Wilberforce's bullying tactics in the debate. 'Speak roughly to your little boy . . .'

As we left the Museum where Huxley outwitted Wilberforce and Owen, we looked back into the glass case where we had seen what remained of the ancient Dodo after Dr Acland had finished with it. There was the dried out, wrinkled specimen of its sole surviving claw. Its museum number was printed on it as on the wrist of a newborn child. It was the yellow, bony wrist of Carroll raised in defiance of all the pepper and the hot air that he had observed on his frequent visits to the Natural History Museum both with and without Alice.

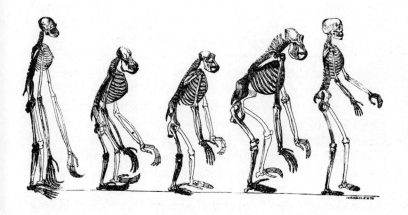

CHAPTER EIGHTEEN

Old Hummums

AS WE DROVE along the North Wales coast one seaside town spread into the next. Where this had not happened, the gaps were filled with caravan sites. Much of this coast consists of a narrow strip of flat land below cliffs and the A55 Expressway for Ireland-bound traffic, which has absorbed even more of the space. It was very different when the Liddells built their large house a mile from Llandudno and came chugging up on the train from Oxford via Crewe and Chester and then along the coastline.

We had come away from Oxford with a strong notion that Henry Acland had inspired the White Rabbit, and we detected the presence of a number of other scientists in 'Alice'. Some characters in the stories we had been unable to fathom at all – the Frog and Fish Footmen, for instance. If George Henry Hudson, the railway magnate, was indeed Humpty Dumpty, as was claimed in an ingenious article by Dr Elizabeth Osborne in *New Scientist* magazine, it was not out of keeping with the entourage of politicians, writers, artists, clergy, scientists and Oxford dons who made appearances in Carroll's world. He dined with a railway magnate at the right time, and was preoccupied with railway matters of every kind since boyhood.

We were at the time, however, on to another track. We had spotted Ruskin again in another fishy joke about seaside and salt-water crustaceans. This reference came in Tweedledee's wonderful song, 'The Walrus and the Carpenter'. Who was the Walrus? Who was the Carpenter and who were the Oysters they disposed of?

We were following the North Wales coast because that was where Alice Liddell, an inland Oxford child, became familiar with the seaside. We were lost, after a fashion. We were not sure if Pen Morfa, the Liddells' house near Llandudno, still existed, although we did know something about it. We knew where once it stood, and how hurt Carroll had been when the Liddells set off there without waving him goodbye. Perhaps he had an inkling that relations with Alice were soon to end because two days earlier – the year was 1862 – he had written:

Aug:6. (Wed). Left the papers at the Delegates' room: we have 250 plucked [i.e. failed] out of 600. In the afternoon Harcourt and I took the three Liddells up to Godstow, where we had tea; we tried the game of 'the Ural Mountains' on the way, but it did not prove very successful, and I had to go on with my interminable fairy-tale of *Alice's Adventures*.

Next came this:

Aug:8. (F) In the morning happened to cross the quadrangle as the two flies from the Deanery were driving out, and so got a last sight of my young friends.

That was all: there was no goodbye. The Liddells went off to the newly-completed Pen Morfa on their first ever visit with the children. Carroll travelled to Worcester and to Putney, photographing children on his list and assisting at Sunday services. Then he went on to lionise Tennyson on the Isle of Wight, not without serious set-backs.

The location which the Dean had chosen for Pen Morfa is beside one of the finest and most spectacular bays in Britain. Pen Morfa lies under the shadow of the Great Orme, the dome-shaped mountain that sticks out into the Irish Sea at Llandudno. Most of the town looks north but Pen Morfa faces south-west. It fronts a beach with a sandy shore, rocks and rock-pools for crabs and, of course, shelter for Gryphons to sun themselves. Carroll knew about the seaside from his many visits since boyhood to the Yorkshire coast and later to Eastbourne, Devon, Brighton and the Isle of Wight. He loved to be beside the sea. In Llandudno, as at the Deanery, little

Alice had what at first amounted to a private beach.

The Liddells had come to Llandudno on their honeymoon and visited it again with the children for Easter in 1861 – some twelve years after the opening of the main-line railway from Crewe to Holyhead, the event to which Llandudno, a Victorian gem, and the resort towns along the coast owe their existence. Dean Liddell, Alice's father, had preached in Trinity Church in the centre of the town. An interior designer we knew told us there was a stair-case in a Llandudno hotel up which the real Alice had walked. To our surprise, the hotel was the former Pen Morfa.

The house was cut right into the cliff, leaving virtually no space behind for any of the drains or services. It is a high villa, its ground floor raised ten feet above the shoreline, built with two projecting fronts and steep slate roofs. The mock-Tudor hotel extensions have not enhanced it. The Gryphon, who might have liked the original, would describe it now as 'Uglified'. Municipal lawns and concrete balustrades at the sea-shore uglify the landscape even more. When first built, it had stood alone. As with Christ Church's Meadow Buildings, there can be no doubt about it – Dean Liddell's Pen Morfa is a house in the wrong style on the wrong site.

Our view was coloured by our reception. We asked if we could have tea or a drink. It was the 'low season' and nothing was open. We asked if there was any relic of the Liddells: the receptionist had never heard of them. After poking around in the lounge we found a plaque which explained that the Dean had leased the plot from the Mostyn Estates, and planned a four storey house of glazed Ruabon bricks. At least the Ruabon bricks had never materialised!

The Dean dismissed the local builders when they did not get on with the work, commissioned another design and finished the building in an enormous hurry between April and August 1862, at which point he celebrated by giving the labourers roast-beef, plum-pudding and beer. So Alice and her sisters *did* learn all about the seaside whilst Carroll was writing 'Alice'.

We left Pen Morfa and walked up to the summit of the Great Orme's Head.

From here, without the clutter of cars and concrete in front of the hotel, it was possible to appreciate what the view from Pen Morfa must have been. Westward, the sea stretched out towards the low form of the Isle of Anglesey, Ynys Mon, in a shimmer of steel and silver, glittering in a lowering afternoon sun. South-west were the Welsh mountains, layered with deepening colours, and to the south was the sandy estuary of the Conwy river as it ran past the old town and little port dominated by the circular towers of its old, stately castle.

How Carroll had hated the extensions and modernisations that Liddell directed at Christ Church! Like Meadow Buildings, Pen Morfa showed lack of sympathy for everything around it. At least with Meadow Buildings, the Dean had a governing body to placate. Pen Morfa was architectural vanity gone mad. What was worse, it was cheaply built. Its design and execution characterised its founder as a man in a hurry, clever, ambitious, above the crowd, unable to put himself in the shoes of his juniors – of whom an irritating mathematics tutor was one.

C.L. Dodgson, alias Lewis Carroll, was as irritating to the Dean as he was hard-working in his attempts to block his improvements and reforms. Among the entries in Carroll's diary for the days when the final touches were being added to Pen Morfa is the following:

Aug: 4. (M). At work at the papers [marking exams] nearly all day, and all night.

Where we stood was the wind-blown site where the twenty-one-year-old William Blake Richmond, the son of George Richmond, had painted his portrait of the three Liddell sisters on this dome-shaped, grass-covered rock. Ruskin complained about the girls being painted with their shoes on: he said he would have preferred them barefoot. Poor Carroll, now rejected as the portraitist to the King and Queen of Hearts, remarked that young Richmond's Alice 'was not quite natural'. He preferred to see her in the Unicorn's words 'large as life and twice as natural'.

As so often with Carroll's artistic criticism, he was right. The Richmond portrait was charming but insipid, coming nowhere near to catching the Alice that Carroll photographed, the real, mischievous, intelligent, logical Alice – her father's favourite daughter.

At least he may have had his revenge. We believed, without being certain, that Carroll had Liddell in mind when he sketched the portrait of the two Kings in 'Alice', of which the Red King in *Looking-glass* was painted more sketchily than the obviously Liddell-like King of Hearts.

We sat looking out towards the Menai Straits and the coast of Anglesey where the submarine H.M.S. *Thetis* had failed to resurface on its trials from Liverpool with total loss of life.

The weather had changed completely. Suddenly the view was crystal clear, suggesting rain, and there was only a single yacht in the whole expanse of bay. It was just possible to see the new gas rig further along the North Wales coast. From the sands in front of us, the tide was going out, and the sea was glistening in the sun which was now low. There were no Oysters, but we could see two figures on the beach, perhaps the unlikely pair, a Walrus and a Carpenter.

The bullying Tweedledee recites the verses about 'The Walrus and the Carpenter' to Alice. It is the only sea poem in the entire *Looking-glass* journey. The poem starts with the sun sinking, just as it was doing in front of us, and continues:

> The Walrus and the Carpenter
> Were walking close at hand;
> They wept like anything to see
> Such quantities of sand:

The Walrus and the Carpenter had eaten up all the Oysters they led along the beach. This shocked Alice.

One of them hid his gluttony behind a handkerchief, the other behind a moustache.

Tweedledee told the poem after he and Alice noticed that the Red King was fast asleep, snoring beneath a tree. Was the Red King truly asleep? Or was he just caught off his guard?

The reforms of Liddell, Acland, Jowett and Stanley had by 1871 allowed John Ruskin and Walter Pater, Oxford's two greatest aesthetes when Carroll was writing 'Alice', to pack their lecture rooms with young disciples of the newly-decadent,

newly-secular Oxford. Their doctrines shocked the High
Church faction. Liddell had spearheaded the reforms and then,
in Carroll's view, had gone to sleep. Carroll considered this
moral negligence reprehensible.

> 'The time has come,' the Walrus said,
>   'To talk of many things:
> Of shoes – and ships – and sealing wax –
>   Of cabbages – and kings –
> And why the sea is boiling hot –
>   And whether pigs have wings.'

> 'But wait a bit,' the Oysters cried,
>   'Before we have our chat;
> For some of us are out of breath,
>   And all of us are fat!'
> 'No hurry!' said the Carpenter.
>   They thanked him much for that.

   John Ruskin, who at first wrote under the pen-name
'Kataphusin', seemed to be the model for the Walrus and Walter
Pater for the Carpenter. (There is no Gryphon in the second
story.) Pater, the aesthete and art critic, was teaching at Oxford
while Carroll wrote *Through the Looking-glass*. Ruskin wrote, in
Modern Painters, a convoluted essay entitled 'Of Many Things'
under a sub-heading 'Realisation'. Carroll's Walrus talked of
'Many Things'. Ruskin's essay contained wonderfully long-
winded passages about Veronese allowing 'cats and monkeys to

join the company of kings', with further Walrus-like talk about 'real angels with real violins' and 'substantial cats'. Carroll took his revenge through Tweedledee's recitation:

While pretending not to do so, the Walrus swallowed its victims whole. So did the Carpenter. The poor Oysters – the undergraduates – were entirely consumed after their strenuous courses in aesthetics, rushing along the seashore hand in hand with their unreliable modern mentors. They had been as foolish to be carried away by two eloquent and captivating aesthetes as Morris had been to dine with the Panther. All the while, the Red King, who had opened the door to reform at Oxford, dreamed away the hours when he should have been alert to the danger he had let into the curriculum. The Walrus and the Carpenter continued their discourse on whether pigs have wings. 'Walrus' contained the 'Wal' of Walter and the 'Rus' of Ruskin. Pater is hidden in 'Carpenter'. The Carpenter was an appropriate symbol for the two men, concerned as they were with applied as well as fine art. The Walrus suggests a fishy joke. In 1865, Walter Pater, known as 'Old Mortality in his Cap and Gown', grew a walrus moustache. Perhaps Carroll had transferred that bushy moustache from the upper lip of Pater as the Carpenter to the Walrus, Ruskin. The two identities continued to fix themselves in front of our eyes like negatives in a bath of developing fluid.

Pater, in his lectures on the Italian Renaissance, liked to compare the portrait of the *Mona Lisa* by Leonardo da Vinci to a Sphinx who ate men's bones in her cavern. Pater and Ruskin, in Carroll's *Looking-glass* skit, led the Oysters, who should have been Anglican undergraduates, along the wilder shores of love. When Carroll published his Pater skit in 1871 the tide of enthusiasm for art and decadence which he spoofed in *Phantasmagoria* as a Cambridge phenomenon had proved irresistible at Oxford too, and threatened the Pusey party. By the end of the ballad the Walrus and the Carpenter 'had eaten every one!'

★

We had lived with an interconnected group of Victorians for eighteen intensive months. We had ploughed through as many of the thirty-nine thick volumes of Ruskin's works as we could and looked with enthusiasm at as many of his drawings as we could locate. As to Cardinal Newman, more than thirty-nine volumes await the interested reader in addition to some of the best hymns in the English language. No fewer than twenty-two volumes of Mr Gladstone's diaries were just published, and we had been invited to a reception at Christ Church to mark this occasion by the Oxford University Press. We crossed Tom Quad in the darkness and walked up the stone stairway under its ceiling of hanging stone vaults and into Wolsey's Hall.

This was where Carroll ate on many days of his life. It was one of the most beautiful rooms in England, with long black polished tables pricked out with standard lamps with little parchment shades, portraits all round the walls and a wooden ceiling embellished with rosettes and other decorations of gold, blues and reds. Up near the High Table was the portrait of Dean Liddell by Herbert Herkomer. The Dean was dressed in his red robe, looking disdainful as ever, bald and red-lipped as if condemned for eternity to sitting at a long, dull committee meeting where his position was being irritatingly challenged. He seemed old and rather tired.

Carroll was there too, as far away from High Table as possible. He had been painted posthumously by the same artist, but in a much smaller portrait. He was shown in profile and looked a bit jowly, wearing a black suit and his white donnish bow tie. He had been portrayed as though he were going to give nothing away but might make a clever remark at the Dean's expense. Or not quite that: because nothing really could be at the all-powerful Dean's expense. Carroll would just fire a little squib. He would be amused and others might too. But it made no difference to the governance of Oxford. Alice dreamed, but finally the Red King commanded the reality. Carroll had no influence, except through his children's books, which were the greatest of the nineteenth century.

Oddly, perhaps predictably, it was after the Dean gave in to Carroll that he really began firing the squibs. Carroll, as part of the old, pre-Reform, Foundation at Christ Church, should have taken full holy orders, which would have banned him from the theatre and involved him in priestly duties. He broke the rule for reasons that he never openly declared, nor even in full analysed for himself. There was the stammer, there was the doctrinal problem he had (like Maurice) over the notion that young children were born in sin. This he could not accept for a moment.

In active doubt about the priesthood as he began to think along the lines that led to 'Alice', he requested a meeting with the Dean on Tuesday 21st October 1862, a month after the summer visit to Pen Morfa. The Dean said he would have to take orders or leave Christ Church. Carroll felt the Dean was being illogical:

> His opinion was that by being ordained Deacon I became a Clerical Student . . . and must take Priest's Orders within four years from my time for being M.A. and as this was clearly impossible in my case [he left it far longer than this] I have probably already lost the Studentship . . . I differed from this view.

The Dean said he would talk to the College Electors, mainly the Canons. Perhaps he wanted to make Carroll quake, and certainly this story throws light on the Mouse's horror of Dogs, but by the very next day Liddell had stepped down. Either he was bored by the whole issue of whether Carroll should be dropped or he was a truly tolerant man and did not wish to force him into the difficult commitment of becoming a full member of the clergy to retain his fellowship. Liddell could be pompous, but he was liberal. With Stanley and Jowett and others he did indeed reform Oxford.

At least, he reformed its substance if not its mannerisms: some of the sniping gossip we heard at the reception could have come from Carroll's Common Room. The day before, Christ Church had been lambasted by an American graduate student and then further attacked in *The Times* by a right wing professor who lashed out, not just at Christ Church but at the whole of Oxford, for being fossilised and missing opportunities for higher learning of a more trenchant kind. The American PhD student who had attacked Christ Church borrowed the title of her attack, possibly unwittingly, from Carroll. She called her polemic, and referred to poor old Christ Church as, 'A Garden of Paper Flowers'.

A good deal of the talk was about political change at Christ Church. Lord Blake, the historian, Disraeli's biographer, who had been of the Trevor-Roper generation of tutors at Christ Church, gave the opening address about the Liberal Mr Gladstone's diaries, and afterwards none of the speeches was as cutting about him as Carroll had been. In fact there was no levity on the subject of any kind. Had the great Victorians grown sacrosanct?

Then we heard his voice. It was an old, very early sound recording of Gladstone addressing Thomas Edison on the occasion of the switching-on of the trans-Atlantic cable. The Grand Old Man's voice came out, as from the tomb, from near his portrait by the Lobster, John Everett Millais. Although we could not hear clearly what he said, we were reminded that the Unicorn called little Alice a 'monster'. His Christ Church ghost was with us again. In fact it was unmistakable. This great worldly-wise Christian Prime Minister who always got a slice of the cake actually croaked at us across the sound-waves.

As we were gazing up at the inscrutable portrait of Carroll, Dr David Butler, the political analyst and broadcaster, approached us very quietly so as not to interrupt our concentration. Three of his great-aunts, he told us, had been child-friends of Carroll's. One of them was called Violet, one of the V's on a much later list of little girls Carroll hoped to photograph than the one dated 1863 which we had studied earlier.

By that late period of his life Carroll took no more photographs, but he wrote a charming poem full of anagrams about butlers and bunches of violets, and the sisters' names, the old routine. Two of them, the country cousins, had taken to him and had a wonderful time staying with him at Eastbourne. One had not. She had run away rather than continuing to keep him company.

We walked from the reception into the shadowy opaque light, down Wolsey's stone stairs, their treads worn to a curve with age. It was dark; a chill, moist Thames mist hung over

Tom Quad so that only the shadow of Wren's tower and Carroll's staircase was visible.

★

We were nearing the end of our quest, and on a late autumn Sunday travelled to London. Carroll came from a background of isolated, rural Northern parsonages, then moved to Oxford, but found the coterie of people who really understood him in London when he was devising the two 'Alice' books. Besides the seaside, this growing Victorian metropolis was where he spent as much leisure time as he could, and we wanted to visit his hideaways there.

First there was Uncle Skeffington Lutwidge's home. It was he, a London figure, Carroll's mother's brother and a bachelor, who provided the level of confidence for Carroll that Croft had done when he was younger. He was Carroll's mentor in the early days. He was ebullient and wore a large watch-chain and spotted waistcoat under his velvet-collared frock-coat. When he lived off Tottenham Court Road, he and Carroll had looked through his telescope at the twinkling stars together. Later, Carroll's visits were to his affluent five-storey house at 101 Onslow Square. Besides being an amateur inventor, Lutwidge was a solicitor and Commissioner for Lunacy who died unfortunately from a blow he received from an inmate in an asylum. He introduced Carroll to photography and to London. To the extent that Carroll agonised with anyone about his love for Alice Liddell in 1863, it was with Lutwidge.

Just south-west of South Kensington station what we thought was 101 Onslow Square appeared still to be a family house. Through a window we could see rich red taffeta covering a ground floor dining-room and roe deer horns on the walls. The marble fireplace was still intact and the chequered tiles on the doorstep looked original. The houses next-door were numbered 98 and 104; and 104 seemed to be several houses converted into one. The number 101 had been removed, and to check that we were at the right place we knocked.

Footsteps came down the stairs. 'Wot you want?' came aggressively through the closed door.

'We are doing historical research.'

'Wot research?'

'Is this number 101?' The sound of chains rattled, then locks, and more locks. A large man in a designer suit opened the door.

'You say market research?' he said with a strong Italian accent.

'We just wanted to be sure this was 101. We couldn't see a number. We're interested in people who lived here in the past.'

'Past research.' His face darkened. 'Weech company you from?'

'We're not working for a company . . .'

A hand was waved from side to side in front of us as the resident shook his head and quickly withdrew, closing the door and securing it in reverse order.

This almost certainly was Uncle Skeffington's house and from a glimpse inside at the stairwell it was possible to imagine it – large as it was for a bachelor – well-staffed, slightly scruffy, with dark ferns in glazed pots and comfortable linen-sheeted beds, well supplied with sherry and tea and cakes.

Carroll discussed the idea of the looking-glass world with Alice Raikes, then nine years old, in the residents' garden at Onslow Square. He traced her parents, who were relatives and neighbours of Lutwidge's, and took her and her sisters to the theatre to see *Goody Two Shoes*. Later he entertained the children of the Marquis of Salisbury at the house and told them parts of what became *Sylvie and Bruno*.

Carroll thought of *Sylvie and Bruno* – to write which he gave up teaching – as his masterpiece, but it never worked with the public. Even when it was first published in 1889 readers felt uncomfortable with it, quite the opposite to 'Alice' which, by and large, both children and adults relish. After 'Alice' Carroll went on trying but he never found the same magic again. The formula that was the root of his great stories puts an adult world in front of a logical child, dresses up Alice's dream as the Red King's dream and explores Carroll's own adult anguish in a children's story.

Uncle Skeffington's was important as a home from home, but in London we wanted to look beyond the family to other

Carroll contacts. From South Kensington we made our way through the cream-coloured pomposity of Eaton Square and into Belgravia. Number 6 Belgrave Place was less grand than most of the houses around it. The bare stone entrance and the windows had a quaintness about them. It was here that Alexander Munro, the sculptor, had had his studio. Sarah Acland gave Carroll the introduction on 22nd February 1858, suggesting he show Munro his photographs. Munro taught with Maurice at the Working Men's College and was a Liberal. He knew a great deal about the clashes of personality in the Christian Socialist Movement.

It was Munro who made the black bust of Acland which we had seen in the Oxford Natural History Museum, perched on a shelf, twenty feet to the right of the Dodo and ten behind the Tuna fish skeleton. Carroll and Munro liked one another, and in exchange for some photography of his sculptures, Munro invited Carroll to keep his camera equipment in Belgrave Place and use it occasionally as a studio. In the summer of 1860, while Munro was carving 'Boy with the Dolphin', Carroll met and befriended young Greville MacDonald who was in the studio posing for the statue. Carroll made a joke with him about how, if he had a stone head like the sculpture, he would not have to brush his hair, a joke he continued with Greville's sister, posing her with her hairbrush in her night-dress. 'It won't come straight' was the title Carroll gave his portrait. Greville was then four, his sister Mary six, and she became one of Carroll's favourite child-friends. She was known as 'blackbird' by her father, George MacDonald, and Wilfred Dodgson was reported to have taught her to box. It was her father who wrote two of the greatest children's classics of the period, *On The Back of the North Wind* and *The Light Princess*, and a series of other children's stories. Even the Tennyson boys were allowed to read these: we never heard that they were allowed to read 'Alice' even though their father was sent a complimentary copy by the author bound in white vellum. Was this a case of satirist's revenge?

Later Carroll helped to fund a bed at Great Ormond Street Hospital for Sick Children, choosing a London, not an Oxford, hospital on which to focus a lasting benevolent concern. He shared this particular interest with George MacDonald, who portrayed Carroll anonymously as the tall, quiet benefactor of a children's ward in *On the Back of the North Wind*. No Dodo in that story, the stranger saves the life of a little crossing-sweeper by providing her with a hospital bed and country air. Carroll, Macdonald, Hughes and Christina Rossetti belonged to a movement of the 1860s to give children's literature a less sentimental direction. Carroll held the ground at each end of the spectrum they mapped out. He was at once the most sentimental and at the other end of the scale, the most acerbic of them all. He was also the greatest.

Munro, with his large airy studio in Belgravia, had been Carroll's conduit to the MacDonald family. He photographed the parents and the children. He also photographed himself stretched out on the lawn among them. Three years after the occasion on which he met Greville and Mary MacDonald, Carroll wrote to Mrs MacDonald from Croft about a day of disasters when he had had Mary MacDonald with him, moving about London on foot and by cab.

He had arrived first at Belgrave Place to be told by Mrs Munro that the Munros were leaving for Inverness. So disappointed was he that he forgot he was still wearing his hat when she greeted him. He shook hands with it on and feared he might 'have made her an enemy for life'. Then Carroll took Mary Macdonald to meet the painter Arthur Hughes, who was on the point of leaving for Brighton. Undaunted, Carroll hurried on to see his *Punch* connection, the playwright, Tom Taylor, in Wandsworth, but he had left for a holiday. So as not to disappoint Carroll, Mrs Taylor suggested that Carroll might like to take a photograph of the only other person available, 'an old gentleman in the house', who refused to co-operate. 'The climax of the day's failures', Carroll noted wryly in his diary, one of the many passages Lancelyn Green left out of the published version.

All this time he had Mary MacDonald with him, now aged ten. He could not track down the Terry sisters, and so went back to Munro's house to see if his chemicals had been delivered, and when he found they had not, took Mary back to the MacDonalds' house off Regent's Park, hoping to stay there for the night. But he found that they had gone away too, leaving the nanny in charge. Carroll left Mary with the other children and the servants, and eventually dropped his cameras at King's Cross for the journey to Croft, still without picking up his chemicals.

Poor old Carroll, wandering round London with cameras and girls in tow, finding places for the little girls to pee, eat and sleep: but this was much more Carroll than the Deanery and its royalty.

We found the MacDonalds' house, Tudor Lodge, (not Tudor but built in an odd gothic style in red brick) on the edge of a Regency terrace just behind Regent's Park. It seemed rather a higgledy-piggledy place. Carroll was happy there, most especially because it was a family environment where theatricals were often in progress.

Instead of going south to Vere Street we walked on north up Kentish Town Road. It was one of those old, knocked-around London arteries that have stood the test of time and the refacings of generations of shops, the scruffy purposefulness of which survives. Just south of Kentish Town Underground station was Caversham Road where Ellen Terry and her family lived. When Carroll took a cab there, which would have been necessary with the camera boxes and developing equipment, it would have turned off by the black and gold window of Dawson and Bryant, the jewellers, established in 1840 and still extant.

Four of the happiest days of Carroll's life were spent here, photographing. This was somewhere for people who were struggling for artistic success, advancing their careers, but still struggling.

The Terrys' house and those around it were three storeys high on raised basements. Some were bombed in the Second World War and almost all are now divided into flats. There were old cars in the street, which gave it a somewhat run-down air, but what the street lacked in polish, it had in pleasantness and quietness. It was lined with pollarded lime trees and there were long thin gardens behind the houses. It was Carroll's kind of place, and here he photographed.

The Terrys and the MacDonalds accepted Carroll and he accepted them. It was possible to imagine him at ease here in North London in a quiet street in sight of Hampstead Heath. Double-decker buses rattled down the Kentish Town Road and the shouts of a domestic quarrel were reminders of how painful Ellen Terry's life had become. Later, she moved quietly to the country in Hertfordshire, raising her two children, Edith, the writer, and Edward Gordon Craig, the stage designer. Their father had been the architect, Edward Godwin, from whom she soon drifted apart. She was eventually lured back on to the stage but after giving up everything for a period of quiet country life with her own little ones. Nobody knew where she had gone.

Carroll, like her other admirers, had lost Ellen Terry at this time, as she intended, but he came forward to welcome her return to the stage with an even more remarkable emotional range when her idyll with Godwin was over. The rules of the church about marriage may have been important to Carroll, but he continued, as he always had been, to be transported by the enticement of the London theatre.

From the Terrys' home we went back to the West End and looked in at the old Macmillan offices at 16 Bedford Street, just off the Strand, a comfortable house for an emerging publisher in a narrow street. It was in a convenient position for Carroll to come and pester Alexander Macmillan about details of book production. At the other end of close-by Henrietta Street it was just possible to see Covent Garden. On the corner of the old piazza stood a high, rather proud regency structure, built of bright red brick with stonework detailing, That had been Old Hummums, Carroll's central London hotel. Now the lower part of it is a brasserie, with the London Transport Museum next door.

Outside a pop group with punk haircuts and black leather jackets was playing to an idling London crowd. Across the square in the direction of the Opera House a 'Punch and Judy' had drawn a crowd of children. A young woman walked up and down dwarfed by a bunch of iridescent helium balloons she was selling. The punk band played on, not very well, but they played on.

Sitting on the ledge of wall opposite what had been Old Hummums we were next to the bookshop where Dr Johnson met James Boswell. Carroll never met a biographer in his lifetime. The clerical constraint of his nature forced him to cover up the wild, witty, and cruel manifestation of his adult humour in the adult squibs he composed and, we believe, their extension in 'Alice'. Watchful he certainly was. What had he seen while he watched the illogical tumult of the adult world around him?

In her journey Alice meets the members of Christ Church locked in dispute with her father over changing College rules, the Professor of Medicine prescribing growth potions, and a new museum built in an overblown architectural style with the result that the roof kept falling in. She encounters the art critic dancing on the beach, full of mad aesthetic vanity, and her own parents conducting a trial at which the adults are 'nothing but a pack of cards'. She enters a world that Roman Catholic prelates seek to divide like squares on a chess-board, where a poet falls on his head, so heavy is the armour of false medievalism that he wears, and where she rows an old sheep-like priest into the waters of death. In his dream the Red King creates nightmares in which the innocent are eaten like oysters for yet more aesthetic pleasure.

There is consistency in Carroll's caricatures. Though they tend to be those individuals a High Church don and mathematician would hold out against, how right Carroll is in his account of their posturing. The Unicorn really is Mr Gladstone with his imperious and cavilling moods. The Gryphon's absurd dialogue perfectly catches John Ruskin and the White Knight is a precise and savage attack on the overblown aspect of Tennyson's verse. There is enough evidence to link the characters and behaviour of the White Rabbit to Henry Acland, the Cheshire Cat to Dean Stanley, the mad Hatter to Charles Kingsley, the Red King and The King of Hearts to Dean Liddell, the Queen of Hearts to Mrs Liddell, Father William to Benjamin Jowett, The Tiger-lily to Ellen Terry.

By the Pool of Tears Alice meets the gentle Duck (Robinson Duckworth), the Mouse (Prout of Christ Church) and the Lizard (surely Disraeli?), the secretive Lory (the young Lorina

Liddell, Alice's eldest sister), and Dodgson the Dodo, with his flightless wings, great curved beak and punky-feathered tail. She then meets the Mock Turtle (Carroll's friend Liddon). We have only just begun to unscramble the Pre-Raphaelite names Carroll planted layer upon layer in the verses about the Lobster and the Panther and the Owl – although Rossetti recognised himself and wrote to Carroll applauding his wit.

In the Duchess (Huxley, with more than a touch of Bishop Wilberforce) and the playful Beagle Puppy (almost certainly Darwin) we have stumbled on Alice's quarrel with evolutionary theory. How could life have arrived in its intricate splendour through processes controlled exclusively by a doctrine Carroll questioned – the survival of the fittest? How did Carroll prefer the doctrine of life to run? Why, like this:

> At last the Dodo said '*Everybody* has won, and *all* must have prizes.'

'Alice' represents the dream-like adventures of a child, but it is the Red King's dream too, an adult dream based on Victorian reality, not just the light airs of fantasy. Indeed when the Red King sleeps, what Alice worries about is the practical matter that 'he will catch cold with lying on the damp grass'. Tweedledee tells her she is only one of the things in his dream: 'You know very well you're not real.'

'I *am* real!' said Alice, and began to cry.

If she is not real, she says, she would not be able to cry, or to laugh at the absurdity of it all. Neither would we; and that is Carroll's legacy.

We were here outside Carroll's favourite hotel on a noisy, ebullient London afternoon. We imagined him going in to change for the theatre and to meet child-friends, looking impassive and poker-like, dressed in black. We pictured him top-hatted, in a stiff collar, followed by a boy with the hand-trolley and his boxes, fastidiously taking off his grey gloves and requesting his room key.

What an odd man, but a wonderful man if you caught his attention as a child, as we have been lucky enough to do through the books. For he spoke to children with a mixture of

adult and child sense that perhaps we have lost in the noisy age
of more passive visual entertainment, at least a kind of quiet
attention that only seems possible now with bedtime stories and
in the lull of a frantic day's ending. He spoke with a stooping
and kind and humourous engagement, with a love of little word
games, of the particles of humour that make England and its
language what they are, with a willingness to give up his time.

His prayers said in the old London hotel, Carroll would
then think about children and what he could give them – his
company, or visits to the theatre, or presents, or puzzles, or a
copy of *Alice's Adventure*. To his nephews, he signed himself
their 'watchful' uncle, indicating that he had a gift of a watch in
mind. It gave him a deep, private pleasure of a kind only his
intimate friends could read in his features. It gave them something beyond the watch which they remembered for years.

To Alice, he offered another kind of reality, a version of the
adventures they had shared and the grotesque and cruel adult
world they had, unrecognised by her, encountered during their
friendship, the one started when Carroll looked down on the
flat green plane of the Deanery garden and saw her below. How
high on our list should he be? With the centennial of his death
in 1898 not far away, perhaps higher than he is, perhaps deserv-
ing more of a memorial than the simple white grave in
Guildford that has been forced a bit crooked by the roots of a
hemlock tree, the scene of his simple funeral that only his
family, his brothers and sisters and a few close friends attended.

Biographical Register

P★ indicates that this character agreed to one or more photographic sessions with Carroll. The drawing on the left is the Reverend Dodgson's own idea of what he looked like when lecturing.

Dodgson, Charles Lutwidge, later Lewis Carroll (1832–1898). Born in Cheshire, moved to Yorkshire as a young boy, educated at Rugby and Christ Church. Student of Christ Church, Assistant Librarian then Tutor in Mathematics. Ordained Deacon in 1861. Photographer, satirist and teller of tales. *Alice's Adventures Under Ground* presented to Alice Liddell in handwritten form in 1863, published in expanded form as *Alice's Adventures in Wonderland* in 1865, illustrated by John Tenniel. Carroll's direct friendship with Alice Liddell lasted from c.1853 to c.1863. In 1868 his father died and he moved his sisters to Guildford. *Through the Looking-glass and What Alice Saw There* published in 1871. In 1881 gave up teaching in order to write. 1882–1892 Curator of the Christ Church Senior Common Room. Published works on mathematics: *Euclid and His Modern Rivals* (1879), *Curiosa Mathematica* (1888–93) and *Symbolic Logic* (1896). From 1877, he took regular holidays at Eastbourne and other favourite seaside resorts, where he sought the company of child-friends. He died at Guildford in January 1898 and was buried there with only small attendance at his funeral at his own insistence. P★

Liddell, Alice Pleasance (1852–1934). Born in Westminster where her father was Headmaster. Soon moved to the Deanery at Christ Church, Oxford. The fourth of ten children, one brother dying at the age of three, another at two months. She married Reginald Gervis Hargreaves (1852–1926) in 1880 and thereafter lived a country-house life, mostly at Cufnalls, which was in flat, wooded countryside between the New Forest and the Solent. Carroll did not attend her wedding, nor she his funeral. Alan, Rex and Caryl were born in 1881, 1883 and 1887. Alan and Rex were killed whilst serving as army officers in 1915 and 1916. In the summer of 1932, a hundred years after Carroll's birth, she came back into the public eye as 'Alice'. She was taken to New York, entertained lavishly and

277

given a Doctorate of Literature by Columbia University. She died in 1934. Her descendants live in Gloucestershire. P★

Characters in alphabetical order:

Acland, Professor Henry Wentworth, (1815–1900). Physician, Public Health Reformer, Fellow of the Royal Society, Honorary Student of Christ Church, Regius Professor of Medicine at Oxford. With Stanley, ally to Dean Liddell in the reform of Oxford University architecture and science. Likely original for the White Rabbit. P★

Bayne, Thomas Vere (1829–1908). Known to Carroll from his very young days in Daresbury. He spent his whole adult life in Christ Church. Among his Christ Church appointments was that of archivist. He left his invaluable scrapbook of Carroll materials and other satires of the Liddell era to the college. P★

Brown, Ford Madox (1821–93). English painter, born in Calais. He settled in England from the age of 24 and remained close to but not a member of the Pre-Raphaelite Brotherhood. Ruskin implacably opposed his work. Carroll did not know him, although their circle of acquaintances intersects. Carroll saw an exhibition of his pictures in 1865. He provided a name joke in 'The Voice of the Lobster'.

Burne-Jones, Edward (1833–1898). Artist and pre-eminent stained glass designer. Employed by Morris and Co., he became one of the most feted painters of the Victorian age. His wife was Georgiana Macdonald, and she taught with him and Ruskin at Winnington School in Cheshire. 'Georgie's' memoirs reveal how intimate the Burne-Joneses were with the Morris, Rossetti and Ruskin circles. 'The Voice of the Lobster' includes a pun on his name.

Cameron, Julia Margaret (1815–1879). From 1864, a photographer of portraits and scenes set in costume. She lived on the Isle of Wight as a neighbour of the Tennysons and gathered around her an influential group of subjects and friends. These included Benjamin Jowett, Charles Darwin, Ellen Terry and, later, Alice Liddell. Carroll inspected and purchased some of her early prints. Her manner, conversational style and dress habits resemble those of the White Queen. (See also Newman.)

Collingwood, Stuart Dodgson (1870–1937). Carroll's eldest male descendant. His mother was Mary Dodgson, the only one of Carroll's seven sisters who married. Literary executor and biographer, he successfully retained the genteel image Carroll wished to convey to the world. Known to Carroll when he was an undergraduate at Christ Church, he became a schoolmaster in adult life.

Combe, Thomas (1792–1872). A key figure in Carroll's life. He prospered as head of the Clarendon – the Oxford University Press – due to the sale of Bibles. He and his wife were patrons and friends of the Pre-Raphaelites, especially Holman Hunt, and introduced Carroll into their circle. For the Press, he purchased a paper mill at Wolvercote, close to Port Meadow on the river Isis where Carroll took Alice and her sisters rowing. There he helped Carroll with the lay-out for the 'Alice' books.

Darwin, Charles Robert (1809–82). Educated at Shrewsbury, Edinburgh and Cambridge. Naturalist and traveller. *On the Origin of Species . . . by Means of Natural Selection* was published in 1859 and defended by Thomas Henry Huxley in Oxford. Carroll photographed his own scientific friends facing monkey skeletons and drew monkeys in his sketch of the Pool of Tears. Carroll's diaries in 1872 note that he was reading Darwin's *The Expression of Emotions in Man and Animals*. This study of human ethology was illustrated by Carroll's mentor, the pioneering photographer, Oscar J. Rejlander. Carroll sent Darwin a photograph of one of his prettiest child friends, smiling broadly. He entitled it: 'No Lessons Today'. Darwin was parodied by Carroll as the clumsy puppy dog who nearly knocks Alice down in *Wonderland*.

Disraeli, Benjamin, M.P. (later Earl of Beaconsfield) (1804–1881). Conservative Chancellor of the Exchequer and later Prime Minister. Opposition Leader during Gladstone's first Liberal Ministry. He was a Sephardic Jewish convert to Anglicanism. An outsider to Oxford and a notable wit, Disraeli warred against agnostics and Roman Catholics. The disapproval with which arch-Conservatives like Carroll viewed him is captured in Carroll's 1864 sketch of Bill the Lizard. Tenniel's cartoons of Disraeli between 1865 and 1871 include the Man in the Paper Suit. Disraeli was source for the gossip Ruskin repeated in his memoirs of being caught by Alice's parents after dark at an unauthorised tea-party at the Deanery.

Dodgson, Frances Menella (1877–1963). Daughter of Carroll's land agent brother, Wilfred, and Alice Jane Donkin. She or her cousin (also Alice) are possible sources for information about Ruskin's dancing at Winnington Hall. She made enterprising attempts to edit and find a publisher for Carroll's manuscript diaries from the time of the centennial of his birth until, while living in Leamington Spa, she contacted Roger Lancelyn Green.

Dodgson, Charles (1800–1868). Carroll's father, rector of Croft in Yorkshire and Canon of Ripon Cathedral. He was the third of four Charles Dodgsons. The first was a bishop, the second an army officer, the fourth was Carroll. He was High Church and published at least one sermon that caused controversy in the High Church/Broad Church debate. He married his cousin, Frances Jane Lutwidge. P★

Duckworth, Robinson (1834–1911). At the time of his acquaintance with Carroll, Duckworth was Fellow of Trinity College, Oxford. He had a fine tenor voice. Later, as royal chaplain, one of the royal princesses fell in love with him. It was he who accompanied Carroll and chaperoned the Liddell girls on several river expeditions. He sang songs while Carroll told stories. Later, Carroll inscribed a copy of *Wonderland* which he gave him: 'From the Dodo to the Duck', one of his few private admissions that there were real people in 'Alice'. P★

Fitzgerald, Edward (1809–1883). Friend of Tennyson, recluse and Arab scholar educated at Cambridge. He translated from the Persian and published anonymously the hedonistic *Rubaiyat of Omar Khayyam*. Its authorship was tracked down after the poem was circulated by D.G. Rossetti. It became an immediate success. There are overlaps between the beliefs and actions of Fitzgerald and the Caterpillar sitting on a mushroom puffing its hookah. (See also Hooker.)

Gladstone, William Ewart, M.P. (1809–1898). Educated at Christ Church, friend of Liddell's, made an Honorary Student. A devout High Church Anglican, Gladstone was closely involved in Oxford University affairs and was M.P. for Oxford. He was Liberal Chancellor of the Exchequer when Carroll was writing *Alice*, and became Prime Minister in 1868. Possibly photographed by Carroll. Carroll made up anagrams on his name and spoofed him as the Unicorn in *Through the Looking-glass*.

Gordon, Osborne (1813–1883). Classics tutor at Christ Church. Tutor to the Prince of Wales. Ruskin described him as 'an Englishman of the olden time', *The Times* said he was able, charming and despotic in a small world, and unconcerned to work hard. Liked by Carroll, who walked with him, learnt how to write squibs with him, out-paced his master, and photographed him. There are some overlaps between Gordon and the Magpie in *Alice*. P★

Harcourt, Augustus George Vernon (1834–1919). Christ Church tutor, Lee's Reader in Chemistry. A chemist of distinction, Harcourt was Fellow of the Royal Society before he was 30. He seconded Dodgson as

Curator of the Common Room after the 'Bread and Butter Row'. Carroll helped Harcourt's wife organise her own photographic studio. It was to the Harcourt estate at Nuneham, with its boathouse and delightful river frontage, that Carroll sometimes took the Liddell and Acland girls on downstream rowing expeditions while he was devising the 'Alice' stories. P*

Hardy, Gathorne (Viscount Cranbrook) (1814–1906). Carroll's candidate, Hardy became M.P. for Oxford when he defeated Gladstone. He was appointed Home Secretary and Secretary for War in Disraeli's and Lord Salisbury's Conservative governments. P*

Hare, Julius Charles (1795–1855). Theologian and writer. Educated at Cambridge and incumbent at Herstmonceux, reportedly the richest living in England. A key figure in the introduction of German theological ideas, he was a financial supporter of the Macmillan brothers when they established their first business in Cambridge. F.D. Maurice married his sister and became leader of a theologically liberal circle that included Jowett and Kingsley. Eccentric, controversial and a prolific writer, Hare once wrote a footnote that was over 200 pages long. The character of the Mad March Hare at the Hatter's Party is in part a name joke. (See also Henry Kingsley.)

Hare, Augustus John Cuthbert (1834–1903). Impoverished nephew to Julius Hare. His biography of Julius' lesser known brother, Augustus, contained many anecdotes about Julius. An undergraduate at University College, Oxford, for a time he was a member of the Christ Church Common Room in the *ex-officio* position of secretary to Dr Stanley. Later in life, Hare became a prolific travel and gossip writer. He served as an important secret source for Carroll about the Liberal Reformers' plans, at Oxford.

Hargreaves, Reginald (1852–1926). Exact contemporary of Alice, who later married her. After graduating from Christ Church, he lived in Hampshire on the proceeds of a northern cotton fortune, played cricket for Hampshire, shot and fished extensively. Two of his and Alice's three sons died in the first World War.

Hawarden, Clementina, Lady (1822–1865). From an aristocratic Scottish background, married Viscount Hawarden in 1845. An important Victorian photographer, she specialized in portraits of women and girls in flowing costumes, generally set in interior poses in large-windowed, mirrored rooms. Carroll admired, purchased and occasionally tried to emulate her work.

Hooker, Joseph Dalton (1817–1911). Botanist, traveller and evolutionist, Hooker was appointed Director of Kew Gardens by the Queen on the death of his father in 1865. Several of his plant-finders acquired the opium habit in China and Sikkim. The Caterpillar smokes a Hookah. Though Hooker was not hooked, one or two of his botanical associates were. He helped Darwin take the difficult decision to publish his evolutionary theories.

Huxley, Thomas Henry (1825–1895). Controversialist and biologist, follower of Darwin. Later espoused Eugenics. From 1856 Huxley popularised science, bringing him in headlong collision with the anti-Evolutionists. His most determined antagonists were Richard Owen and Samuel Wilberforce, William Ewart Gladstone and Benjamin Disraeli. There is a strong facial resemblance between Huxley and the Ugly Duchess in 'Alice'. P★

Jelf, Richard William (1798–1871). Reactionary Canon of Christ Church. From 1844 he was also Principal of King's College, London. He banned Pusey from preaching from 1847–1849. Afterwards, he sacked the Professor of Theology F.D. Maurice for stepping over the opposite side of the theological line. He married Emmy, Countess of Schlippenbach, lady-in-waiting to a plain royal Duchess. His brother, William Edward, was a Student at Christ Church with him, and like him, was intolerant of undergraduates. P★

Jowett, Benjamin (1817–1893). Pre-eminent university reformer and translator of Plato, Jowett was a close friend of Cameron, Swinburne, Nightingale and the Tennysons. As Christ Church was home to Carroll, so Balliol was to Jowett. Initially High Church, Jowett withstood repeated accusations of religious scepticism. For years he was forbidden to preach in the University Church. His forum became the pulpit of Westminster Abbey and the national press. His alliance with Stanley and Liddell led him to become Master of Balliol College and University Vice Chancellor, appointments which signalled the eclipse of the High Church party. Alice's 'Father William' ballad depicts Jowett's uncompromising manner when cross-examined, with some precision.

Kingsley, Charles (1819–1975). Attended London University and Cambridge. From the age of 25 he was Rector of Eversley in Hampshire. From 1860 to 1869 he held the Professorship of Modern History at Cambridge. At first the author of Christian Socialist tracts and sermons, Kingsley turned to novels and stories for children (such as *The Water Babies*) and young people (*Hereward the Wake*). He married Fanny Grenfell in 1844. He and his friend Tom Hughes with their love of the outdoors, rowing and acts of schoolboy heroism, were evolutionists, 'Muscular Christians' and Christian Socialists. The one recorded meeting between Carroll and Kingsley took place at Macmillan's on 7th January 1869. Kingsley has to be a model for the Hatter.

Kingsley, Henry (1830–1876). Younger brother of Charles Kingsley. Henry was educated at Oxford but failed to take his degree. Instead he went to Australia in disgrace for opium-smoking. Here he failed to prosper, but turned his adventures to advantage when he came back, living at first at Eversley and becoming a novelist whose popularity briefly rivalled that of his brother. He married his second cousin, Maria Kingsley, in 1864 and spent his honeymoon on the Isle of Wight, where Carroll called on him. He bought a house at Wargrave on the Thames, where Carroll came to an untidy tea-party in the garden under a tree. Like his brother, Henry was over-energetic and smoked heavily. He admired Carroll and helped persuade Macmillan to publish 'Alice'. Has to be an original for the Hare. P★

Kitchin, G.W. (1827–1912). Student of Christ Church. Censor from 1861–63. A friend of Carroll's, Kitchin was initially a mathematician. Handsome and energetic, he left Christ Church to marry in 1863. Kitchin continued to live in Oxford where he brought up his children, of whom 'Xie' – Alexandra – was, with Alice, one the most beautiful of all Carroll's child models. P★

Liddell, Henry George (1811–1898). Student and Fellow of Christ Church, Liddell married Lorina Hannah Reeve in 1846. From that year until 1855 he was Headmaster of Westminster School. Dean of Christ Church until his retirement in 1891, he was co-compiler with Robert Scott (Master of Balliol during the Jowett controversy) of the Greek-English *Lexicon*. Liddell preceded Jowett as Vice-Chancellor from 1870–74. Elements of his character can be traced in Carroll's portrait of the King of Hearts and in the sketch of the dreaming Red King. His papers were not preserved for posterity but Carroll immortalised him. P★

Liddell, Lorina Hannah, born Reeve (1826–1910). Fifteen years younger than her husband, Alice's mother was six years older than Carroll. She married at the age of 20. Ina and Harry were born in 1847. James died young in 1850. Alice was born in 1852. The last of her ten children was born when she was 42. After leaving Christ Church on the Dean's retirement, she lived at Ascot but continued to dominate Oxford functions. Determined and socially ambitious, the Queen of Hearts with her croquet parties and (social) executions resembles the woman who removed her daughter from Carroll's doting presence and destroyed their letters – to Alice's lasting regret. P★

Liddon, Henry Parry (1829–1890). Carroll's closest friend at Christ Church. They travelled together to Russia via Cologne in 1867. A disciple of Pusey, he was a famous High Church Anglican orator who would practise preaching against the roar of breaking waves in his native Pembrokeshire. From 1854 to 1859, he was Vice Principal at Cuddesdon Theological College. He resigned at Wilberforce's request to become Principal of St Edmund's Hall. An uncompromising Puseyite, he refused Dean Stanley's invitations to preach at Westminster Abbey. The Mock Turtle with its 'Lid On' must have been closely acquainted with Carroll's conscientious position on 'Alice', and perhaps persuaded him to publish 'An Easter Greeting' to present it. P★

Lutwidge, R.W. Skeffington (Uncle Skeffington) (1802–1873). Brother of Carroll's mother, his favourite uncle and family confidant. Interested in telescopes, photography and other inventions, he lived near Tottenham Court Road and then, in considerable style, in Onslow Square. He was a barrister who became a government Commissioner for Lunacy. P★

MacDonald, George (1824–1905). Scottish author and poet, now best known for his children's books, *At the Back of the North Wind* (1871 in book form), *The Princess and the Goblin*, etc. MacDonald and his wife Louisa had eleven children. Carroll became friends of both parents and children and attended Maurice's services at Vere Street Chapel with them when he was in London. A charming if stiff photograph of Carroll shows him lying in the midst of this happy family on the lawn of their house in Regent's Park. P★

MacDonald, Greville (1856–1944). Son and biographer of *George MacDonald and his Wife*, befriended by Carroll when he (Greville) was modelling at Alexander Munro's studio. Loved 'Alice' on an early reading of the manuscript. Later a doctor. P★

Macmillan, Alexander (1818–96). Carroll's patient publisher in a beneficial relationship. Carroll paid all up front costs and Macmillan took a commission on sales. The Macmillan business was first established in Cambridge when Alexander and his brother showed themselves sympathetic to Julius Hare's theological ideas. Thereafter he published the works of Maurice, Hughes, the Kingsley brothers and Carroll, by which time his expanding business had moved to London. He was introduced to Carroll by Henry Kingsley, a talent-scout for him.

Manning, Henry Edward (1808–1892). A leading Anglican theologian until he was forty, Manning was an intimate of Gladstone's and worked with Pusey, Newman and Keble to create The Oxford Movement. In 1850 he became a Roman Catholic, causing shock waves through the Anglican Church. His success in making converts, rivalled only by that of Newman, led to his election as Cardinal in 1865. He was brilliant, demanding and intolerant of rivals including Newman, whose conversion preceded his. He provides a compelling model for the Red Queen.

Maurice, Frederick Denison (1805–1872). Theologian, historian and social reformer. He was forced to resign both his Chairs at King's College, London, by the High Church Canon Jelf for his controversial views on eternal damnation. He also resigned (although later took up working there again) as Principal of Queen's College, the pioneering girls' school. He was a close friend of Tennyson's. His bestselling writing on issues of Christian Socialism and Christian unity were published by Macmillan. Carroll admired him and officiated with him after his disgrace at services at St Peter's, Vere Street in London. In 1866 Maurice was elected Professor of Moral Philosophy at Cambridge. Known as 'Master' by Kingsley, Hughes, Woolner, Rossetti, Maurice served as model for the Dormouse in 'Alice'. P★

Millais, (Sir) John Everett (1829–1896). At the age of 19 Millais was a founder of the Pre-Raphaelite Brotherhood with D. G. Rossetti, Holman Hunt and others. An Associate of the Royal Academy in 1853, Millais married Effie Gray in 1854 after she had divorced Ruskin on grounds of non-consummation. Later Carroll photographed the Millais at their Kensington house. As the steam went out of the Pre-Raphaelite movement, Millais became wealthy by choosing commercially appealing subjects for his paintings. Carroll parodied Millais' self-seeking in Alice's Royal Academy skit, 'The Voice of the Lobster'. P★

Morris, William (1834–1896). Poet, artist, designer and socialist commentator, Morris was committed to medieval design, art and craftsmanship. Befriending Rossetti and Burne-Jones as an Oxford undergraduate, he worked with them on the murals at the new Oxford Union. He funded the design and manufacturing firm of Morris, Marshall, Faulkner & Co in 1861 and is parodied as the Owl consumed by a Panther in the poem Alice recites to the Gryphon.

Munro, Alexander (1825–1871). Sculptor, friend of the Aclands' who owned a bust of Dante by him. Carved a bas-relief of King Arthur for the Oxford Union. Lived in Belgravia where Carroll had 'carte blanche' to photograph sculptures and store photographic equipment. Without the Munro connection via the Aclands, the reserved though stage-struck Carroll would have lacked a London artistic and literary base. P★

Newman, John Henry (1801–1890). College Tutor at Oriel College, Oxford, and author of *Tract XC* of the tracts which started the Oxford Movement, Newman was ordained a Roman Catholic priest in 1847. Charles Kingsley attacked him as 'a liar' in 1864. In response to this attack he published an *Apologia* for his own religious transformation. His highly personal faith and practice delayed his election to Cardinal until 1879. His personality and literary styles are recognisable in the White Queen. He acknowledged a gift of Carroll's stories sent by one of Carroll's child-friends by noting that Carroll's theology was in keeping with that of the Oxford Movement.

Owen, (Sir) Richard (1804–1892). Key figure in the development of the systematics of vertebrate anatomy and a Fellow of the Royal Society. Controversial, virulent in his arguments, Owen was a favourite of the Queen. He was interested in extinct birds, including Dodos, and a photograph of him shows a balding man in academic robes half the height of the skeleton of *Dinornis Maximus* but still smiling. He was an opponent of Darwin and Huxley, but his dismissive attitude to their evidence backfired on him when his briefing failed to protect Bishop Wilberforce from Huxley's powers of induction. There is a close facial and personality likeness between Owen and the Cook in the Duchess's kitchen.

Pater, Walter (1839–1894). Aesthete and scholar, Fellow of Brasenose, and proponent of the doctrine that the intense experience of art for its own sake must be the goal of human life, as he taught it had been in Classical Greece. Carroll cut Pater down to size as the Carpenter in *Alice*. (See also Ruskin.)

Prout, Thomas Jones (1824–1909). Student of the Old Foundation of Christ Church, like Carroll. Leader of the movement which began in 1857 for Christ Church tutors to wrest more rights from the Dean and the Canons. Like Liddell, Prout came from Westminster School. The Christ Church Reform Bill passed through Parliament in 1867. The complaints of The Mouse with the Long Tail in *Alice* match his arguments against the Dean and Canons as drafted in part by Carroll. P★

Pusey, Edward Bouverie (1800–1882). Canon of Christ Church and Regius Professor of Hebrew from the age of 28. Key figure in the Oxford Movement. His notoriety increased when a sermon, *The Holy Eucharist,*

A Comfort to the Penitent, he preached in the University Church at Oxford led to his suspension. 18,000 copies of the sermon sold in pamphlet form. Supported by Liddon and Carroll and opposed by Maurice, he attempted to have Jowett condemned for heresy. His entrenched Anglicanism led him to public opposition to the Roman Catholic revival led by Cardinals Newman and Manning. He is the likely original for the Sheep. P★

Rejlander, Oscar (1813–1875). Victorian photographer patronised by Prince Albert. He specialised in large, composite set pieces and vivid portraits. A mentor to Carroll who collected his photographs, he also agreed to teach Carroll his technical secrets for a fee. His best portrait photography has an immediacy which Carroll quickly mastered.

Richmond, George (1809–1896) & his son, William Blake (1842–1921). The father painted in watercolour delicate portraits of Victorians and their children, including Liddell, Swinburne, some of the Gladstones and Jowett. The son, named after Willam Blake whom his father knew, was a follower of Ruskin's. He posed the Liddell girls at the Great Orme's Head as his first formal commission and succeeded Ruskin as Professor of Art at Oxford.

Rossetti, Christina (1830–1894). Two years younger than her brother, D.G. Rossetti, she, like him, was a poet from a young age. As a girl she posed for her brother, Holman Hunt, Millais and other Pre-Raphaelites. Her children's poetry was admired by Carroll and she was photographed by him with other members of her family. Like Carroll, she never married. Like him, she was a High Church Anglican with religious scruples. Carroll probably knew this reserved woman better than his diary entries suggest. P★

Rossetti, Dante Gabriel (1828–1882). One of the founders of the Pre-Raphaelite Brotherhood, painter and poet, he married Acland's patient, Elizabeth Siddal, who later died of laudanum poisoning after the loss of her new-born child in 1862. Photographed by Carroll, who took pictures of Rossetti's drawings and drawing collections, he wrote limericks about his friends for their amusement. It was he who discovered Edward Fitzgerald's *Rubaiyat of Omar Khayyam*. He may have seen that he and other Pre-Raphaelites were spoofed by Alice when she recited 'The Voice of the Lobster' to the Gryphon. P★

Ruskin, John (1819–1900). Philosopher, art critic and artist. An early patron of the Pre-Raphaelites, he broke with Millais in 1861 and with Rossetti thereafter. He was an intimate of Acland's in the 1850s. He became Slade Professor of Fine Art at Oxford in 1871 but left over the vivisection issue. Appears in *Wonderland* as the Gryphon and in *Looking-glass* as the Walrus. P★

Salisbury, 3rd Marquis of (R.A.T. Gascoyne-Cecil) (1830–1903). Two years older than Carroll and at Christ Church as an undergraduate. Chancellor of Oxford and Prime Minister. Gladstone's chief opponent after the death of Disraeli. The Salisburys liked *Wonderland* and that led to photography of Salisbury, his wife and children and a friendship as privileged as any enjoyed by Lorina Liddell. Salisbury asked Carroll's help in finding a mathematics tutor for one of his sons in 1870. Though the Liddells avoided Carroll at Royal Academy opening exhibitions, the Cecils enjoyed them in his company. P★

Stanley, Arthur Penrhyn (1815–1881). First cousin to Lord Stanley, pupil of Dr Arnold of Rugby before Lewis Carroll and his brothers went there. He became Arnold's biographer and Canon of Christ Church. His diplomatic pull in high places made him invaluable to Dean Liddell as a university reformer. In 1863, he married Lady Bruce, the Queen's Lady in Waiting and became Dean of Westminster. He held advanced views. His brother, Owen Stanley, a naval surveying captain, took T. H. Huxley on board the *Rattlesnake* to Australian waters as a biologist at the start of his distinguished scientific career. Carroll, Pusey and Liddon feared Stanley's influence with the Queen and in Parliament with some justification. He is one likely original for the mysterious Cheshire Cat. P★

Swinburne, Algernon Charles (1837–1909). One of Jowett's brilliant protégés at Oxford, Swinburne the poet later lived in Rossetti's house on Cheyne Walk in Chelsea at the time Carroll was writing 'Alice'. He modelled for the Arthurian murals in the Oxford Union with his halo of flying red hair. By 1865, his carnal, rhythmic verses were widely read to the scandal of many.

Taylor, Tom (1817–1880). Lawyer, contributor to *Punch* and prolific writer of light plays, he became editor of *Punch* in 1874 and retained the position until his death. Helpful to and tolerant of the exacting Carroll, he became his conduit to *Punch* and to Tenniel. He lived in Wandsworth. His wife was a composer of theatrical music. His farces and domestic comedies were enjoyed by Carroll and child friends. He posed in American Civil War uniform for Carroll and, for Carroll, his little son dressed up as a tiny King Henry VIII at a children's party. P★

Tenniel, (Sir) John (1820–1914). Illustrator and leading political cartoonist for *Punch*, Tenniel was responsible for the weekly 'big-cut' cartoon in that satirical journal was paid by Carroll to illustrate both 'Alice' books. Contrary to common supposition, Tenniel admitted late in life that he had always been a Tory, like Carroll. He was knighted by Gladstone.

Tennyson, Alfred, Lord (1809–1892). Poet and Poet Laureate from 1850. Born in Lincolnshire, educated at Cambridge. In 1834 he wrote T*he Two Voices*, parodied by Carroll as *The Three* . . .). From 1853 he rented, then purchased Farringford on the Isle of Wight. Offered a peerage by Gladstone after the two of them went on a cruise of northern waters in 1882. Photographed on several occasions by Carroll, as was his wife Emily and their two pampered sons, Lionel and Hallam. Portrayed by Carroll as the White Knight. P★

Terry, Ellen Alice (1848–1928). English actress whose acting ability was first noted in Carroll's diaries at the time she reached the age of eight. He spent four days photographing her with her sisters in their home in London at the time that her marriage to George Frederick Watts collapsed. Carroll continued to write poems and riddles with allusions to her histrionic grace. She appeared with her elder sister Kate in benefits for *Punch* in the 1860s and 1870s. Carroll's sketch of the Tiger-lily in 'Alice' was inspired by his years of secret observation of her burgeoning talent as an actress. P★

Thackeray, William Makepeace (1811–1863). In Thackeray, founder editor of *Punch*, novelist and humorist, two circles familiar to Carroll when he wrote 'Alice' intersect. The Isle of Wight circle round Cameron and Tennyson, of which Thackeray and his daughters were members, could explain the facial likeness between Thackeray and the White King and Queen, a 'cover' for Carroll's spoof of Newman and Cameron. As Tenniel worked with Thackeray weekly on *Punch* until 1863, their workaday *Punch* connection could equally well have inspired the White King and Queen's likeness.

Victoria Regina (1819–1901), Queen of England. Diarist, Mother of the Empire, Queen of England and amateur photographer, the Queen was an early exponent of the cross-word puzzle. She mourned her late husband, the Prince Consort from 1861, when he died, with full formality. *Punch* criticised her joylessness after the official mourning had run its course in 1877. Carroll did not ingratiate himself with her. He wrote a spoof letter purporting to be from her to a child-friend. The elaborate court she travelled with gave Carroll and Alice personal experience of the royal paraphernalia he portrayed in *Wonderland*.

Watts, George Frederick (1817–1904). Painter and sculptor. Hard working and reclusive, often in bad health, he married Ellen Terry in 1864. He abandoned her, but did not divorce her until 1877. He did not marry again until 1886. He was a portraitist like Millais, of Gladstone and Tennyson. His London base was Little Holland House, where he painted Terry in her wedding dress in 'Choosing'. 'The Briary' at Freshwater on the Isle of Wight was his country home from 1873. He may be portrayed as the unsupportive Willow in the 'Garden of Live Flowers'.

Wilberforce, Samuel, (1805–1873). Fox-hunting Bishop of Oxford, later Bishop of Winchester Son of the Emancipator, William Wilberforce. Consecrated Bishop of Oxford in 1845, at the time Pusey was banned from preaching and Newman defected to the Roman Catholic Church with several members of Wilberforce's own family. A tireless diocesan administrator and debater in the House of Lords, he could not keep his finger from many pies. In his attack on evolutionary theory he underestimated Huxley's skill in debate. In his attempt to revive Church courts, he fell foul of Benjamin Jowett. His style of rhetoric was captured by Carroll in the slippery, illogical opinions of the Ugly Duchess. P★

Woolner, Thomas (1825–1892). Sculptor, radical and founder Pre-Raphaelite. He left England in 1852 for the Australian gold fields, a departure depicted in Ford Madox Brown's *The Last of England*. He returned to England two years later when his bust of Tennyson helped make his name. Woolner advised Carroll to take life-classes if he wished to be an illustrator, having examined his sketches for 'Alice' in 1863. The list of people who sat for Woolner included Combe, Acland, Gladstone, Kingsley, Maurice, Newman and the Queen. The engraving of his bust of Kingsley, frontispiece to Fanny Kingsley's memoirs, led to our identification of the Mad Hatter. P★

Sources and Bibliography

This list of printed sources refers mainly to biographies, not to general Victorian histories, nor to histories of children's literature or books about Victorian photography. Specific literary works discussed in the text, such as Tennyson's poems or Kingsley's novels, are not included. Nor is this a complete list of all books relating to Carroll and his period. It is rather a list of the books that led us to the identity of some of the characters concealed in 'Alice'. *Punch* illustrations from 1855–1875 also provided vital sources for individuals caricatured in Carroll's world, but are not listed. Source notes for Carroll's diary entries and letters are given first and the bibliographical list follows.

CARROLL'S DIARIES AND LETTERS

Reference page in this text is given at the start of each entry and the source reference at the end. 'LG' are the Lancelyn Green edited Diaries (volumes I and II). Letters refers to Morton Cohen's edited *Letters*. BL stands for the British Library MS diaries.

15. **After early failures** . . . LG I, 83–86.
16. **Mayor of Leeds** . . . Letters I, 4.
18. **Gladstone** . . . LG I, 231.
21. **Gathorne Hardy** . . . LG I, 254–5, 260.
24. **He had sent** . . . LGII, 266.
26. **Wild Agitator**. LG I, 277.
31. **I had a** . . . LG II, 128–9.
32. **Dean Liddell's early years.** LG I, 51.
33. **Syllabus reform** LG I, 209.
33. **Professor of Medicine, Henry Acland** . . . LG I, 128.
33. **Hiawatha** . . . LG I,129–30.
35. **Mrs Liddell cut Carroll off** . . . LG I, 215, also 228.
42. **Rejlander** . . . LG I, 194.
43. **Alice Donkin** . . . LG I, 187.
43. **Crown Prince of Denmark**, LG 1, 207.

43. **Weld** . . . LG I, 118.

43. **Xie Kitchin** . . . LG II, 281.

44. **In the main Library** . . . LG I, 124–8

56. **Alice Jane Donkin** . . . GLI, 303

56. **Alice Donkin** . . . LG II, 583 (Index).

58. **On each occasion** . . . BL diary.

65. **Royal grandees** . . . LG I, 163, 197–8, 207.

69. **April 25** . . . LG I, 83, 84.

74. **My dear Mrs Hargreaves,** Letters II, 876.

84. **Rejlander** . . . LG I, 194.

90. **Called on** . . . LG I, 140.

91. **Carroll's second** . . . LG II, 405.

91. **. . . took to Prout's** . . . LG II, 405.

95. **Carrolliana** . . . LG I, 227.

100. **Continuing** . . . LG II, 321.

103. **. . . in 1862** . . . LG I, 181.

108. **Thomas Combe** . . . LG I, 180.

108. **. . . arranged the layouts of Wonderland,** LG I, 199.

110. **Christmas in 1891** . . . LG II, 488.

110. **Called on the Stevens** . . . LG II, 491.

114. **All passengers** . . . ms from Houghton Library, Harvard

115. **Dined** . . . LG I, 97.

115. **Visited** . . . LG I, 98.

118. **First exhibition** . . . LG I, 99.

119. **Now at** . . . LG I, 99.

123. **Charles . . . had rebuffed** . . . LG I, 188.

129. **Finished Alton Locke** . . . LG I, 71.

129. **Finished Hypatia** . . . LG I, 100.

142. **Read Maud** . . . LG I, 65.

142. **I . . . walked** . . . LG I, 186.

143. **We talked** . . . LG I, 187.

144. **I have seen** . . . Letters I, 53.

144. **On the 1864** . . . LG I, 220.

145. **The sale** . . . BL.

151. **I was shown** . . . LG I, 125.

153. **. . . he purchased prints** . . . LG I, 200.

156. **During his 1862** . . . Letters I, 55.

156. **Called on Mrs** . . . LG I, 221.

156. **In the evening** . . . Letters I, 66.

157. **The next two** . . . Letters I, 67

157. **. . . a few days later** . . . LG I, 221.

162. **Carroll knew** . . . LG I, 220.

165. **For eight years** . . . LG I, 88.

165. **For that pose** . . . LG I, 223.

166. **With the Terrys** . . . LG I, 261; LG II, 326.

167. **The Needles Hotel** . . . LG I, 221

169. **My dear Maggie** . . . Letters I, 115.

170. **This was** . . . LG I, 178.

175. **'should you be disposed . . . '** Letters I, 63.

178. **'Little Jack'** . . . LG I, 228, also 231 & 233.

180. **Two books** . . . LG I, 243.

181. **Promulgation** . . . LG I, 165.
197. **There is** . . . BL
197. **Three days** . . . LG I, 196.
197. **These entries** . . . LG I, 196.
200. **a Full Priest** . . . LG I, 188.
202. **May 19** . . . BL.
206. **Carroll made** . . . BL.
206. **An idea** . . . BL.
209. **. . . Liddon.** LG I, 216.
210. **. . . Church Mission** . . . LG I, 261. (see also *The Russian Journal*, full title in Bibliography).
218. **. . . This small figure . . .** LG I, 179.
222. **. . . Of the Mice** . . . LG II, 297, (also Decision to write about Ch affair)
224. **27th July** . . . LG I, 201.
225. **Apparently** . . . LG I, 192, 200, 244, 253; LG II, 266
227. **Tenniel** . . . LG I, 210
227. **Taylor** . . . LG I, 201, 202.
227. **MacDonalds** . . . LG I, 154, 184, 200 (also see LG II, index)
228. **During the winter** . . . LG I, 139
229. **Saw Millais'** . . . LG I, 177
229. **Took Mr Holman Hunt** . . . LG II, 324

230. **'Her First'** . . . LG I, 213.
231. **'Sir Isumbras** . . . LG I, 114.
232. **Rossetti** . . . LG I, 201–5.
233. **Alice's perverted** . . . see note 1 in Letters I, 81.
235. **It was the Aclands** . . . LG I, 133.
235. **The first recorded** . . . LG I, 94.
236. **Madeira** . . . LG I, 98
237. **Dr Acland called** . . . LG I, 111.
239. **Invented and wrote** . . . LG I, 210.
259. **Left the papers** . . . LG I, 185.
259. **In the morning** . . . LG I, 186.
261. **At work at** . . . LG I, 185.
261. **Richmond** . . . LG I, 228.
266. **His opinion was** . . . LG I, 188.
268. **Skeffington** . . . LG I, 232.
269. **Alice Raikes** . . . LG II, 272.
270. **Belgrave Place** . . . LG I, 142.
270. **Greville MacDonald** . . . LG I, 154.
271. **Munro** . . . LG I, 201–3
271. **Belgrave Place** . . . Letters I, 58–60.
272. **Four of the happiest** . . . LG I, 233.

BIBLIOGRAPHY

Abbott, Evelyn and Campbell. Lewis, *The Life and Letters of Benjamin Jowett. M.A., Master of Balliol College, Oxford*, two volumes, E.P. Dutton, New York, 1897
Annan, Noel, *Leslie Stephen: The Godless Victorian*, Weidenfeld and Nicholson, London, 1984

Sources and Bibliography

Ashwell, A.R., *Life of the Right Reverend Samuel Wilberforce, D.D. with Selections from his Diaries and Correspondence*, 3 volumes, John Murray, London, 1880

Atlay, J.B., *Sir Henry Wentworth Acland, Bart. KCB. FRS. Regius Professor of Medicine in the University of Oxford: A Memoir*, Smith, Elder & Co, London, 1903

Batey, Mavis, *Alice's Adventures in Oxford*, Pitkin Pictorial, London, 1980

Bill, J.F.A. and Mason, J.F., *Christ Church and Reform, 1850–67* Clarendon Press, Oxford, 1970

Blake, Robert, *Disraeli*, St Martin's Press, New York, 1966

Bloomfield, Paul, *William Morris*, Barker, London, 1934

Bowman, Isa (et al.), *The Story of Lewis Carroll Told for Young People*, J.M. Dent, London, 1899

Browne, Janet, *Charles Darwin: Voyaging*, Jonathan Cape, London, 1995

Burd, Van Aken, *John Ruskin and Rose La Touche: Her unpublished diaries of 1861 and 1867*, Clarendon Press, Oxford, 1979

Burne-Jones, Georgiana, *Memorials of Edward Burne-Jones*, 2 volumes, Macmillan, New York, 1904

Caine, Hal, *Recollections of Rossetti*, Cassell, London, 1928 (re-issued with an introduction by Jan Marsh, Century, 1990)

Carroll, Bibliographical Reference: *The Lewis Carroll Handbook, being a New Version of: The Literature of the Rev. C.L. Dodgson* by Sydney Herbert Williams and Falconer Madan revised and augmented by R. Lancelyn Green, 1962 and further revised by Dennis Crutch, Dawson, Archon Books, for the Lewis Carroll Society, 1979 (This gives a full listing of Carroll's works)

Carroll, Diaries: *The Diaries of Lewis Carroll*, in two volumes, edited by Roger Lancelyn Green, Oxford University Press, Oxford, 1954.

Carroll, Diaries: see Collingwood for three 'lost' entries.

Carroll, Diaries: *The Private Journals of Charles Lutwidge Dodgson*, Vol I, edited by Edward Wakeling, 1993. This publication by the Lewis Carroll Society marks the beginning of the project to make available in printed form an unexpurgated version of the manuscript diaries.

Carroll, Diaries: *The Russian Journal and Other Selections from the Works of Lewis Carroll*, edited by John Francis McDermott, E.P. Dutton, New York, 1935

Carroll, Letters: *A Selection from the Letters of Lewis Carroll to His Child-Friends*, edited by Evelyn M. Hatch, Macmillan, London, 1933

Carroll, Letters: *Lewis Carroll and the House of Macmillan*, edited by Morton N. Cohen & Anita Gandolfo, Cambridge University Press, 1987

Carroll, Letters: *The Letters of Lewis Carroll* in two volumes, edited by Morton N. Cohen, Macmillan, London 1979

Sources and Bibliography

Carroll, Papers about: *Aspects of Alice: Lewis Carroll's Dreamchild as seen through the Critics' Looking-glasses, 1865–1971*, Gollancz, London, 1972

Carroll, Papers about: *Alice in Wonderland: Lewis Carroll/Alice's Adventures in Wonderland, Through the Looking Glass, The Hunting of the Snark: Backgrounds, Essays in Criticism* edited by Donald J. Gray (Norton Critical Edition series) 1971. (Note: these include the hard-to-find articles by William Empson, Shane Leslie and Alice herself, together with essays or sections of essays by Virginia Woolf, W. H. Auden, Walter de la Mare and others.)

Carroll, Papers about: *Jabberwocky: The Journal of the Lewis Carroll Society*, edited by Selwyn Goodacre. Ongoing papers about Lewis Carroll's life and works.

Carroll, Photographs: *Lewis Carroll, Photographer of Children: Four Nude Studies*, pamphlet by Morton N. Cohen, Clarkson Potter, New York, 1978.

Carroll, Photographs: *Lewis Carroll Observed: A Collection of Unpublished Photographs, Drawings, Poetry and New Essays* edited by Edward Guiliano, Clarkson Potter, New York, 1976.

Carroll, Photographs: *Lewis Carroll: Victorian Photographer*, introduction by Helmut Gernsheim. Thames and Hudson, London, 1980. Includes many of the important child photographs.

Carroll, Photographs: *Lewis Carroll at Christ Church*, introductory note by Morton M. Cohen, reproduces some of the Christ Church Album photographs, National Portrait Gallery, 1974.

Carroll, Works: *The Annotated Alice: Alice's Adventures in Wonderland & Through the Looking-glass* with an Introduction and Notes by Martin Gardner, Clarkson Potter, New York, 1960

Carroll, Works: *The Complete Works of Lewis Carroll*, Introduction by Alexander Woollcott, Nonesuch Press, London, 1939. Not complete, but extensive.

Carroll, Works: *Lewis Carroll's Games and Puzzles*, edited by Edward Wakeling, Dover, New York, 1992

Carroll, Works: *The Pamphlets of Lewis Carroll*: Volume I. The Oxford Pamphlets, edited by Edward Wakeling, University Press of Virginia, Charlottesville, 1993

Carroll, Works: *Symbolic Logic Parts I and II*, 1896, reprinted by Dover Publications, New York. The best edition was annotated by William Warren Bartley and published by Clarkson N. Potter, New York, 1977

Chadwick, Owen, *Newman*, in 'Past Masters' series, Oxford University Press, 1984

Cheshire, David F., *Portrait of Ellen Terry*, Amber Lane, Oxford, 1989

Chitty, (Lady) Susan: *The Beast and the Monk: A Life of Charles Kingsley*, Mason Charter, New York, 1974

Sources and Bibliography

Clark, Anne, *The Real Alice*, Schocken, New York, 1981

Clark, Anne, *Lewis Carroll: A Biography*, Schocken, New York, 1979

Clark, Ronald W., *The Huxleys*, Heinemann, London, 1968

Cohen, Morton, N. (Ed.), *The Letteres of Lewis Carroll* (2 vols.), Macmillan, London, 1979

Collingwood, Stuart Dodgson, *The Life and Letters of Lewis Carroll (Rev. C.L. Dodgson)*, T. Fisher Unwin, London, 1898

Colvin, Howard, *Unbuilt Oxford*, Yale University Press, New Haven, 1983. Describes much that was built as well, including the Natural History Museum.

Daly, Gay, *Pre-Raphaelites in Love*, Ticknor & Fields, New York, 1989

Darwin, Charles, *Journal of Researches into the Geology and Natural History of the Various Countries Visited by HMS Beagle*, with Fitzroy, Captain Robert, *Narrative of the Surveying Voyages of HMS Adventure and Beagle and the Beagle's Circumnavigation of the Globe*, Henry Colburn, London, 1839

Darwin, Charles, *The Descent of Man* (2 vols.), 1871; reprinted, Princeton University Press, 1981

Davies, Rev. J. Llewellyn (Ed.), *The Working Men's College, 1854–1904*, Macmillan, London, 1904. (Davies was the father of the boys James Barrie adopted, for whom *Peter Pan* was written.)

de Maré, Eric, *The Victorian Woodblock Illustrators*, Gordon Fraser, London, 1980

Desmond, Adrian and Moore, James, *Darwin*, Michael Joseph, London, 1991

Ellis, S.M., *Henry Kingsley: Towards a Vindication, 1830–1876*, Grant Richards, London, 1931

Empson, William, 'The Child as Swain' in *Some Versions of the Pastoral*, Chatto and Windus, London, 1935

Engen, Rodney, *Sir John Tenniel: Alice's White Knight*, Scolar Press, Aldershot, 1991

Faber, Geoffrey, *Jowett: A Portrait with a Background*, Faber, London, 1957

Feiling, Keith, *In Christ Church Hall*, Macmillan, London, 1960. Includes essays on Pusey and Ruskin.

Fitzgerald, Edward, *Letters of Edward Fitzgerald* edited by J.M. Cohen, University of Illinois Press, Champaign, 1960

Fitzgerald, Penelope, *Edward Burne-Jones*, Michael Joseph, London, 1975

Foister, Susan, *Cardinal Newman 1801–90: A Centenary Exhibition*, National Portrait Gallery, London 1990

Fuller, Hester Thackeray, *Three Freshwater Friends*, 1933, pamphlet, reprinted by Hunnyhill Publications, Isle of Wight, 1992 (for Cameron, Tennyson and Watts on the Isle of Wight).

Gattégno, Jean, *Lewis Carroll: Une Vie*, Editions du Seuil, Paris, 1974

Gernsheim: See also Carroll, Photographs.

Gernsheim, Helmut, *Lewis Carroll: Photographer*, originally published in 1949 by Max Parrish, London, expanded in 1969 and still in print, Dover Books, New York. This reprints many of the important photographs held in Texas and discusses Carroll as a photographer. It also lists many, but not all, of the figures of the day who sat for Carroll. There is no complete book of Carroll's photographs.

Gernsheim, Helmut, *Julia Margaret Cameron: Her Life and Photographic Art*, Aperture Press, New York, 1987

Gielgud, John, *An Actor and His Time*, Sidgwick and Jackson, London, 1979. Contains personal reminiscences of Kate and Ellen Terry by their most distinguished descendant.

Gladstone, Penelope A., *Portrait of a Family: The Gladstones*, Lyster, Lancashire, 1989

Gordon, Colin, *Beyond The Looking-glass*, Hodder and Stoughton, London, 1982. On the Liddell and Hargreaves families.

Grant Duff, Right Hon. Sir Mountstuart E., *Out of the Past: Some Biographical Essays*, 2 volumes, John Murray, London, 1903.

Graves, Charles L., *Life and Letters of Alexander Macmillan*, Macmillan, London, 1910

Green, Roger Lancelyn, see Carroll, Diaries.

Hare, Augustus and Julius C., *Guesses at the Truth by Two Brothers*, Ticknor and Field, Boston, 1865 edition.

Hare, A. J. C., *Memorials of A Quiet Life*, Strahan, New York, 1873. The quiet life is Augustus Hare's, but Augustus' brother Julius' noisier life is also reported.

Hinton, Brian, *Immortal Faces: Julia Margaret Cameron on the Isle of Wight*, Isle of Wight County Press, 1992

Hodnet, Edward, *Image and Text: Studies in the Illustration of English Literature*, Scolar Press, London, 1982

Hudson, Derek, *Lewis Carroll*, Constable, London, 1954. (Illustrated, 1976.)

Huxley, Francis, *The Raven and the Writing-desk*, Harper & Row, New York, 1976

Huxley, T.H., *Man's Place in Nature and Other Anthropological Essays*, Macmillan, London, 1894

Huxley, Leonard, *Life and Letters of Sir Joseph Dalton Hooker OM GCSI*, John Murray, London, 1918

Johnson, John Octavius, *Life and Letters of Henry Parry Liddon DD, DCL, LLD, Canon of St Paul's Cathedral, and sometime Ireland Professor of Exegesis in the University of Oxford*, Longmans, London 1904

Jowett, Benjamin, *Essays and Reviews: Recent inquiries in theology by eminent English Churchmen*, 5th edition, Longmans, London, 1861. Jowett's long essay is 'On the Interpretation of Scripture'.

Jowett, Benjamin, *College Sermons by the Late Benjamin Jowett, M.A., Master of Balliol College*, edited by the Very Rev. The Hon. W.H. Freemantle, M.A., 2nd edition, John Murray, London, 1895

Ker, Ian, *John Henry Newman: A Biography*, Oxford University Press, 1988

Kingsley, Charles, *Cheap Clothes and Nasty*, 1850, reprinted in *Prose Masterpieces from Modern Essayists*, Putnam, New York, 1893

Kingsley, Henry, *Tales of Old Travel re-Narrated . . .*, 5th edition, Macmillan, London, 1876

Kingsley, Charles, *Charles Kingsley: His Letters and Memories of his Life* 'edited by his wife', viz by Fanny Kingsley, (2 vols.), Kegan Paul, London, 1877

Kitchin, G. W., *Ruskin in Oxford and Other Studies*, John Murray, London, 1904

Leslie, Shane, *Henry Edward Manning: His Life and Labours*, Burns and Oates, 1921

Liddell, H.G. and Scott, R., *A Greek-English Lexicon*, Clarendon Press, various editions, and still in use.

Lilly, W .S., *Characteristics, Political, Philosophical and Religious of Henry Edward, Cardinal Archbishop of Westminster*, Burns and Oates, London, 1885

MacDonald, Greville, *Reminiscences of a Specialist*, George Allen and Unwin, London, 1932

Magnus, Sir Philip, *Gladstone: A Biography*, John Murray, London, 1954

Manning, Henry Edward, *Sermons* in 2 volumes, 2nd edition, James Burns, London, 1846

Manning, Henry Edward, *The Unity of the Church*, 2nd edition, John Murray, London, 1845

Martin, Robert B., *Tennyson: The Unquiet Heart*, Clarendon Press, Oxford, 1980

Maurice, Frederick, *The Life and Correspondence of Frederick Denison Maurice*, 2 volumes, Scribners, New York, 1884

Maurois, André, *Disraeli*, translated by Hamish Miles. Penguin Books, London, 1938

Milner, Frank, *The Pre-Raphaelites: Pre-Raphaelite paintings and drawings in Merseyside Collections*, National Galleries and Museums of Merseyside, 1985

Mitford, Nancy, (ed.): *The Stanleys of Alderly: Their Letters between the Years 1851–1865*, Hamish Hamilton, London, re-issued 1968

Moneypenney, W.F. and Buckle, G.E., *The Life of Benjamin Disraeli, Earl of Beaconsfield*, 6 volumes, 1910–1920

Morley, John, *The Life of William Ewart Gladstone*, 3 volumes, John Murray, London, 1903.

Norman, Edward, *The Victorian Christian Socialists*, Cambridge University Press, 1987

Sources and Bibliography

North, F.J., *Sir Charles Lyell: Interpreter of the Principles of Geology*, Arthur Barker, London, 1965

Oman, Sir Charles, *Memories of Victorian Oxford*, Methuen, London, 1941

Ovenden, Graham, (ed.), *Pre-Raphaelite Photography*, Academy, London, 1972

Owen, Rev. Richard, *The Life of Richard Owen by his Grandson*, 2 volumes, John Murray, London, 1894

Pattison, Mark, Late Rector of Lincoln College Oxford, *Memoirs of an Oxford Don*, re-issue edited and introduced by Vivien H.H. Green, Cassell, London, 1988

Peters, Cuthbert, *Thackeray's Universe: Shifting Worlds of Imagination and Reality*, Oxford University Press, New York, 1987.

Prothero, R.E. (Lord Ernle), *Life and Letters of Dean Stanley*, John Murray, London, 1894

Pusey, Edward Bouverie, *Selections from the Writings of Edward Bouverie Pusey, D.D.*, Rivingtons, London, 1883

Pusey, Edward Bouverie, *First Letter to the Very Rev. J.H. Newman in Explanation chiefly in regard to the Reverential Love due to the Ever-Blessed Theotokos and the Doctrine of Her Immaculate Conception*, Rivingtons, London, 1869

Raven, Charles E., *Christian Socialism, 1848–1854*, Macmillan, London, 1920

Read, Benedict, *Millais*, Medici Society Pamphlet, 1983

Reid, T. Wemyss, *The Life, Letters and Friendships of Richard Monckton Milnes, first Lord Houghton*, 2 volumes, 3rd edition, Cassell, London, 1891

Rose, Andrea, *Pre-Raphaelite Portraits*, Oxford Illustrated Press, Somerset, 1981

Ruskin, John, *The Works of John Ruskin*, Library Edition, 39 Volumes, edited by E.T. Cook and Alexander Wedderburn, George Allen, London, 1903–12. (The illustration of Griffins is opposite page 140 in Vol V. Ruskin's discussion of Griffins is either side of this page. *Praeterita* is published in volume XXXV of the *Collected Works*. An interesting modern edition of *Praeterita* is that commented upon by Kenneth (Lord) Clark, Hart-Davis, London, 1949.)

Ruskin, John, *Winnington Letters: John Ruskin's Correspondence with Margaret Alexis Bell and the Children at Winnington Hall*, edited by Van Akin Burd, Beknap Press, Harvard, 1969

Strachey, Lytton, *Eminent Victorians* (includes essays on Manning and Dr Arnold of Rugby), re-issued by Chatto and Windus, London, 1966

Strachey, Lytton, *Queen Victoria*, Harcourt Brace, London, 1921

Taylor, Una, *Guests and Memories: Annals of a Seaside Villa*, Oxford University Press, 1924

Tenniel, Sir John, *Tenniel's Alice: Drawings by Sir John Tenniel for Alice's Adventures in Wonderland and Through the Looking-glass*, pamphlet, Harvard/ Metropolitan Museum of Art, 1978

Sources and Bibliography

Tennyson, Hallam, *Alfred Lord Tennyson: A Memoir by His Son*. 2 volumes, Macmillan, London, 1897

Tennyson, Charles, *Alfred Tennyson by His Grandson*, Macmillan, London, 1950

Tennyson, Charles, and Dyson, Hope, *The Tennysons: Background to Genius*, Macmillan, London, 1974

Tennyson, Emily, *The Farringford Journal of Emily Tennyson, 1853–1864* edited by Richard J. Hutchings and Brian Hinton, Isle of Wight County Press, 1986

Thackeray, William Makepeace, *The Letters of William Makepeace Thackeray* edited by Gordon N. Ray. Harvard University Press, 1946

Thompson, Rev. Henry L., (student and censor of Christ Church) *Henry George Liddell, D.D.: A Memoir*, John Murray, London, 1899

Tollemache, L.A., *Benjamin Jowett: Master of Balliol*, Edward Arnold, London, 1895

Trail, H.D., *The Marquis of Salisbury*, 4th ed, J. M. Dent, London, 1906

Trevor-Roper, Hugh, *Hermit of Peking: The Hidden Life of Sir Edmund Backhouse*, Macmillan, London, 1976

Tuckwell, Rev. W., *Reminiscences of Oxford*, Smith Elder. London, 1907

Vance, Norman, *The Sinews of the Spirit: The Ideal of Christian Manliness in Victorian Life and Thought*, Cambridge University Press, 1985

Victoria Regina, *Letters of Queen Victoria*, edited by Arthur C. Benson and Viscount Esher, 3 volumes, John Murray, London, 1907

Vidler, Alec R., *Witness to the Light: F.D. Maurice's message for today*, Scribners, New York, 1948

Wheatcroft, Alexander, *The Tennyson Album; A biography in original photographs*, Routledge, Kegon Paul, London 1980

Whiteley, Jon, *Pre-Raphaelite Paintings and Drawings in the Ashmolean Museum*, Ashmolean, Christie's Handbook, 1987

Wilberforce, Reginald G., 'Bishop Wilberforce', in *Leaders of the Church 1800–1900*, Mowbray, Oxford, 1905

Wimperley, Arthur, *Lewis Carroll and Cheshire*, pamphlet, Overcoat Publications, Cheshire, 1991

Acknowledgements

The following have helped with encouragement, comment, and advice; with the location and lending of source material; with guidance on various journeys; and we wish to thank them. They are: Andrew and Jackie Best, Peter and Win Campbell, Max Cooksey, Linda and Mark Courthoys, John and Louisa Craddock, John de Cuevas, Kirsty Dunseath, Graham Fuller, Elwyn Gladstone, Penelope Gladstone, Sir William and Lady Gladstone, Patrick Griffin, Brian Griffiths, Linda Homphray, Felicia and Ben Kaplan, Robert Loder, James Marquand, J. F. A. Mason, Bruce and Neva Mazlish, Peter McGhee, Janet McMullin, Erica Schumacher, Louisa C. Spencer, Roderick Taylor, Edward Wakeling, Patsy Williams, John Wing, Stephen Wood, Jo and Derek Wyatt.

The late John Clive gave us generous academic backing, while the late Isla M. Gladstone and the late Polly Binder provided uncanny support to the project without emphasising the depth of their involvement in it. Our editor, Tony Colwell, brought a lifetime of experience to the shaping of this book. His interventions have been faultless and tireless and the book could not have happened without his wise guidance.

We are most grateful for help from the Librarian and Archivist at Christ Church, the staffs at the London Library, St Deiniol's Library, the New York Public Library, the Widener Library at Harvard University, the Morris L. Parrish Collection at Princeton University, the staff at the Guildford Muniments Room, and the Harry Ransom Research Center at the University of Texas. For permission to quote material in their possession we owe a considerable debt to the Governing Body of Christ Church, Mrs M. J. St Clair, the Trustees of the C. L. Dodgson Estate, the Harry Ransom Research Center, the New York Public Library (Henry W. and Albert A. Berg Collection), the Houghton Library at Harvard University, and the Alfred C. Berol Collection at New York University.

For permission to reproduce photographs in their possession, the authors and publishers are particularly grateful to the Governing Body of Christ Church, Oxford, and Mrs M. J. Sinclair. For providing photographs and other illustrative material, they also wish to thank the Gernsheim Collection, Harry Ransom Humanities Research Centre, University of Texas at Austin, USA; the Morris L. Parrish Collection, Princeton University, USA; the National Portrait Gallery, London; and the Sarah Acland Memorial Hospital, Oxford.

Index

As Lewis Carroll and his two 'Alice' books are referred to on almost every page of the text they are not included in this index, though the Reverend C. L. Dodgson is listed where Carroll is given his 'real' name. Oxford, as a University or a city, is listed under more specific entries, such as Christ Church or Balliol, Carfax or Peckwater. Themes are generally excluded as they thread their way through the book and should not be disentangled one from another by means of quick consultation via the index. A few names that are not central to the theme are omitted.

Index

Students (dons at Christ Church), 33, 65, 68-9, 88-91, 94, 198

Swinburne, A.C., 228, 231, 235, 241

Sylvie and Bruno (Lewis Carroll), 269

Symbolic Logic, Part I, Elementary (Lewis Carroll), 139

Taylor
Henry, 155-8
Una, 157-8, 205
Thomas, 227, 239, 272

Tea-party, 54, 91, 121-2, 125, 128-9, 132-8, 222-3

Tenniel, John, 9, 18, 19, 25, 31, 46, 98, 108, 125, 147-8, 152, 159-60, 185-6, 192, 216, 227, 239, 253, 255-6; *see also Punch*

Tennyson
Album, The, 45
Alfred Lord, 27, 42, 45, 71, 140-61, 164, 167-8, 195, 197, 225, 228, 233-4, 254, 259, 274
Charles, 144, 145, 152,
Emily, 45, 141, 142-4, 146, 153, 204
Hallam and Lionel, 43-5, 141, 143-4, 146, 152-3, 270

Tent Lodge, Coniston, 142-3

Terry
Ellen, 12, 161-6, 195, 218, 220, 225, 271-4
sisters, 163-6, 205, 271

Texas, University of, 38-41, 57, 80

Thackeray, William Makepeace, 159-60

Three Freshwater Friends (Emily Tennyson), 141

Tiger-lily, 12, 161-4, 195, 274

Tories, 12, 18, 20, 21, 24-6, 97

Train, The, 142, 145

Trevor-Roper, Professor Hugh, 193-4, 267

Trial of the Knave of Hearts, 133, 242, 274

Tuna fish, *see* Acland

Tweedledee and Tweedledum, 9, 44-5, 63, 72, 99, 141, 146, 148, 153, 159, 195, 258, 262-3, 275

Twiss, Quintin F., 79, 199

'Two Voices', The (Alfred Lord Tennyson), 142, 145

Ugly Duchess, 12, 63, 78, 103, 163, 199, 208-11, 215, 247, 255-7, 275

Unicorn, 18-28, 31, 37, 46, 63, 72, 84, 149, 170, 261, 274

Union, *see* Oxford Union

Vere Bayne, *see* Bayne, Rev. Thomas Vere

vivisection, 90-1, 176, 198, 243

Victoria, R.I., *see* Queen Victoria

Wall, Henry S. (Oxford University Treasurer) 240, 249

Walrus, 12, 258, 262-4

Water Babies, The (Charles Kingsley), 123, 133-5, 138

Watts, George Frederick, 141, 161-5, 195

Weld Agnes Grace, 44-5, 204

Westbury, Lord Richard Bethell, 189-90

Westmacott, Alice, 43

White, Sir Dick, 193-4

White King, 18, 132-3

White Knight, 9, 43, 63, 146-53, 159-60, 168, 195-6, 228, 274

White Queen, 27, 63, 159, 160, 212-4, 216-8

White Rabbit, 12, 63, 108, 159, 241-4, 248-9, 251, 258, 274

Alice. Pleasance. Liddell.